Concentrate

Free online study and revision support

Visit the online resource centre at:

www.oup.com/lawrevision/

Take your learning further:

➤ Multiple-choice questions

➤ An interactive glossary

➤ Outline exam answers

➤ Flashcards of key cases

➤ Download our free ebook, *Study and Exam Success for Law Students*, which includes:

• Guidance on how to approach revision and prepare for exams

• Guidance on how to use a statute book

'I always buy a Concentrate revision guide for each module and use the online resources. The **outline answers are particularly helpful** and I often use **the multiple-choice questions to test my basic understanding** of a topic'

Alice Reilly,
Cardiff University

'The Online Resource Centre has been **exceptionally useful**. In my first year, I used the resources to **quiz myself**, to **test my knowledge and understanding** of cases, and to **pick up extra pointers that could give me a few extra marks**'

Kelly Newman, University of Exeter

D0544093

consolidate knowledge ❯ **focus revision** ❯ **maximise potential**

New to this edition

New coverage in this edition includes:

- Tables outlining judicial directions on good character in *R v Hunter* [2015] 2 Cr App R 116 (9)
- Supreme Court majority decision on implied statutory abrogation of the privilege against self-incrimination in *Beghal v DPP* [2015] UKSC 49
- The Court of Appeal case *R v Lubemba* [2014] EWCA Crim 2064 which set out procedures for cases involving vulnerable witnesses
- Tables on admissibility of expert opinion in criminal cases involving defendants exhibiting mental instability

Evidence
Concentrate

5th
edition

Maureen Spencer

Associate Professor of Law
Middlesex University

John Spencer

Barrister

OXFORD
UNIVERSITY PRESS

OXFORD

UNIVERSITY PRESS

Great Clarendon Street, Oxford, OX2 6DP,
United Kingdom

Oxford University Press is a department of the University of Oxford.
It furthers the University's objective of excellence in research, scholarship,
and education by publishing worldwide. Oxford is a registered trade mark of
Oxford University Press in the UK and in certain other countries

Second edition 2012
Third edition 2013
Fourth edition 2015

Impression: 2

Public sector information reproduced under Open Government Licence v3.0
(http://www.nationalarchives.gov.uk/doc/open-government-licence/open-government-licence.htm)

Published in the United States of America by Oxford University Press
198 Madison Avenue, New York, NY 10016, United States of America

British Library Cataloguing in Publication Data
Data available

Library of Congress Control Number: 2017933301

ISBN 978-0-19-880386-7

Printed in Great Britain by
Ashford Colour Press Ltd

Contents

Table of cases

Table of cases

✳✳✳✳✳✳✳✳✳✳

Table of cases

✳✳✳✳✳✳✳✳✳✳✳

Table of cases

Table of legislation

Table of legislation

✳✳✳✳✳✳✳✳✳✳✳

Table of legislation

✳✳✳✳✳✳✳✳✳✳

Table of legislation

✳✳✳✳✳✳✳✳✳✳✳

#1
Introduction, principles, and key concepts

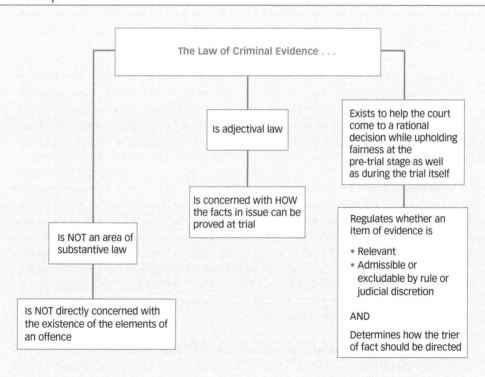

The Law of Criminal Evidence . . .

Is adjectival law

Exists to help the court come to a rational decision while upholding fairness at the pre-trial stage as well as during the trial itself

Is concerned with HOW the facts in issue can be proved at trial

Is NOT an area of substantive law

Regulates whether an item of evidence is

- Relevant
- Admissible or excludable by rule or judicial discretion

AND

Determines how the trier of fact should be directed

Is NOT directly concerned with the existence of the elements of an offence

Due process, fair procedure, the rule of law, and natural justice are interrelated principles which are fundamental to a civilised society. Achieving them in practice, however, involves complex considerations. This book examines the way that the law of evidence protects the right to a fair trial. This right applies of course to the participants in the trial but also to society as a whole. We all have an interest in justice being done and also being seen to be done. Achieving the correct outcome of the trial whether civil or criminal is crucial, otherwise resentment, disaffection, and agitation may follow.

In this book we concentrate primarily on criminal evidence because that is where the most complex issues in evidence law lie. Civil law will also be examined where appropriate.

Law of evidence

Glover (2015) draws a distinction between the law of evidence and evidence itself. The latter is defined (at p2) 'as any material which has the potential to change the state of a fact-finder's belief with respect to any factual proposition which is to be decided and which is in dispute'. It is the material out of which the events which led to the trial will be reconstructed in court and may consist, eg of eyewitness accounts, forensic samples, or objects such as weapons. The law of evidence is the system of rules and judicial discretionary practice which regulates how such material may be presented at the trial. This system was historically largely concerned with exclusion of evidence at trial. One reason for this was that a lay jury was held not to be able to evaluate certain types of evidence such as hearsay. At an extreme level evidence may be excluded because its admissibility would undermine the integrity of the system, such as evidence obtained by torture. Evidence law is based on several underlying assumptions including the need for trials to be fair, to uphold standards of a civilised society, and to achieve as accurate an outcome as possible, given that the truth of what happened may be elusive. The adversarial nature of the common law system is important also in determining the shape of evidence law since the parties aim to convince the court of the justice of their case and the law acts to control their submissions, which might otherwise be overlong or reflect superior or inferior resources. The rules differ according to whether the case is a civil or a criminal one, in part of course because the consequences of a wrong outcome of the latter are more serious.

Lack of fairness might involve wrongful acquittals as well as wrongful convictions. For example, the failure to secure convictions for the murder of Stephen Lawrence formed part of the background to proposals to remove the rule on **double jeopardy**, whereby acquitted defendants could not be prosecuted again for the same offence (see *Macpherson Report* Cm 4262–1, 1999). In recent years, the thrust of government policy has been to redress the balance of the criminal justice system to be more advantageous to victims. This has been one of the main objectives of the Criminal Justice Act 2003 (CJA).

Evidence law could be seen as a mass of rules, but it is better, at least to start with, to look at its underlying principles, traditionally derived largely from case law, but in modern times increasingly flowing from statute.

There is now a growing body of evidence scholarship which examines critically the theoretical underpinnings of the key doctrines and procedures, particularly in relation to criminal trials. A leading text is Roberts and Zuckerman (2010). Scholars have expressed the significant contribution made to evidence law by the late Mike Redmayne, who was a leading exponent of the importance of interdisciplinarity. His published work includes penetrating studies of the privilege against self-incrimination, the right to confrontation, forensic probability, and bad character evidence.

ECHR and fair trial procedures

A good starting point in understanding what is meant by a fair trial is Art 6 European Convention on Human Rights (ECHR), now part of English law as a result of the Human Rights Act 1998.

The common law equivalent is the doctrine of natural justice, which, like Art 6 ECHR, applies in both a civil and a criminal law context. Article 6 is a natural progression from Art 5, which sets out the procedure under which a person may lawfully be deprived of personal liberty, in many cases in anticipation or as a result of a civil or criminal hearing. The provisions of the two Articles, therefore, to some extent overlap. The wording of Art 6 is complex and some of the terminology needs to be analysed carefully before transposing into English law. Article 6(1) applies to both civil and criminal proceedings and calls for 'fair and public hearing within a reasonable time by an independent and impartial tribunal established by law'. Article 6(2) and (3) apply only to criminal proceedings. These latter two are supplementary and give some specific but not exhaustive instances of requirements of a fair criminal trial. These provisions apply to the law of civil and criminal procedure with which the law of evidence is closely associated. Procedural and evidence law are known as 'adjectival law' to distinguish them from the substantive law of crime, tort, land, equity, and so on, which form the basis of a prosecution or a suit in civil law.

Criminal and civil procedure

Procedural law is a separate area of study from evidence and will not be covered in this book, although you should be aware of the importance of the Civil Procedure Rules 1998 and Criminal Procedure Rules 2015. The latter sets out the practices the parties should follow as well as proclaiming the 'overriding objective' of the Rules. Paragraph 1.1(2)(a) states that this includes 'acquitting the innocent and convicting the guilty'. It refers (para 1.1.(2)(c)) to 'recognising the rights of a defendant, particularly those under Article 6 of the European Convention on Human Rights' and also (para 1.1(2)(d)) to 'respecting the interests of witnesses, victims and jurors and keeping them informed of the progress of the case'. It is important to recognise also that Art 6 applies to pre-trial as well as trial procedures and therefore influences the way the police gather evidence at the investigative stage.

Key concepts

The following are the main provisions, explicit and implicit, which are likely to occur in your study of evidence.

Foundational principles

The presumption of innocence

A fundamental aspect of a fair criminal trial is the requirement of the state to prove its case against the defendant. The state should run the risk of losing. However, presumptions of law or fact in favour of the prosecution, such as the principle of strict liability, are acceptable 'within reasonable limits'. Parliament may expressly shift the burden of proof. See Chapter 2.

Privilege against self-incrimination

This is a very broad concept of which the right to silence is just one part. It includes the question of how far a citizen should be required to cooperate with the state in the investigation of crime. However, the right not to incriminate oneself is not specifically included in the Convention. See Chapters 3 and 11.

The right to examine witnesses

This right is intimately related to the equality of arms principle which is enshrined in Art 6. In some cases the court has found a violation where the testimony of anonymous witnesses was permitted, such witnesses being unavailable for questioning by the defence. However, this is a difficult area particularly in view of the need to protect vulnerable witnesses, especially victims. See Chapter 7.

Admissibility of evidence: covert surveillance

Sometimes the investigatory authorities, including the police, resort to undercover methods. The case law suggests that the provisions of the Article require similar considerations to be raised, as in the operation of s78 Police and Criminal Evidence Act 1984 (PACE), which provides discretion to exclude prosecution evidence. The Strasbourg court stresses that the admissibility of evidence is essentially a matter of national law. See Chapter 4.

Admissibility of evidence: entrapment

If it is difficult to catch offenders the police may set traps or even encourage the committing of offences. They may act here as *agent provocateurs*.

English law does not allow a defence of entrapment but in principle such evidence may be excluded under s78 PACE or alternatively the prosecution could be stayed. The key element in deciding whether the police have acted improperly is causation—has the accused been persuaded to do something he would not otherwise have done? See Chapter 4.

Admissibility of evidence: disclosure

In order for a trial to be fair it is necessary for evidence to be exchanged pre-trial between the parties. This is particularly important in an adversarial trial because evidence is only gathered by the parties themselves. There is no investigating magistrate.

See Chapter 10 for some aspects of this complex area. It is not covered in detail in this book.

Revision tip

You are unlikely to be asked a question about fairness in general. However, in assessing, eg whether the rules on hearsay or character are fair it is useful to have in your mind academic comment on the matter. Roberts and Zuckerman (2010, pp19–22) identify 'five foundational principles of criminal evidence'. They are listed as

- accurate fact-finding,
- protecting the innocent from wrongful conviction,
- the principle of liberty or minimum state intervention,
- the principle of humane treatment, and
- the principle of upholding standards of moral propriety in criminal adjudication.

The authors argue that these provide a framework for an understanding of fair trial procedures. It would be a useful exercise for you to consider whether the current operation of the law of evidence meets these standards or indeed whether you would identify any additional principles to be added to this list.

Relevance

The account so far has introduced the key legal concepts which make up the expectations of a fair trial. However, equally important for achieving a just outcome is the presentation of the facts of the case in a rational, logical, and intelligible way. As Twining (1990, p23) put it:

> The serious study of reasoning in regard to disputed matters of fact is at least as important and can be at least as intellectually demanding as the study of reasoning in respect of disputed questions of law.

A crucial concept is that of relevance. Which of the facts are relevant to the case as presented by the prosecution or claimant or the defence?

> Relevant evidence means evidence having any tendency to make the existence of any fact that is of consequence to the determination of the action more probable or less probable than it would be without the evidence. *(Rule 401 US Federal Rules of Evidence)*

Although not all relevant evidence is admitted, in order to be admissible evidence must be relevant. Relevance is largely a matter of logic and common sense while admissibility is a matter of law. Thus, some relevant evidence may be excluded because it is more prejudicial than probative or because it would undermine the integrity of the trial to admit it. There are competing issues of fairness and relevance:

> Although relevant, evidence may be excluded if its probative value is substantially outweighed by the danger of unfair prejudice, confusion of the issues, or misleading the jury, or by considerations of undue delay, waste of time or needless presentation of cumulative evidence. *(Rule 403 US Federal Rules of Evidence)*

Law and facts

All legal disputes involve a mixture of fact and law. The parties may disagree over

- what happened,
- what are the relevant facts,
- what inference(s) can be drawn from even agreed facts, and
- how the law should be applied to the facts.

The evidence has to be relevant to a matter at issue in the trial. This means it must shed light on at least one of the following:

Facts in issue

These are based on the substantive law and in a criminal case are

- those which the prosecution must establish to prove the defendant committed the offence, which include, eg the *actus reus* and *mens rea* of murder, and
- those which the defendant denies, which might include issues such as lack of intent.

Facts relevant to facts in issue/collateral facts

These are side issues, eg evidence relevant to a fact in issue, such as the obtaining of a disputed confession and that relating to the credibility or the competence of a witness.

What is relevant, however, is sometimes a matter of subjective assessment and thus dispute. However, it is important to approach the matter in a rational way, starting with generalisations based on experience. Take this example from the case of Barry George who was first convicted and then acquitted on a retrial of murdering the television presenter Jill Dando.

Premise/generalisation

Part of the prosecution case was based on the following arguably questionable reasoning:

- People who obsessively collect large quantities of photographs of celebrities are more likely to be involved in their murder than those who do not collect such photographs.
- BG collected such photographs.
- BG is therefore more likely to have committed the murder than someone who did not collect such photographs.

The prosecution argument was that this evidence was relevant in that it increased, albeit minimally, the likelihood that BG was involved in the murder. The jury in the retrial was not persuaded to convict by the reasoning from this generalisation.

Forms of evidence

Evidence may be categorised in a number of different ways:

Direct and circumstantial evidence

Direct evidence is based on first-hand knowledge, eg A saw Y shoot Z.

Circumstantial evidence falls short of directly establishing a fact in issue, eg A saw Y running away from the scene of the shooting of Z, or Y was seen to buy a shotgun the day before the shooting of Z.

Real and testimonial evidence

Real evidence is an object, such as the gun in the above example or Barry George's photographs. Difficulties arise when the object may include a piece of writing such as a ticket. This may bring into play the rule against hearsay evidence because it then becomes a piece of documentary evidence. Testimonial evidence is the spoken evidence of a witness at trial.

Admissibility

Once the evidence is judged to be relevant then the court has to decide if there is any bar to its admissibility. This may be a rule of exclusion such as legal professional privilege or the rule against hearsay, or it may be based on the exercise of judicial, common law, or statutory discretion to exclude evidence. The common law discretion to exclude evidence which is more prejudicial than probative and the discretion under s78 PACE only apply to prosecution evidence. If there is a dispute over admissibility the judge will decide the issue in a trial within a trial known as a *voir dire*, where the jury will not be present.

Weight

Obviously, the judge is to a certain extent considering the strength or **weight** of the evidence when deciding on admissibility, but once evidence is admitted it is for the jury to decide whether they believe it or not, ie what weight to attach to it. In a civil trial the judge performs both functions. The matter is often expressed as that it is for the judge to decide on the law and the jury to decide on the facts. Naturally, in a *voir dire* the judge is deciding on both law and facts in assessing whether there is sufficient evidence and a case to answer to go to trial. The prosecution might be halted if, for example, the only evidence presented at trial is weak identification evidence or tainted hearsay evidence.

Conclusion
✻✻✻✻✻✻✻✻✻

Rules versus discretion

The sources of the law of evidence are to be found in common law precedents and increasingly in statute. The law is a mixture of rules and the exercise of judicial discretion either under the common law or authorised by statute, particularly s78 PACE. The difference between rules and discretion is largely marked by the approach of the Court of Appeal. It is more likely to overturn a decision which is based on a breach of a rule than one based on judicial discretion to exclude evidence. There is no common law discretion to include evidence but the CJA does introduce an inclusionary discretion for hearsay evidence (see Chapter 6).

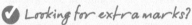 Looking for extra marks?

Your answers to essay questions will be much improved if you demonstrate knowledge, where appropriate, of key theoretical debates in the discipline. To give one example, there is currently much scholarly debate on whether the current practice of evidence law is concerned too much with values other than getting at the truth. The American author Larry Laudan (2008) argues that some rules such as the standard of proof are overly concerned with making it more difficult to convict the innocent than with the overall establishment of truth. Yet other rules, such as spousal privilege, are based on protecting certain relationships rather than seeking the truth. What is clear at least is that the law has no one single objective.

 Conclusion

The following ten chapters aim to give you the leading principles which govern the specific areas of evidence law and also try to demonstrate the relationship between the topics covered. Textbooks and undergraduate evidence courses vary in the order in which they cover these topics. Chapter 2 covers the foundational issue at a trial, namely who has the burden of proving the case. Chapters 3 and 4 review evidence gathering during the investigation before trial, particularly in relation to police undercover activity and interrogation of suspects. Chapters 5 and 6 cover hearsay and character. These are the two of the four traditional common law exclusionary rules of evidence now largely modified and codified in the CJA. Chapters 7 and 8 cover various areas concerned with treatment of witnesses at trial and the final three chapters cover the remaining common law exclusionary rules, opinion evidence, and public interest immunity/privilege, the latter embracing the privilege against self-incrimination and legal professional privilege.

At the end of the material in each chapter you will find a summary of some of the leading cases which have been examined in the text. The chapters end with Exam Questions, with some Answers at the back of the book, providing a succinct guide to success in problem-based and essay assessments, which are covered in more detail in the companion volume, Spencer and Spencer (2016).

 Key debates

Topic	How evidence law has been affected by the implementation of the Human Rights Act
Authors	J Jackson and S Summers
Viewpoint	Examines and contrasts the way the UK and Swiss courts have applied the rulings of the European Court of Human Rights (ECtHR) on evidence law. The authors argue that the ECtHR needs to give fuller explanations of the principles on which its decisions are based.
Source	'Confrontation with Strasbourg: UK and Swiss Approaches to Criminal Evidence' [2013] *Crim LR* 114

Topic	Contribution of Mike Redmayne to evidence scholarship
Authors	P Roberts and J Doak (eds)
Viewpoint	This special edition of the journal includes nine articles by leading scholars reviewing the body of work of a leading evidence theorist. It highlights particularly Redmayne's contribution to analysing inferential reasoning.
Source	'Mastering Evidence and Proof: A Tribute to Mike Redmayne' (2016) 20/2 *E&P* 89

#2

Burden of proof and presumptions

Key facts

In criminal cases

- The presumption of innocence is specifically enshrined in **Art 6 European Convention on Human Rights (ECHR)** but it is not recognised as an absolute since legislatures may **reverse the burden** of proof within reasonable limits which take account of the importance of what is at stake and of maintaining the rights of the defendant.

- In English law the principle of placing the burden of proof on the prosecution was acknowledged under the common law, although it was not until *Woolmington v DPP* (1935) that the courts fully acknowledged that this applied to the *mens rea* as well as the *actus reus*.

- A criminal offence may contain several elements and there may be therefore several different allocations of the burden of proof.

- Where the prosecution bears the burden of proof, the standard is beyond reasonable doubt. If the defence bears the burden the standard is the balance of probabilities.

- The term burden of proof should strictly be reserved for the legal or persuasive burden which is determined at the end of the trial when the jury decides whether to convict or not. The party that has the legal burden usually has the evidential burden, ie the burden of adducing sufficient evidence to make the issue a live one at the trial. (It also known as the burden of passing the judge.) Exceptions to this are certain common law defences where the defendant has the evidential burden before the judge will allow them to be considered by the jury.

- Misdirection by the judge on burden or standard of proof is likely to lead to an appeal.

- The Human Rights Act 1998 (HRA) has had considerable influence in this area. Reverse burdens will only be acceptable if they are proportionate and preserve the interest of the defendant. The court may read down a statutory provision in order to comply with Art 6.

In civil cases

- The principle in civil cases is he who asserts must prove. The placing of the burden of proof would therefore be apparent from the statement of claim and any counterclaim or specific defence, such as reference to an exclusion clause in contract or to contributory negligence.

Presumptions

- Presumptions work on occasion to remove the need for proof. They are mostly of significance in relation to civil cases.

- Factual presumptions are common sense logical inferences from a state of affairs.

- Irrebuttable presumptions of law are provisions of the substantive law, such as the provision that a child of 10 and over has criminal liability.

- Rebuttable presumptions of law cover situations where, once foundational facts have been proved by a party, a particular state of affairs will be assumed to exist.

Chapter overview

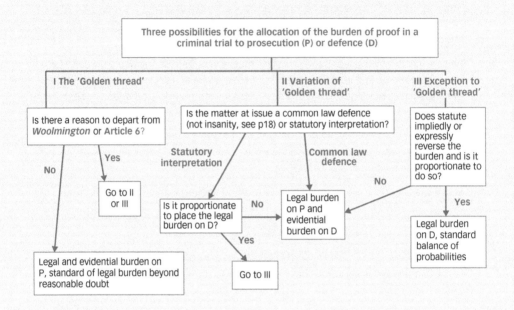

Related areas

The allocation of the burden of proof is intrinsic to all trials, criminal and civil. It has particular resonances with the privilege against self-incrimination in that it could be argued that the undermining of the right to silence impacts on the allocation of burden of proof. Under statute there may now be a permissible presumption of guilt for failure to respond to questions or failure to testify (see Chapter 3). More specifically, it has been argued that placing the legal burden or even the evidential burden on the accused violates the privilege against self-incrimination in that the accused is at a disadvantage if he does not testify. This is, however, probably an untenable argument since the presumption of innocence in itself does not specify that obtaining proof of guilt in any particular way is a prohibited activity. The debate on this involves quite sophisticated doctrinal argument. At a more concrete level you will see that references to the burden and standard of proof occur throughout your consideration of the production of evidence at trial. Note, for example, in the discussion in Chapter 3 on confessions that there are differing rules for the standard of proof for the prosecution and for the co-defendant under ss76 and 76A Police and Criminal Evidence Act 1984.

The assessment: key points

This is primarily a case law subject and you should be familiar with the details of the argument in the leading cases, which are set out in the tables later in this chapter. The issue of the allocation of the burden of proof in criminal cases raises both principled constitutional questions and practical problem-solving ones. As far as the former is concerned, you need to have read widely on what has been a fertile area for academic comment of late. As for the latter, you may be asked specifically to advise on the burden and standard of proof or you may assume that it forms an indispensable part of any question which gives you a scenario and asks you to 'advise on evidence'. A common feature of such questions is to give you an imaginary statute which includes an apparent reverse burden and to ask you how the courts will approach this. Watch out also for references to common law defences, such as self-defence. They give you an opportunity to display your knowledge of evidential burdens.

Questions on civil trials are likely to concentrate on two areas. These are the question of whether the standard of proof ever approaches the criminal standard and also the shifting of the burden during the trial as claimant and defendant put claim and counterclaim, such as relying on an exclusion clause in a contract.

Revision tip

You need to refresh your memory about the meaning of key terms which you will have also studied in criminal law. These include the elements of an offence, *actus reus* and *mens rea*, common law and statutory defences.

Key features and principles

This topic is really about who will bear the risk of losing a trial. A simple example from civil trials explains the point. Suppose that the claimant, C, sues the defendant, D, on the grounds that he failed to perform a contractual obligation to deliver some goods. D claims he did deliver. C is not able to provide proof to convince the court on the balance of probabilities that the goods were not delivered. Should the court:

Decide in favour of C

OR

Decide in favour of D

OR

Split any award between C and D?

In fact it will decide in favour of D here since in civil cases, 'He who asserts must prove' is the principle. It was C who initiated the case so he bears the risk of losing if he cannot produce proof to the required standard: the balance of probabilities, as Fig 2.1 illustrates.

In a criminal case the 'presumption of innocence' has the effect of placing the burden of proof on the prosecution, who also of course initiate proceedings. This is a principle of the common law enshrined specifically also in Art 6 ECHR. If the prosecution cannot prove the case against the defendant to the standard of beyond reasonable doubt the defendant is acquitted. Legally he does not have to produce evidence of innocence, although tactically he will be advised to do so. See *R v Bentley* (2001) on directions to the jury.

Figure 2.1 Who runs the risk of losing in a civil trial?

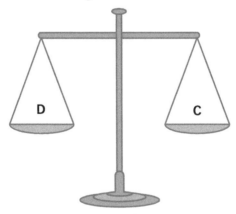

The scales are in balance. The claimant loses since
he/she initiated the case and has not proved it

There are three problematic areas in relation to the burden of proof which will be reviewed in this chapter. The first two relate specifically to criminal trials. They are first, the terminology, particularly the difference between the legal and the evidential burdens; second, the rationale behind reverse burdens; and third, the contentious subject of the standard of proof in civil cases where the allegation by the claimant is of a quasi-criminal act such as fraud. The standard of proof in criminal cases is more straightforward and will be covered in outline. The chapter concludes with a brief examination of presumptions.

Legal and evidential burdens

You must be careful how you use language in this area, which is a terminological minefield. You need to understand clearly the difference between the legal and evidential burdens. In particular, bear in mind that it is best to reserve the term 'burden of proof' for the legal (or persuasive) burden.

Legal/persuasive burden of proof: This is the burden which is discharged at the end of the trial when the jury gives its verdict or the civil court makes a decision.

Evidential burden: This is the burden of adducing sufficient evidence to convince the judge there is an issue to put before the court. Chronologically, it occurs at an earlier stage of the trial than the discharging of the legal burden. For the prosecution the task is to establish that there is a prima facie case. The test is set out in *R v Galbraith* (1981).

Note that Lord Bingham in *A-G's Reference (No 4 of 2002); Sheldrake v DPP* (2004) stated (at para 1):

> An evidential burden is not a burden of proof. It is a burden of raising, on the evidence in the case, an issue as to the matter in question fit for consideration by the tribunal of fact. If an issue is properly raised, it is for the prosecutor to prove, beyond reasonable doubt, that that ground of exoneration does not avail the defendant.

There are two preliminary keys to understanding this area, which some students take time to grasp:

- first, be aware that there may not be one burden of proof in a trial but several according to the various elements of the offence and any statutory or common law defences; and
- second, it may help to consider how the burdens may shift over time as the trial progresses.

The prosecution or claimant initiate the case and they have the initial evidential burden of 'passing the judge', ie convincing the court that there is enough evidence on which a trial can go ahead in the sense that there is a case to answer. The prosecution also has the legal burden of convincing the jury of the defendant's guilt on the charge.

The defendant legally at this stage does not have any burden. A not guilty plea is enough to make every matter a fact in issue, including the identity of the defendant. Tactically, of course, it would be wise for the defendant to produce some evidence which might raise a reasonable doubt in the mind of the jury, but legally there is no requirement to do so. The general rule is that the party which has the legal burden has the evidential burden but there

Legal and evidential burdens

✳✳✳✳✳✳✳✳✳✳✳

are a number of exceptions. The situation changes if the defendant plans to raise a particular defence or if the statute purports to reverse a burden. In such situations the defendant may have only an evidential burden, or, if the court considers it reasonable and proportionate in the light of the provision of Art 6(2), the evidential *and* the legal burden. How the courts decide how to allocate the burden is reviewed in the next section.

Joan is accused of growing an illegal drug in a window box in her flat, contrary to ss5 and 28 of the Misuse of Drugs Act 1971. She pleads not guilty, arguing that she thought the plants she was growing were tomato plants since they looked similar to a picture she had in a gardening book, *Growing Tomatoes in Small Spaces*. See Table 2.1.

Cowboys Ltd are contracted by Sam Sloan to transport Diana, his racehorse, from the stables to the racecourse. The contract specifies that Cowboys will not be liable for any harm caused to Diana in transit if Sloan had failed to have her given a clean bill of health by a veterinary surgeon before the journey. Diana dies of heart failure during the journey. Sloan sues Cowboys Ltd for breach of contract. See Table 2.2.

Table 2.1 Example of the allocation of the burden of proof in a criminal case

Elements of the offence	Who has the evidential burden?	Who has the legal burden?	What is the standard of proof of the legal burden?
1. Possession of window box	Prosecution	Prosecution	Beyond reasonable doubt
2. Defendant's knowledge of possession of window box	Prosecution	Prosecution	Beyond reasonable doubt
3. Identity of plant as cannabis	Prosecution	Prosecution	Beyond reasonable doubt
4. Defendant's knowledge of identity of plants	Defence*	Prosecution*	Beyond reasonable doubt

*Following *R v Lambert* (2002)

Table 2.2 Example of the allocation of the burden of proof in a civil case

Fact in issue	Who has the legal burden?	Who has the evidential burden?	What is the standard of proof of the legal burden?
Existence of contract	Sloane	Sloane	Balance of probabilities
Death of Diana	Sloane	Sloane	Balance of probabilities
Absence of veterinary surgeon's examination	Cowboys	Cowboys	Balance of probabilities

Placing the burden in criminal cases

Generally, the party which has a legal burden also has the evidential burden. There are two situations where the legal and the evidential burden may be split:

Common law defences

You will have come across the details of these leading cases in your criminal law course and most Evidence courses will require you to be able to cite an authority for the placing of the evidential burden of a common law defence on the defence. Remember that the defence of accident is not a common law defence. As *Woolmington* (1935) decided, it acts to negative *mens rea*.

See Table 2.3. Remember that the legal burden in these cases remains on the prosecution. Missing from the list now is 'provocation'. This has been replaced by a statutory defence of loss of self-control. Section 54(5) of the Coroners and Justice Act 2009 provides that, if sufficient evidence is **adduced** to raise an issue with respect to this defence, the jury must assume that the defence is satisfied unless the prosecution prove beyond reasonable doubt that it is not. The burden on the defence is still evidential only.

Table 2.3 Evidential burden and common law defences

Common law defence	Burden	Authority
Self-defence	Evidential burden on D	*R v Lobell* (1957); *R v O'Brien* (2004)
Duress	Evidential burden on D	*R v Gill* (1963)
Non-insane automatism	Evidential burden on D	*Bratty v A-G for Northern Ireland* (1961)
Drunkenness	Evidential burden on D	*R v Groark* (1999)

Statutory defences or elements of the offence

See the following discussion for a consideration of the principles of statutory interpretation.

The legal burden and the golden thread

Every law student will know by heart the passage from *Woolmington v DPP* (1935) referring in reverential terms to the golden thread while even then acknowledging two sets of exceptions, one, the defence of insanity, based on common law and the other based on statute, either by express or implied provision.

Legal and evidential burdens

✳✳✳✳✳✳✳✳✳✳

Woolmington v DPP (1935)

FACTS: Reggie Woolmington was convicted of the murder of his wife by shooting. He claimed the gun had been fired accidentally. The trial judge and the Court of Appeal had held that the defence of proving lack of *mens rea* was on him.

HELD: The House of Lords allowed the appeal and stated that at common law in criminal proceedings the burden of proving, beyond reasonable doubt, the *actus reus* and the *mens rea* is on the prosecution. The only two exceptions to this rule were the defence of insanity and statutory provisions. Viscount Sankey stated (at pp481–482):

> Throughout the web of English criminal law one golden thread is always to be seen, that it is the duty of the prosecution to prove the prisoner's guilt . . . No matter what the charge or where the trial, the principle that the prosecution must prove the guilt of the prisoner is part of the common law of England and no attempt to whittle it down can be entertained.

Revision Tip

Woolmington recognised one common law exception to placing the burden of proof (legal and evidential) on the prosecution. An accused who raises insanity bears the legal burden of proving it, see *McNaghten's Case* (1843). In such cases remember that the standard is the balance of probabilities (see more on this later). This is a controversial requirement since, in effect, the accused is asked to prove the absence of *mens rea*. You should demonstrate in any question on this that the case raises questions about two presumptions: that of innocence and that of sanity. In *H v UK* (1990), the European Court of Human Rights ruled that the insanity exception did not breach Art 6(2) since the rule did 'not concern the presumption of innocence, as such, but the presumption of sanity'. The Law Commission (2013) has proposed reform of the defences of insanity and automatism.

The common law approach to the burden of proof continued after *Woolmington* with the flurry of academic commentary arising from the two cases, *R v Edwards* (1975) and *R v Hunt* (1987). Most evidence courses include a review of the reasoning in these cases, which is still pertinent in relation to regulatory offences. This reasoning was much criticised by academics as marking a retreat from principle to public policy considerations which were very loosely expressed in both judgments.

R v Edwards (1975)

FACTS: E was convicted of selling alcohol without a licence. He appealed on the grounds that the prosecution had not produced evidence that he had not been granted a licence. His appeal was dismissed.

HELD: The Court of Appeal held that under the common law, where a statute prohibited an act save in specified circumstances, the court could construe the statute such that the burden of proving the existence of the circumstances, including the granting of a licence, could lie on the defendant.

> ### *R v Hunt* (1987)
>
> **FACTS:** H was convicted of being in unlawful possession of a Class A drug, morphine. One issue at the trial was the composition of the alleged drug. The statute provided that if the proportion of morphine was not more than 0.2 per cent the substance was not unlawful under the regulations. The prosecution had not adduced evidence on the proportion of morphine; the judge would not allow a defence submission of no case to answer. The applicant pleaded guilty.
>
> **HELD:** The Court of Appeal upheld the conviction but the House of Lords allowed the appeal. On the facts, the composition of the morphine was an essential element of the offence, which it was for the prosecution to prove.

It could be argued that *Hunt* and *Edwards* are of mainly historical interest and have been overtaken by the enactment of the HRA. On the other hand some academics such as Dennis see a reappearance of the factors discussed in *Hunt* in the current preliminary approach under the HRA (see 'Reverse Onuses and the Presumption of Innocence' [2005] Crim LR 901). The cases are also cited in recent leading judgments such as *R v Lambert, Ali and Jordan* (2002). It is therefore useful for you to have some knowledge of them. *Hunt* primarily concerns the interpretive approach in the case of implied statutory exceptions. It is not applicable in cases where the burden has been expressly shifted by statute.

In essence the decision in *Edwards* attempted to address how to interpret the precursor of what became s101 Magistrates' Courts Act 1980. This covers the situation where an otherwise unlawful act may become lawful if the perpetrator falls within a category of persons 'with an exception, exemption, proviso, excuse or qualification'. Thus, it is an offence to drive unless the driver has a licence. Following *Edwards*, it was for the accused to prove he fell within these categories, ie had a licence etc. The difficulty still existed, however, of distinguishing such specific defences and the elements of the offence where the burden remained on the prosecution. *Hunt* added additional factors to statutory interpretation, to be considered whether, in cases where the statute was unclear, Parliament had intended the burden to be on the defence. Both cases referred to an earlier civil case, *Nimmo v Alexander* (1968), which is still extensively cited as authority in criminal cases involving health and safety issues particularly. Table 2.4 summarises the combined aspects of the rulings in *Hunt* and *Edwards*.

Table 2.4 Key aspects of the judgments in *Hunt* and *Edwards*

Edwards (1975) (approved in *Hunt* (1987))	
• Examine the wording of the statute to see if it creates an exception, exemption, etc.	• Examine what the **mischief** was that the statute was addressing.
• The approach should be the same whether the offence is tried summarily or on indictment.	• Examine the practical problems in allocating the burden of proof, including who would find it easier to discharge.
• Where the legal burden is on D the standard of proof is the balance of probabilities.	• Examine the seriousness of the offence, which could resolve ambiguity in favour of the defence.

Human Rights Act and burden of proof

There is probably no area of evidence law which has been more affected by the implementation of the HRA than that of the allocation of the burden of proof in criminal cases. The presumption of innocence is specifically enshrined in Art 6(2) but the Strasbourg court has not taken it to be an absolute principle. In *Salabiaku v France* (1988) the European Court of Human Rights found there was no principled objection to the imposition of strict liability in a criminal case involving violation of customs regulations. This should be applied 'within reasonable limits' and subject to the test of proportionality in that the courts should balance the interests of the community and the rights of the individual.

The ECHR and English law

At first it seemed that the English courts in applying the ECHR were adopting a more robust approach to upholding the presumption of innocence. In *R v Lambert, Ali and Jordan* (2002), the House, in a majority decision, held that it was not justifiable to use s28 Misuse of Drugs Act 1971 so as to transfer the legal burden on the accused and to require him to prove that he did not know the bag he was carrying contained a controlled drug. The section should be read down to impose only an evidential burden. Lord Hutton dissented stating (at para 194) that 'it is not unprincipled to have regard to the practical realities where the issue relates to knowledge in a drugs case'.

There are to date several House of Lords cases on the subject; a number of them reversing decisions of the Court of Appeal. It is an indication of the significance of the controversial nature of this area of law that a number of the decisions are majority decisions, suggesting the fluid state of the law. The Court of Appeal in *A-G's Reference (No 1 of 2004) (2004)*, a case involving five conjoined appeals, identified a conflict between the House of Lords decisions of *Johnstone (2003)* and *Lambert (2002)*. This was held not to be the case, however, in *A-G's Reference (No 4 of 2002); Sheldrake v DPP (2004)*, where the House stated that both *Lambert* and *Johnstone* were the primary domestic authorities and *Johnstone* did not depart from *Lambert*.

Navigating your way through this conflicting scenario therefore is not easy. The following account will act as a compass. You will perhaps be tempted in addressing a problem to repeat the mantra that each decision is made on its own facts and that it is impossible to derive principles to apply to the problem. This will not get you many marks. Rather, you should familiarise yourself with the judgments and their nuances and consider them in the context of the question you have to address.

✅ Looking for extra marks?

In order to perform well in your assessment you should show evidence of wider reading than the standard texts and the notes you have taken from lectures. You should keep up to date with the academic discussions in key journals such as the *Criminal Law Review* and the *International Journal of Evidence and Proof*. The article by Dennis (2005) cited earlier provides an excellent framework ➔

➡️ with which to approach either an essay or a problem question in this area. In particular, it contains an extremely helpful table examining the key features of the leading cases. A very useful exercise would be for you to add the additional judgments which have been pronounced since the article was written.

Reverse burdens and statute

Consider the following provisions of the Health and Safety at Work Act 1974 (HSWA 1974):

- s2(1) It shall be the duty of every employer to ensure, so far as is reasonably practicable, the health, safety and welfare at work of all his employees.

- s3(1) It shall be the duty of every employer to conduct his undertaking in such a way as to ensure, so far as is reasonably practicable, that persons not in his employment who may be affected thereby are not thereby exposed to risks to their health or safety.

- s37 Where an offence under any of the relevant statutory provisions committed by a body corporate is proved to have been committed with the consent or connivance of, or to have been attributable to any neglect on the part of, any director, manager, secretary or other similar officer of the body corporate or a person who was purporting to act in any such capacity, he, as well as the body corporate, shall be guilty of that offence and shall be liable to be proceeded against and punished accordingly.

These provisions place on the defendant, an employer, or a corporation, a duty to provide a safe place of work, the breach of which is a criminal offence. A separate section gives the defendant employer a possible defence:

- s40 In any proceedings for an offence under any of the relevant statutory provisions consisting of a failure to comply with a duty or requirement to do something so far as is practicable or so far as is reasonably practicable, or to use the best practicable means to do something, it shall be for the accused to prove (as the case may be) that it was not practicable or not reasonably practicable to do more than was in fact done to satisfy the duty or requirement, or that there was no better practicable means than was in fact used to satisfy the duty or requirement.

R v Chargot Ltd (2009)

FACTS: Chargot was charged with breaching the Health and Safety at Work Act 1974 following an accident in which an employee who was driving a dumper truck was killed when the lorry-load fell on him.

HELD: The House of Lords considered where the burden of proving the defence under s40 lay. It held that the legal burden was on the defendant employer to prove that it was not reasonably practicable to provide the safe conditions. The employer was convicted.

Reverse burdens and statute

✱✱✱✱✱✱✱✱✱✱

The outcome of this case is illustrated in Table 2.5.

Table 2.5 Outcome of *R v Chargot Ltd* (2009)

Element of offence/statutory defence under HSWA 1974	Evidential burden	Legal burden	Standard of proof of legal burden
Employee harmed by exposure to risks to health and safety	P	P	Beyond reasonable doubt
Not reasonably practicable for employer to do more than was done; s40	D	D	Balance of probabilities

Contrast this judgment with that of *A-G's Reference (No 4 of 2002); Sheldrake v DPP* (2004). This was two conjoined appeals. The contested statutory provisions in the first of the conjoined appeals were contained in the Terrorism Act 2000. Section 11 covers membership of organisations which are listed as **proscribed** by the government as having terrorist associations:

(1)   A person commits an offence if he belongs or professes to belong to a proscribed organisation.

(2)   It is a defence for a person charged with an offence under subsection (1) to prove—

(a)   that the organisation was not proscribed on the last (or only) occasion on which he became a member or began to profess to be a member, and

(b)   that he has not taken part in the organisation since it was proscribed.

The defendant was charged with belonging to the proscribed organisation, Hamas. He relied on s11(2) in his defence. The House held that (by a majority judgment on this point), notwithstanding that it was Parliament's intention to impose a legal burden on the defendant, he should only bear the evidential burden.

The outcome of this case is set out in Table 2.6.

Table 2.6 Outcome of *A-G's Reference (No 4 of 2002)* (2004)

Element of offence/statutory defence under Terrorism Act 2000	Evidential burden	Legal burden	Standard of proof of legal burden
Belonging to a proscribed organisation; s11(1)	P	P	Beyond reasonable doubt
Proof that the organisation was not proscribed at the time of joining; s11(2)(a)	D	P	Beyond reasonable doubt

Element of offence/statutory defence under Terrorism Act 2000	Evidential burden	Legal burden	Standard of proof of legal burden
Proof that has not taken part in organisation since it was proscribed; s11(2)(b)	D	P	Beyond reasonable doubt

Applying the Human Rights Act on burden of proof

This section will try to expand on the jurisprudential considerations which underpin these two contrasting judgments. Dennis's penetrating 2005 article, cited at p19, is the basis of the following account. He identifies several stages in the judicial deliberations on whether a reverse burden should apply. First of all, there is the question of statutory interpretation, and it is here that *Edwards* and *Hunt* could be applied. Then the courts move on to considering whether a reverse burden is justified as proportionate. It is here that the policy considerations in *Hunt* may be developed. At this stage Dennis considers that there are six factors which can be derived from the cases.

Factors to consider, according to Dennis (pp908–916) are:

1. Judicial deference
2. Classification of offences
3. Construction of criminal liability: element of offences and defences
4. Significance of maximum penalties
5. Ease of proof and peculiar knowledge
6. Presumption of innocence

We have based the following tables (Tables 2.7 to 2.12) on the account in Dennis's article and added comment as some of the cases have been decided since its publication.

Judicial deference

Table 2.7 The courts and the will of Parliament

Cases cited by Dennis	Comment and additional cases
For a deferential stance see Lord Hope's judgment in *Kebilene* (2002), Lord Nicholls in *Johnstone* (2003) and Lord Woolf CJ in *A-G's Ref (No 1 of 2004)* (2004). But contrast this with Lord Bingham in *Sheldrake* (2004), who argued that this approach might result in too little consideration of the presumption of innocence.	Dennis (p909) distinguishes between legitimate aim, which it is the task of Parliament to pronounce on when making an enactment, and proportionality. In *R v Foye* (2013) a reverse burden on diminished responsibility was justified.

Reverse burdens and statute

✳✳✳✳✳✳✳✳✳

Classification of offences

Table 2.8 Can the courts distinguish truly criminal and regulatory offences?

Cases cited by Dennis	Comment and additional cases
See Lord Clyde in *Lambert* (2002).	Dennis (p911) points out the difficulty in determining the moral quality of criminal offences and in particular that it does not necessarily follow that a statutory defence to a regulatory defence will be any easier for a defendant to prove.
	See now *R v Chargot* (2009), applying *R v Davies* (2002) in placing a legal burden on the defendant employer for breach of health and safety law leading to the death of a worker.

Construction of criminal liability: element of offences and defences

Table 2.9 Can the courts distinguish elements of offences from defences?

Cases cited by Dennis	Comment and additional cases
Lord Hope in *Lambert* (2002), referring to *Edwards* (1975) and Lord Rodger in *Sheldrake* (2004) suggested that the courts can distinguish between the elements of the offence and any defences.	The burden should more properly be on the prosecution for an element of the offence. However, Dennis (p913) observes that it may be acceptable on occasion to place a reverse burden for an element of the offence in the sense that not having a licence is an essential element of the offence of unlicensed driving.
Lord Steyn in *Lambert* and the Court of Appeal in *A-G's Ref (No 4 of 2002)* (2003) suggested that discovering the **'gravamen' of the offence** may blur the distinction. It is better to concentrate on the nature of the moral blameworthiness.	Note that in *R v G (Secretary of State for the Home Department)* (2008) the House of Lords upheld the presumption of strict liability in a charge of rape of a minor by a 15-year-old. The Strasbourg case *Salabiaku v France* (1991) on that point was disregarded. The content of the substantive law did not engage **Art 6**.

Significance of maximum penalties

Table 2.10 The nature of the penalty

Cases cited by Dennis	Comment
See Lord Steyn in *Lambert* (2002) and *A-G's Ref (No 4 of 2002)* (2004). But contrast *Johnstone* (2003), where a reverse burden was approved where the maximum penalty was ten years.	Dennis (p914) writes that the application of this principle has been 'patchy to say the least'.

Ease of proof and peculiar knowledge

Table 2.11 Ease of proof, peculiar knowledge, and *mens rea*

Cases cited by Dennis	Comment and additional cases
Lord Hope in *Ex parte Kebilene* (1999), Lord Nicholls in *Johnstone* (2003), Lord Clyde in *Lambert* (2002), and the Court of Appeal in *A-G's Ref (No 1 of 2004)* (2004) all referred to peculiar knowledge.	'Peculiar/special knowledge' relates to state of mind. Dennis (p915) points out that *Edwards* (1975) had rejected the approach to peculiar knowledge which had earlier been a feature of the common law allowing reversal of the burden of proof. The current common law position is that peculiar knowledge in relation to certain common law defences places an evidential burden only. Note that in *R v Keogh* (2007) the Court of Appeal 'read down' the reverse onus defences in **ss2(3) and 3(4) Official Secrets Act 1989** because they related to *mens rea*. In *DPP v Barker* (2004) the Divisional Court held it was proportionate for the accused to have the legal burden under **s37(3) Road Traffic Act 1988**. Under this a disqualified driver may hold a provisional licence and drive in accordance with its conditions. In *DPP v Wright* (2009), by contrast, it was disproportionate to impose a legal burden on the accused under **s1 Hunting Act 2004**. This section gives an exemption for hunting with dogs in the categories specified in **Sch 1**. An evidential burden was appropriate. In *L v DPP* (2003), *Lambert* was distinguished. This concerned the defence to a charge of possession of a bladed article in a public place under **s139 Criminal Justice Act 1988**.

Presumption of innocence

Table 2.12 Procedural and substantive aspects of the presumption of innocence

Cases cited by Dennis	Comment
Lord Steyn in *Lambert* (2002) and Lord Bingham in *Sheldrake* (2004) identified substantive as well as procedural aspects to the principle of the presumption of innocence. Lord Bingham in *A-G's Ref (No 4 of 2002)* (2004) identified the risk of a wrongful conviction.	Dennis (p917) points out that concentration on outcomes rather than processes is a feature of the approach of the UK courts.

Table 2.13 Legal and evidential presumptions (see p32)

Name of presumption and type	Conditions
Legitimacy: legal	Once it is established that the woman was married at the time the child was born or conceived, the child is presumed to be fathered by the husband. The party challenging the presumption will have to convince the court to the standard of beyond reasonable doubt. **s25 Family Law Reform Act 1969** Case: *S v S* (1972)

Reverse burdens and statute

✳✳✳✳✳✳✳✳✳✳✳

Marriage: legal	There are three aspects to this presumption: (i) if a marriage has been celebrated there is a presumption that legal formalities have been followed. Applies to foreign as well as UK marriages; (ii) the marriage is presumed to have essential validity in that the parties have the capacity to marry and their consent is genuine; and (iii) if a couple have cohabited they did so as man and wife. The party challenging the presumption has the burden of proof to the high standard of beyond reasonable doubt in (i) but to the lower standard of the balance of probabilities in (ii) and (iii). Case: *Mahadervan v Mahadervan* (1964)
Regularity: evidential	There are two aspects to the concept of 'regularity': 1. public acts have been properly performed and public officials have been properly appointed; and 2. mechanical devices are working properly. Cases: 1. *Campbell v Wallsend Slipway & Engineering* (1978). This concerned the actions of a health and safety inspector. (NB in a criminal case the prosecution may not be able to rely on the presumption to establish facts in issue, eg that escaped prisoners had been lawfully in a police officer's custody: see *Dillon v R* (1982)). 2. *Nicholas v Penny* (1950). This involved the operation of a police speedometer.
Death: evidential	If someone is not heard of for seven years, by people who might be expected to have heard of him during that period, he will be presumed to have died. NB there is no presumption about the date of death. Case: *Bullock v Bullock* (1960)
Res ipsa loquitur: evidential	Applies in a civil case where a state of affairs is under the control of the defendant and an accident occurred which would not normally happen in the absence of negligence on the part of the defendant. There is a presumption of negligence on the part of the defendant if there is no other plausible explanation. Current approach is that it is an evidential presumption, see *Ng Chun Pui Lee Chuen Tat* (1988) and *Royal Bank of Scotland v Etridge* (2001). See also *Scott v London and St Katherine Docks Co* (1865), *Widdowson v Newgate Meat Corp* (1988), and *George v Eagle Air Services Ltd* (2009).

Dennis continues his analysis by identifying additional principles which he argues should be considered. A more structured approach, he suggests (p919), would be achieved by elevating ease of production of proof, which, following *Edwards*, would 'require a defendant to prove a formal qualification to do an act that is otherwise prohibited by legislation'. However, questions of moral blameworthiness, particularly questions of *mens rea*, should be on the prosecution. Dennis's analysis on this point in some ways has been confirmed by the decision in *Keogh* (2007), where the court was not prepared to shift the burden on *mens rea* in a case concerning the Official Secrets Act.

The exception to the 'foundational principle' (p920) that in cases involving moral blame the burden should be on the prosecution is to be seen in cases such as *Johnstone* (2003) and the health and safety cases such as *Davies* (2002). In these cases the perpetrator engaged in a regulated activity but one which arguably involved moral blameworthiness, such as breaching the Trade Marks Act 1994. However, since in such cases the alleged offender obtained a benefit, he and not the prosecution should prove exculpation from the apparently wrongful acts. Dennis (p920) calls this the 'voluntary acceptance of risk' principle and likens it to what Roberts and Zuckerman call 'the duties of citizenship' (2010, p244).

Sheldrake v DPP (2004)

Finally, Dennis turns to Lord Bingham's speech in the case of *A-G's Reference (No 4 of 2002); Sheldrake v DPP* (2004) and calls for an examination of not only moral blameworthiness in the definition of the offence in question but of how far the alleged conduct itself is properly criminal. He refers (p922) to Lord Bingham's observation in the case of *A-G's Reference (No 4 of 2002)* (2004) that the definition of the offence under s11(1) Terrorism Act 2000 was sufficiently wide and uncertain as to include persons whose conduct could not reasonably be regarded as 'blameworthy or such as should properly attract criminal sanctions', namely belonging to an organisation which was not at that time proscribed. If the only defence available to the defendant was s11(2), to show that he had not taken part in the activities at any time while it was proscribed, he should only have an evidential burden.

As Dennis himself acknowledges (p923), it is difficult to overcome problems even in this structured approach. The nature of moral blameworthiness is historically and socially conditioned. Dennis points out (p925) that allowing reverse burdens for statutory defences to actions which are presumptively morally blameworthy, under the 'voluntary acceptance of risk' principle, contrasts with common law defences to serious crimes. There the burden is only evidential.

These first two stages of judicial decision-making, according to Dennis (p927), establish whether a reverse onus is 'justified as proportionate to a legitimate aim'. If it is not so justified the courts move on to the third stage and examine whether the section can be 'read down' to impose only an evidential burden (see pp925–927). Dennis comments (p927), 'On the basis of *Sheldrake* it seems that it will almost always be possible to do this ... Accordingly a declaration of incompatibility of a reverse onus will almost never be necessary.'

We have set out as a flow chart, Fig 2.2, the three-stage process, with some overlap between the stages, identified by Dennis.

Reverse burdens and statute

✳✳✳✳✳✳✳✳✳✳

Figure 2.2 Diagram based on the analysis in Dennis (2005)

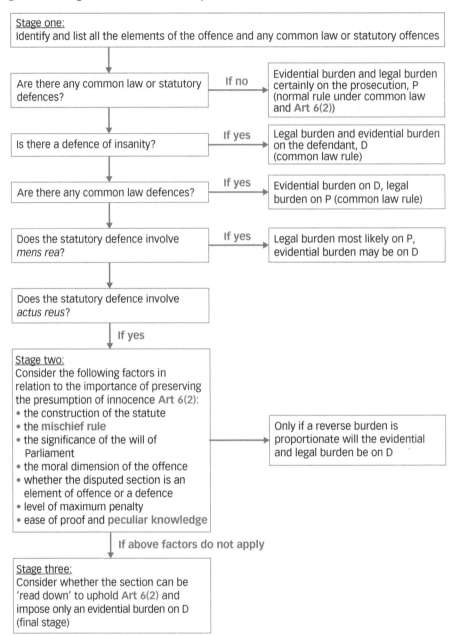

Note that some cases may encompass several of the factors listed by Dennis.

R v Williams (Orette) (2012)

FACTS: W was found in violation of **s5(1) Firearms Act 1968**, namely possession of a device that could be converted to firing live ammunition. It was a defence under **s1(5)** that the defendant neither knew nor had any reason to suspect that the device was readily convertible.

HELD: A reverse legal burden was proportionate. The grounds for this were (i) the seriousness of the problem of firearms offences which is reflected by the (legitimate) creation by Parliament of a number of strict liability offences in this context; (ii) that the elements of the **s1(5)** defence involved facts readily available to the defendant but which it might be very difficult for the prosecution to disprove; (iii) the lack of obvious unfairness or unreasonableness, where the prosecution had first proved to the criminal standard that the defendant had been in possession of an imitation firearm which was readily convertible into a lethal firearm, in requiring the defendant then to justify his possession of it; and (iv) to the maximum sentence of ten years' imprisonment.

You will find in reading the judgments for yourself that the speeches in *Lambert* have been open to review by the Court of Appeal. Glover (2015, p100) suggests that the Court of Appeal observed that in too many subsequent cases only an evidential burden was imposed on the defence. He refers to an 'assault on Lord Steyn' by the Court of Appeal in *A-G's Reference (No 1 of 2004)*. He argues (p105), however, that in the light of *A-G's Reference (No 4 of 2002); Sheldrake v DPP*, 'the House of Lords has now made the position clear, and that the way is open for a case-by-case development of the law on the important question of the presumption of innocence and the relationship of a reverse legal burden in a particular case to the requirements of art 6 of the Convention'.

Revision tip

Identify closely the facts in issue in a problem scenario. This may include all the elements of the offence and also any statutory or common law defences. Note that statute may expressly place an evidential burden on the defence—see **s54(5) Coroners and Justice Act 2009** and the defence of 'loss of control' on a charge of murder.

Burden of proof in civil cases

With regard to civil common law cases the allocation of the burden is apparent from the statement of claim. If the claimant fails to prove any essential element of his claim, such as duty of care in a negligence suit, the defendant will be entitled to judgment. Some statutes specify where the burden of proof should lie in civil cases, such as unfair dismissal.

Of course, there may be difficulties in determining who bears the legal burden if it is not clear whether the defendant's denial is simply negativing an essential element of the claim or takes the form of putting forward new information. The position will depend on the construction of the contract and the legal burden may shift with each claim or counterclaim.

Joseph Constantine Steamship Line Limited v Imperial Smelting Corporation (1942)

FACTS: The plaintiff corporation (P) claimed damages for breach of contract when the ship owners could not carry out a charter voyage because the ship was damaged by an explosion. The ship owners (D) claimed frustration in their defence. The question arose as to whether the ship owners had to prove that the frustrating event was not caused by negligence.

HELD: The House of Lords decided the case as follows:

- legal and evidential burden of proving breach of contract on P,
- legal and evidential burden of proving defence of frustration on D, and
- legal and evidential burden of proving negligence which obviated the frustration on P.

✅ Looking for extra marks?

Knowledge of the case of *Rhesa Shipping Co SA v Edmunds* (1985) will enhance your answers on civil cases. This case demonstrates the crucial significance in civil cases of deciding whether to initiate proceedings or not. On some, admittedly rare occasions, the outcome can be decided by the allocation of the burden of proof. The case involved the sinking of a cargo ship, where the insurance policies required proof that the loss was caused by perils at sea. The plaintiff ship owners claimed the cause was a collision with an unidentified submarine. The defendant insurers argued the cause was wear and tear. The House of Lords held that the ship owners had the task of proving that their explanation was more probable than not rather than more probable than that of the defendant. The court did not have to decide which of the explanations was the least improbable. For a recent commentary on the reasoning in this case, see *Rizan v Hayes* (2016).

Standard of proof

Criminal cases where legal burden is on the prosecution

An incorrect direction may give grounds for appeal. There are a number of cases which give guidance on the form of words to be used to convey the meaning of beyond reasonable doubt. One example is that of *Miller v Minister of Pensions* (1947). This was a civil case but Lord Denning's words (at p372) have been often cited: 'If the evidence against a man is so strong as to leave only a remote possibility in his favour, which can be dismissed with the sentence "of course it is possible but not in the least probable", the case is proved beyond reasonable doubt'. See now *R v Majid* (2009).

Revision tip

Essay questions will usually require you to make a critique of the law and to back up your points with jurisprudential evidence. One often raised debate is about the relationship between the presumption of innocence and the erosion of the right to silence in **ss34–38 Criminal Justice and Public Order Act 1994 (CJPOA)**. In a powerful judgment the Court of Appeal has drawn attention to this. *T v Webster* (2010) concerned offences under the **Public Bodies Corrupt Practices Act 1889**, the issue being whether the presumption of corruption which prevailed when a gift is given to a ➡

➡ person employed by a public body 'unjustifiably infringes the presumption of innocence.' The court held that it was a violation of Art 6(2). They went on to observe that ss34 and 35 CJPOA may have made reverse burdens unnecessary.

Criminal cases where legal burden is on the defence

The case law establishes that here the standard is the lower civil one of the balance of probabilities.

The evidential burden requires adducing sufficient evidence to convince the judge to allow the matter to be raised at trial, see *Jayesena v R* (1970). Recent case law has addressed the issue of the standard of proof. Thus, in *R v Majid* (2009) the trial judge had distinguished 'being sure' from 'being certain', which the Court of Appeal held should be avoided, as should the words 'beyond reasonable doubt'. The Judicial Studies Board (*Crown Court Bench Book: Directing the Jury* (2010)) recommends being 'sure'. The European Court of Human Rights referred to convictions being 'on the basis of direct or indirect evidence sufficing in the eyes of the law to find [the defendant] guilty' (*Barbera, Messegue and Jabardo v Spain* (1989)).

Civil cases

Here, again, Lord Denning's *dictum*, this time on the civil standard in *Miller v Minister of Pensions* (1947) (at p372) is worth memorising: 'If the evidence is such that the tribunal can say, "we think it more probable than not", the burden is discharged, but, if the probabilities are equal, it is not.'

There has been considerable controversy over whether there are differing standards in civil cases, in particular those where the allegation is a quasi-criminal one, such as fraud or assault on a child. In *Re H (Minors)* (1996) the House of Lords considered the standard in the case of allegations of sexual abuse in child care proceedings and confirmed that the standard was the balance of probability, rejecting a third standard of proof. The same approach was followed in *Re Docherty* (2008) and in *Re B (Children) (FC)* (2008). In the latter case Lord Hoffmann (at para 5) stated: 'I think that the time has come to say, once and for all, that there is only one civil standard of proof and that is proof that the fact in issue more probably occurred than not.' Dennis (2013, p489), however, is critical of this decision and suggests that the rejection of a third standard 'was perhaps over-hasty'.

In *Re Docherty* (2008) the House also stated that there was one civil standard but applied with some flexibility according to the seriousness of the allegations, such as sexual abuse. Lord Carswell (at p1509) referred to 'the application of good sense'.

Revision tip

It is possible that you will have an essay question on the debate on the civil standard of proof. You should be aware of the exceptions to the general rule that the standard of the balance of probabilities applies in civil cases. The criminal standard of proof applies for civil contempt of ➡

➡ court. In addition some statutes specify that proof beyond reasonable doubt may be required for some civil proceedings.

Thus, in *R v Chief Constable of Avon and Somerset* (2001) Lord Bingham stated (p354) that the proof of conditions for making a sex offender order under s2 Crime and Disorder Act 1998 should be to 'a civil standard of proof which will for all practical circumstances be indistinguishable from the criminal standard'.

✅ Looking for extra marks?

The first class and upper second class student will demonstrate more than an outline knowledge of the key cases. Thus, for example, although it is true to say that the HRA has had a profound impact on the approach of the English courts to the allocation of the burden of proof, a more scholarly approach would be to show the significance in the judgments of Commonwealth as well as Strasbourg cases. See, for example, the citation of South African cases in *Lambert*.

In addition, you should read the commentaries by leading academics and be aware of the nuances of the arguments. Thus, Ashworth (2001) in his article in the Criminal Law Review, 'Criminal Proceedings after the Human Rights Act: The First Year' is critical of the judgment in *Salabiaku v France* (1988). Commenting on the differing approaches to the presumption of innocence he has written (p865) that it 'must be said that the Strasbourg jurisprudence on art 6(2) is underdeveloped, not to say flaccid, and it is British judges, taking their cue from Commonwealth constitutional courts, who have sought to give greater sharpness to the right and any exceptions'.

Presumptions

Not all evidence courses include a review of this topic and those that do tend to concentrate on rebuttable presumptions of law. They can take two forms in civil cases, namely legal or persuasive presumptions, which place a legal burden on the party challenging the presumption, and evidential presumptions, which place an evidential burden. See Table 2.13 (pp25–26).

Rebuttable presumptions of law

- derive their authority from common law and statute; and

- place on the party relying on the presumption, the burden of presenting the basic facts, which will then be presumed unless the other party presents some countervailing facts.

✅ Looking for extra marks?

In discussing the nature of the presumption of innocence you need to make the examiner aware that you understand the distinction between the substantive criminal law and the adjectival law of evidence. In the light of the reticence of both the Strasbourg and domestic courts to address this fully, the law is in a fluid state. Roberts (2002, p36) suggests that it was unwise for the House of Lords in *Lambert* to use the presumption of innocence, which is an evidentiary principle, to undermine the substantive criminal law of strict liability. It is always open to Parliament to extend the scope of the strict liability principle. See also *G v UK* (2012).

Key cases

Case	Facts	Principle and comment
Nimmo v Alexander Cowan & Sons Ltd [1968] AC 107	The House of Lords held that in a prosecution under **s29(1) Factories Act 1961** the burden of proving that it was not reasonably practicable to make and keep a place of work safe rested upon the defendant employer.	Where the text of a statute did not make clear where the burden of proof lay, the court should take into account the mischief at which the statute was directed and the ease or difficulty that the different parties would face in discharging the burden of proof.
R v Bentley (Deceased) [2001] 1 Cr App R 307	B (19 yrs), and C (16 yrs), were cornered by police on the roof of a warehouse. B was held by police on the roof. C produced a pistol and shot one of the policemen. It was alleged that B had shouted 'Let him have it, Chris' before the fatal shot was fired. Both were convicted of murder and B was sentenced to death and executed in 1953 despite widespread pleas for clemency. In 1993 he was posthumously pardoned.	A clear and unambiguous direction on the burden of proof was a cardinal requirement of a properly conducted trial. The direction in this case was not satisfactory. By stressing the abundant evidence calling for an answer in support of the prosecution case and by suggesting that that case had been 'established' and that there was a burden on C to satisfy the jury that the killing had been accidental (however little, on the facts of the case, the injustice caused to C thereby) the jury could well have been left with the impression that the case against B was proved and that they should convict him unless he had satisfied them of his innocence.
R v Chargot Ltd [2009] 1 WLR 1	C was convicted of health and safety breaches following a dumper truck accident in which an employee died. Their appeal was dismissed in the Court of Appeal and they appealed to the House of Lords.	The prosecution had to prove that C had not ensured the employee's health and safety or prevented exposure to risk. This established breach, unless the defendant could establish that it had not been reasonably practicable to do so. The prosecution did not have to identify and prove specific breaches of duty; the overriding test was whether or not defendants had been given fair notice of the claim against them.
R v Edwards [1975] QB 27	E was convicted of selling alcohol without a licence. He appealed on the grounds that the prosecution had not produced evidence that he had not been granted a licence. His appeal was dismissed.	Under the common law where a statute prohibited an act, save in specified circumstances, the court could construe the statute such that the burden of proving the existence of the circumstances, including the granting of a licence, could lie on the defendant.

Key cases

✳✳✳✳✳✳✳✳✳

Case	Facts	Principle and comment
R v Hunt [1987] AC 352	H was convicted of being in unlawful possession of a Class A drug, morphine. One issue at the trial was the composition of the alleged drug. The statute provided that if the proportion of morphine was not more than 0.2 per cent the substance was not unlawful under the regulations. The prosecution had not adduced evidence on the proportion of morphine, the judge would not allow a defence submission of no case to answer.	The House acknowledged the principle that the burden of proof on an element of the defence could be placed on the defendant. Courts should examine the linguistic construction of the statute and if that is ambiguous take into account policy considerations and also the relative ease with which defence or prosecution could discharge the burden. The same approach should be taken whether the offence was a summary one or a trial on indictment. *Edwards* was approved. *Hunt* and *Edwards* have been largely overtaken by the post-*HRA* cases such as *Lambert*.
R v Johnstone [2003] 1 WLR 1736	J was convicted of violations of the **Trade Marks Act 1994**. He had relied on **s92(5)**, whereby it was a defence for the accused to show he believed on reasonable grounds that the use of the sign in question did not infringe the statute. The Court of Appeal, upholding the conviction, had not made it clear where the burden of proof on this section lay. The House of Lords refused the appeal and pronounced on the burden of proof.	**Article 6(2) ECHR** permitted reverse burdens provided they were kept within reasonable limits which took account of the importance of what was at stake and maintained the rights of the defence. In this instance there were compelling policy reasons to place the legal burden of the specific defence on the accused to the standard of the balance of probabilities.
R v Keogh [2007] EWCA Crim 528	A civil servant was charged under the **Official Secrets Act 1989**, having handed to an MP's researcher a copy of a letter from the PM to the US President. The Act required the defendant to prove that he did not know and had no reasonable cause to believe the disclosure of the secret information would be damaging. The judge concluded that the Act infringed the presumption of innocence but this was justified in the circumstances. The Appeal Court allowed the defendant's appeal.	The Act could operate effectively without obliging the defendant to prove that he did not have a guilty state of mind. Given its natural meaning, the Act was incompatible with **Art 6 ECHR**, and the relevant sections should be 'read down' by applying a similar interpretation to that achieved by **s118 Terrorism Act 2000**. That provides: 'If the person adduces evidence which is sufficient to raise an issue with respect to the matter the court or jury shall assume that the defence is satisfied unless the prosecution proves beyond reasonable doubt that it is not.'

Case	Facts	Principle and comment
R v Lambert [2002] 2 AC 545	L was convicted of being in possession of a controlled drug. The judge directed the jury that the prosecution had to prove that L knew he had the bag in his possession and that the bag contained the controlled drug. If L wanted to rely on the defence in **s28(3)(b)(i)** that he did not believe or suspect or have reason to suspect that he was in possession of a controlled drug he had to prove on the balance of probabilities that he did not know the bag contained a controlled drug. His conviction was upheld by the Court of Appeal and the House of Lords. L could not rely on the **HRA** since it was not in force at the time of trial. When the **HRA** was in force, **s28 of the 1971 Act** should be read as imposing an evidential burden.	In order to comply with **s3(1) HRA** it may be necessary to read down a statutory provision which imposes a legal burden of proof on the defendant. Given the seriousness of the offence, if the **HRA** had been in force, the court should have imposed only an evidential burden on the accused in relation to **s28(3)(b)(i)**.
R v Lobell [1957] 1 QB 547	On a charge of wounding with intent to cause grievous bodily harm, the accused argued that he was acting in self-defence. The trial judge held that the burden of proving this lay on him. The Court of Appeal allowed the appeal.	The prosecution had the legal burden of disproving self-defence. The issue should only be put to the jury if the accused produced sufficient evidence to make it possible for a reasonable jury to acquit. This is an instance of what are known as common law defences where the accused has the task of producing sufficient evidence to make the issue a live one before the jury but the legal burden remains on the prosecution.
A-G's Ref (No 4 of 2002); *Sheldrake v DPP* [2004] UKHL 43	The House of Lords considered two conjoined appeals. *Sheldrake* concerned **s5(1)(b) Road Traffic Act 2000** and the *A-G Ref* concerned **s5(2) Terrorism Act 2000**. Both provisions imposed reverse burdens on the accused. The House held that the task of the court was not that of deciding whether a reverse burden should be imposed on the defendant but whether a burden that Parliament had enacted unjustifiably infringed **Art 6(2)**. The **Road Traffic Act** provision imposing the burden was justifiable but not in the case of the **Terrorism Act provision**.	The House acknowledged that the decision in relation to the **Terrorism Act** meant flouting the clear will of Parliament in relation to the allocation of the burden of proof.

Key debates

✱✱✱✱✱✱✱✱✱

Case	Facts	Principle and comment
Woolmington v DPP [1935] AC 462	W was convicted of the murder of his wife by shooting. He claimed the gun had been fired accidentally. The trial judge and the Court of Appeal had held that the defence of proving lack of *mens rea* was on W. The House of Lords allowed the appeal.	At common law in criminal proceedings the burden of proving, beyond reasonable doubt, the *actus reus* and the *mens rea* is on the prosecution. The two exceptions to this rule were the defence of insanity and statutory provisions.

⑤⑤ Key debates

Topic	Standard of proof in criminal cases
Author	F Picanali
Viewpoint	Argues that the standard 'beyond reasonable doubt' is better understood as a form of reasoning on the part of the jury rather than a threshold to be achieved. Concentration on the concept of a threshold indicating the quality and quantity of evidence sufficient for a finding of fact encroaches on the role of the fact-finder. The paper reviews the philosophical dimension of the proposed change and concludes with practical recommendations for devising a new judicial instruction on the standard of proof.
Source	'The Threshold Lies in the Method: Instructing Jurors about Reasoning beyond Reasonable Doubt' (2015) 19/3 *E&P* 139

Topic	Is it a satisfactory response to the placing of a reverse burden in regulatory offences to decriminalise such activity?
Author	N Padfield
Viewpoint	Argues for a category of administrative regulations which would carry little stigma and for which strict liability or reversing the burden of proof would be acceptable.
Source	'The Burden of Proof Unresolved' [2005] *CLJ* 17

⑦ Exam questions

Essay question

'There is a paradox at the heart of all criminal procedure in that the more serious the crime and the greater the public interest in securing convictions of the guilty, the more important do constitutional protections of the accused become' (*State v Coetzee* 1997 (3) SA 527, per Sachs J, p612).

Explain, whether, in your view, the protection of the presumption of innocence in current English law would satisfy the standard articulated by Sachs J in this quotation.

To see an outline answer to this question visit www.oup.com/lawrevision/

Problem question

a. Harold is facing prosecution under the (imaginary) Pest Eradication Act 2008. Under s1 PEA, 'It is an offence for householders to use traps to kill rats if there is a risk that a human being will be harmed'. Harold set a trap in his front yard. He wishes to argue that there was no risk to humans since his yard was fully protected from access by others. The penalty for the offence is six months' imprisonment. The offence is triable either way.

Advise Harold on the burden and standard of proof.

b. Jane is charged with grievous bodily harm. The prosecution case is that she punched Roger, a stranger to her, while waiting for a bus. She claims in her defence that Roger had tried to push her into the road and that she 'lashed out' to protect herself. The judge in her summing-up tells the jury that the defence had the legal burden of proving that Joan had acted in self-defence. Jane is convicted.

Advise her defence team.

See the Outline Answers section in the end matter for help with this question.

Concentrate Q&As

For more questions and answers on evidence, see the *Concentrate Q&A: Evidence* by Maureen Spencer and John Spencer.

Go to the end of this book to view **sample pages**.

#3

Confessions and the defendant's silence

Key facts

Confessions

- A defendant may be convicted on the evidence of a confession alone, although in practice this is not common.

- The definition of a confession is contained in **s82(1) Police and Criminal Evidence Act 1984 (PACE).**

- A confession proffered by the prosecution may be excluded by rule under **s76(2)(a) and (b) PACE** and one proffered by a co-defendant under **s76A(2)(a) and (b).**

- A confession that has been proffered by the prosecution may be excluded by operation of statutory discretion under **s78 PACE.**

- **Section 82(3) PACE** preserves the common law discretion to exclude evidence.

- **PACE Codes of Practice C, E, and F** govern the procedure for police interrogation of suspects.

Pre-trial silence

- A suspect's failure to give an explanation when questioned by a constable under **caution** may allow the jury at trial to draw an inference of guilt under **ss34, 36, and 37 Criminal Justice and Public Order Act 1994 (CJPOA).**

- **Sections 34, 36, and 37 CJPOA** only apply if the suspect is questioned at an authorised place of detention and has been allowed an opportunity to consult a solicitor prior to being questioned, charged, or officially informed he might be prosecuted.

- The fact that the suspect relied on legal advice to remain silent does not of itself prevent **adverse inferences** being drawn at trial.

- **Article 6 European Convention on Human Rights (ECHR)** does not specifically include the right to silence or the privilege against self-incrimination. These have been recognised as international standards which lie at the heart of the notion of fair procedures but not as absolutes.

- Inferences of guilt permissible under **ss34, 36, and 37** are not sufficient without additional evidence to establish a case to answer or a finding of guilt.

- If the suspect and interrogator are on 'even terms', silence on the part of the former may amount to an admissible confession under the common law.

Chapter overview

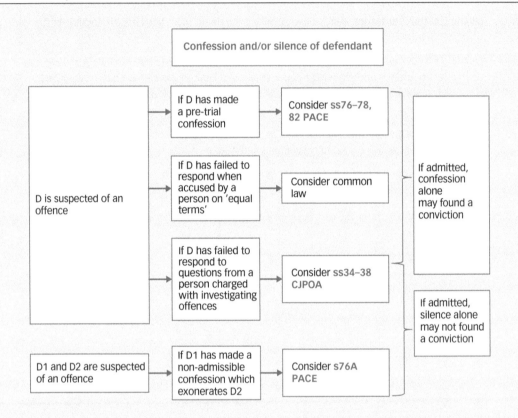

Related areas

There are aspects to this complex area in a number of other chapters. In Chapter 4 we look at the law relating to improperly obtained evidence other than confessions. There is considerable overlap with this area, particularly because the discretionary exclusion of evidence plays a large part in both. The law on privilege is discussed in Chapter 10, where the broader aspects of the privilege against self-incrimination, of which the right to silence is part, are discussed. Note the importance of legal professional privilege, which may be called into question if a suspect claims that he or she has failed to respond to questioning by a constable on legal advice. The effect of the accused's failure to testify is covered in Chapter 7. Chapter 8 covers the use that can be made of defendants' out of court lies as evidence. Finally, it should be stressed that confessions form arguably the biggest exception to the rule against hearsay, see Chapter 6. In that chapter you will find an examination of the conditions under which confessions by third parties may be admitted.

The assessment: key points

This large area remains one of considerable debate and case law, and must obviously form a key part of your revision plan. Since it raises principled questions about the relationship between the individual and the state, it is likely to form the subject of researched essay questions as well as problem-based questions. There is a considerable amount of case law to get to grips with, including a number of important decisions of the European Court of Human Rights. The key statutory sections are:

Police and Criminal Evidence Act 1984

ss76 and 76A: inadmissibility of confession by rule
s77: confessions by mentally handicapped persons
s78: exclusion of unfair evidence, including confessions and silence, by judicial discretion
s82: definition of confession

Criminal Justice and Public Order Act 1994

s34: effect of accused's failure to mention facts when questioned or charged
s36: effect of accused's failure to account for objects, substances, or marks
s37: effect of accused's failure to account for presence at a particular place
s38: interpretation and safeguards

Key features and principles

This chapter covers two areas which are closely related but which have developed their own body of case law. They are confession evidence and the evidential consequences which may arise for the defendant arising from a failure to respond to pre-trial questioning. There are two main assumptions underpinning the law.

- *People do not as a rule make statements which are against their own interests.*

It follows that an out of court confession to involvement in an offence should in principle be admitted at trial even if the suspect then wants to retract the confession and plead not guilty.

- *The law should protect the individual from intrusive and oppressive questioning which might lead to unreliable evidence being obtained.*

To do otherwise would violate individual autonomy and jeopardise the moral integrity of the trial and the verdict. Thus, confessions have historically been regarded as powerful evidence of guilt and they have played an influential role in the development of Western criminal justice culture since the late Middle Ages, influenced in part by religious models. It was also recognised that official interrogation may be abusive and thus controls were needed. Following the exposure of a number of miscarriages of justice in the 1970s arising from the admission of false confessions obtained by the police, a Royal Commission was established which recommended the introduction of an elaborate set of legislative controls on the obtaining of confessions, replacing the system which had operated under non-statutory Judges Rules. The outcome was PACE 1984.

Defendant's silence

The privilege against self-incrimination, of which the right to silence is a part, has been acknowledged since the excesses of the **Court of Star Chamber** in the seventeenth century to be vital to protect the individual from an abuse of state power. Pressure mounted in the 1980s to limit the right to silence under certain conditions, one argument being that it was being abused by career criminals. The CJPOA has eroded this long-standing principle to the extent that, although a suspect is not compelled by law to respond to questioning under official interrogation, he or she may face adverse evidential consequences from such a failure under certain circumstances.

Note the distinction between the weight of evidence of a pre-trial confession and of pre-trial silence. Under the common law the former does not need corroborative evidence, on which see criticisms by Pattenden (1991) who argues that some of the most notorious miscarriages of justice might have been avoided if there had been a requirement to corroborate confessions. By contrast, silence alone is not sufficient to found a conviction, see s38 CJPOA.

Human Rights Act 1998

The Human Rights Act has had considerable influence on the application of ss34–38 CJPOA but less so in relation to confessions. One exception is *R v Mushtaq* (2005).

R v Mushtaq (2005)

FACTS: The appellant was charged with fraud. The trial judge had held on a *voir dire* that an inculpatory statement made to police was admissible since it was not obtained by oppression or other

---

improper means in violation of **s76(2) PACE**. At the trial police officers were cross examined about the way the confession was obtained.

The appellant accepted he had made the statement. He was convicted. The Court of Appeal upheld the conviction and the following question was certified for consideration by the House of Lords:

Whether in view of article 6 of the Convention for the Protection of Human Rights and Fundamental Freedoms, a judge, who has ruled pursuant to section 76(2) of the Police and Criminal Evidence Act 1984 that evidence of the alleged confession has not been obtained by oppression, nor has it been obtained in consequence of anything said or done which is likely to render unreliable any confession, is required to direct the jury, if they conclude that the alleged confession may have so been obtained, they must disregard it.

HELD: The majority of the House answered the question in the affirmative. The jury should be directed that if they considered the confession was or may have been obtained in violation of **s76** they should disregard it.

Definition and content of a confession

Note the key aspects of the definition of a confession in **s82(1) PACE**:

[C]onfession includes any statement wholly or partly adverse to the person who made it, whether made to a person in authority or not and whether made in words or otherwise.

This definition follows that of the common law so many of the earlier cases will still be good law. It is important to determine whether the proffered or disputed statement falls within this definition for two reasons: to determine if (i) it will be admissible by the prosecution as an exception to the rule against hearsay or (ii) it will be inadmissible against the defendant since, if it is a confession, he or she would be entitled to protective measures, the absence of which could result in the statement being excluded.

Points to note:

- 'wholly or partly adverse' means 'adverse' at the time it was made *not* at the time of trial—see *R v Hasan* (2005), where a defendant whose statement was **exculpatory** at the time it was made could not be covered by the provisions of **ss76 and 78 PACE** when the prosecution proffered the statement at trial; and

- mixed statements are those that are partly incriminatory and partly exculpatory. They may be admissible and the **fact-finder** may treat both aspects as evidence of truth—see *R v Sharp* (1988). In *R v Tine* (2006), the Court of Appeal held that only the Crown might adduce a mixed statement.

How do the safeguards operate?

The tests for inadmissibility under s76(2) and discretionary exclusion under s78 and s82(1)

The statute sets out four tests whereby a confession may be held inadmissible (see Fig 3.1). In order to understand them it is necessary (i) to have a knowledge of the specifications set out

How do the safeguards operate?

✱✱✱✱✱✱✱✱✱

for a properly constituted interrogation since breaches of these *may* lead to exclusion; (ii) to understand what the tests are. These will be discussed in more detail later but they have to be understood as an integral system.

Section 76(2)(a) PACE: the oppression test

The test for oppression is included in s76(2)(a) PACE and a partial definition of oppression is given in s76(8): '"oppression" includes torture, inhuman or degrading treatment, and the use or threat of violence (whether or not amounting to torture).'

The key elements of this test are:

- the confession is obtained by oppression, ie there is a causal connection between the action complained of and the confession;
- 'oppression' should be given its ordinary dictionary meaning, see *R v Fulling* (1987);
- there would generally need to be bad faith on the part of the investigating authorities, see *R v Fulling* (1987);
- verbal as well as physical abuse may amount to oppression, see *R v Paris; R v Abdullahi; R v Miller* (1994);
- the burden of proof is on the prosecution to prove beyond reasonable doubt that the confession was not obtained by oppression;
- the particular characteristics of the suspect will be taken into account in deciding if the questioning had been oppressive, see *R v Spens* (1991); *R v Heibner* (2014).

R v Heibner (2014)

FACTS: H, who had a criminal record for serious offences, had been convicted of murder in 1978 and appealed through the Criminal Cases Review Commission (CCRC) 38 years later. One of the nine grounds of appeal was that his confession had been obtained by oppression. He had been detained in custody for 42 hours before a series of four interviews; he claimed he had been denied a solicitor and that if given a direction on the lines of *R v Mushtaq* the jury's attention would have focused on the real issue of whether he provided a partially dishonest confession because of pressure. They would have disregarded the confession, notwithstanding that they believed it was true.

HELD: The Court of Appeal dismissed the appeal. The judge had correctly directed the jury that either the confession was genuine or it was a fabrication because of oppression and anxiety. There was no third option of a conclusion that it was true but born of oppression. Even the Crown did not suggest it was wholly true. Additionally, examination of what is said to amount to oppression reveals more than 42 hours in custody before beginning to confess, tiredness, and anxiety about his family. Those factors must be viewed with a sense of reality. Heibner had been committing crimes for 15 years. He knew the system and told the jury he had just been sitting there relaxing 'I've been in that situation like hundreds of times'. The court did not accept that even if all the complaints were made out it had been established that they would so have oppressed this experienced criminal as to prompt him to make the confession recorded.

Section 76(2)(b) PACE: the reliability test

The test for unreliability is s76(2)(b) PACE. A confession may be inadmissible if it is represented to the court that it was obtained 'in consequence of anything said or done which was likely, in the circumstances existing at the time, to render unreliable any confession which might be made by him in consequence thereof'.

The key elements of this test are:

- there is no need for bad faith on the part of the police, see *R v Harvey* (1988);
- the 'something said or done' must be done by someone other than the suspect, see *R v Goldenberg* (1989);
- the 'something said or done' need not be done by the police, see *R v Harvey* (1988). In *R v Roberts* (2011) the defendant confessed to theft after his employer told him that if he did so the matter would be dealt with internally. The employer called the police. The Court of Appeal held that the confession should have been excluded under s76(2)(b).
- the section has been restrictively interpreted by the courts so that the provision 'circumstances existing at the time' has usually meant that the defendant must have been in a vulnerable mental or emotional state, see *R v Harvey* (1988);
- see *R v Barry* (1991), where the court set out the reasoning which must be applied in s76(2)(b);
- a confession may be excluded 'notwithstanding that it may be true';
- the test relates to 'any confession' that may have been obtained in this way; the truth of the actual confession is a matter for the jury; and
- the burden of proof is on the prosecution to prove beyond reasonable doubt that the confession was not obtained by this means.

There must be a causal connection between the 'something said or done' and the confession, *R v McGovern* (1990). 'Something said or done' may include omissions, see *R v Doolan* (1988), where there was a failure to caution, to keep a contemporaneous note, and to show the record to the suspect.

Section 77 PACE: confessions by mentally handicapped persons

Where the prosecution case against an accused who is a mentally handicapped person depends wholly or substantially on a confession which is not made in the presence of an independent person, the jury should be warned of the special need for caution.

Section 78 PACE: the fairness test

The discretionary test for fairness is in s78(1) PACE, whereby 'In any proceedings the court may refuse to allow evidence on which the prosecution proposes to rely to be given if it appears to the court that, having regard to all the circumstances, including the circumstances in which the evidence was obtained, the admission of the evidence would have such an adverse effect on the fairness of the proceedings that the court ought not to admit it.'

The key elements of the operation of this test are derived from the case law:

- breaches of the Code or s58 PACE, particularly if accompanied by bad faith on the part of the police are the most common causes; failure of the police to caution the suspect and to give an indication of the level of offence with which he may be charged, as required by Code C, may mean that a confession should be excluded, see *R v Kirk* (2001);

- again there must be a causal connection between the breach or impropriety and the making of the confession;

- evidence will not be excluded by virtue of the breaches only, but there must be such an adverse effect on the fairness of the proceedings that justice required exclusion, see *R v Walsh* (1989); and

- the importance the courts attach to the exercise of bad faith on the part of the police is illustrated by the use of trickery in *R v Mason* (1988).

Revision Tip

Examiners will be impressed if you show you are aware of situations where there may be conflicting authorities. Glover (2015, p359) claims that it 'is virtually impossible to reconcile' the differing approaches taken in *R v Goldenberg* (1989) and *R v Walker* (1998). In the former, the drug withdrawal symptoms suffered by the suspect were held to be self-induced and not covered by s76(2)(b). However, in *Walker*, Glover comments, 'the Court of Appeal seems to have accepted the fact that the accused had ingested cocaine before making a confession was a circumstance relevant to the question of whether any confession he might have made might be unreliable'.

Section 82(3) PACE: the common law test

This will apply if evidence is held to have been wrongly admitted at trial and the judge directs the jury not to take account of it.

Think of the above tests as providing a series of filters whereby the disputed confession is to be screened. In order for them to apply, there has to be some flaw in the operation of the interrogation. Most often this involves a breach of the statute or accompanying Codes. To some extent the tests overlap and cases which fall under s76(2)(a) or (b) might also fall under s78. It would be advisable to seek inadmissibility of a confession under s76 rather than exclusion under s78 if the conditions suggest both, since the misapplication of a rule of law by the trial judge is more likely to give grounds of appeal than the operation of discretion. Note that if the question facing the court is whether the confession was made or not, rather than whether it was improperly obtained, that is a question of fact which it is for the jury to decide. See, however, *Thongai v R* (1998), where the Privy Council held that if, because of police impropriety, it is difficult to prove that the confession was made then that may be a question of admissibility and a *voir dire* needed.

Access to legal advice

Section 58 PACE and PACE Code C para 6 relate to an accused's right of access to legal advice. But note that the statute provides that it may be lawfully delayed under certain circumstances in cases involving indictable offences. Thus, a confession is not necessarily inadmissible if it had been obtained in the absence of a solicitor, a contrast to the position in relation to pre-trial silence under the CJPOA (see later in this chapter).

Revision tip

Questions in this area will often ask you to assess the consequences of wrongly denying the suspect access to a solicitor under s58 PACE. It is important to appreciate that the court will be looking for a causal connection between the wrongful denial and the obtaining of a confession. Thus, in *R v Alladice* (1988) the court declined to exclude the confession on the grounds that the defendant had been improperly denied access to a solicitor. The police had been concerned that the solicitor might advise A to remain silent. A made a number of admissions at the interview. There was no ground for inadmissibility under s76 or s78 since, as the suspect had a criminal record and knew his rights the presence of a solicitor would have made no difference. By contrast, in *R v Samuel* (1988), the Court of Appeal considered that the right to legal advice was 'one of the most important and fundamental rights of a citizen' and denial led to exclusion under s78.

The importance of access to legal advice is illustrated in appeals from Scotland to the Supreme Court. In *Cadder v HM Advocate* (2010), Cadder was denied legal advice at interview although the police had told him that a solicitor could be told he was being detained. Appeal against conviction was allowed. In the conjoined appeals *Ambrose v Harris* (2011) the Supreme Court held that Arts 6(1) and 3(c) could require access to legal advice to be available even before the suspect was formally charged or taken into custody. The moment the person moved from being a witness to a suspect was a good guide.

Note that under the Terrorism Act 2000 a suspect may be properly interviewed without a solicitor in a 'safety interview', see *R v Ibrahim* (2009). In that case the Court of Appeal held that the question of whether material gained in the interviews was admissible at trial was 'delicate'. The provisions of PACE applied but the 'legislative structure does not preclude the use of evidence obtained in safety interviews' (para 36). The court, in *Cadder*, cited *Salduz v Turkey* (2009), where the Grand Chamber held that procedural safeguards to the privilege against self-incrimination require early access to a lawyer. This was particularly important in the case of children.

The Codes

PACE Code C: this contains detailed guidance on how a properly conducted police interview should take place. It ranges from elementary provisions, such as adequate food and rest, and significant information, such as the need to caution suspects. It needs to be read in conjunction with the statute. Thus, for example, Part IV PACE deals with periods of detention before charge as does the whole of Code C.

PACE Code D: identification of persons by police officers.

How do the safeguards operate?

✽✽✽✽✽✽✽✽✽✽

PACE Code E: audio recording interviews with suspects charged with indictable offences and subject to further questioning.

PACE Code F: visual recording with sound of interview with suspects.

Figure 3.1 Statutory rules governing inadmissibility of a confession

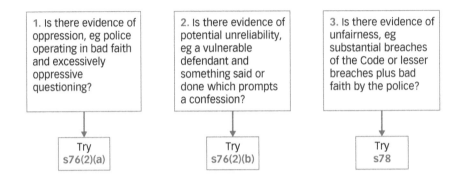

1. Is there evidence of oppression, eg police operating in bad faith and excessively oppressive questioning?

Try
s76(2)(a)

2. Is there evidence of potential unreliability, eg a vulnerable defendant and something said or done which prompts a confession?

Try
s76(2)(b)

3. Is there evidence of unfairness, eg substantial breaches of the Code or lesser breaches plus bad faith by the police?

Try
s78

Revision tip

You may be asked about the admissibility of confessions where the defendant has made more than one. Remember that if an earlier confession is ruled inadmissible under s76(2)(a) or (b), then even a later properly obtained confession may be inadmissible since there may be a causal link between the earlier tainted confession and the making of the subsequent one. See *R v McGovern* (1990), where the defendant was a pregnant young woman with a low IQ. She was improperly denied access to a solicitor and confessed to the charge of murder. In a subsequent, properly conducted interview she again confessed. Both sets of statements should have been excluded since the later admissions may have been made in consequence of the earlier ones.

See also *R v Singleton* (2002).

Fruit of the poisoned tree

This is an area where you need to be very familiar with the details of the statute. Some questions on confessions may slip in a reference to real evidence being found as a result of information being given in a confession where the problem sets out the circumstances in which the confession was obtained. You are expected then to consider not only whether the confession is admissible but whether the finding of the real evidence may be divulged at trial if the confession is inadmissible. Thus, for example, D confesses to murder and says he hid the murder weapon, a gun, on Hampstead Heath. His confession is ruled inadmissible under s76(2)(b); can the jury know about the finding of the gun? Answer, yes, but they must not be told *how* the police came to know it was there. See s76(4)–(6). It would probably impress the examiners if you referred to *A v Secretary of State for the Home Department (No 2)* (2005), where the House of Lords ruled that, although a confession obtained by torture was inadmissible, this did not affect the admissibility of real evidence obtained as a result of the confession.

Revision tip

It is worth making sure that you have fully understood the complexities of the law relating to confessions by drug addicts. In order to avoid too simplistic an interpretation of the decision in *Goldenberg* (1989) it should not be taken to mean that the effects of drug withdrawal can be discounted in deciding on the admissibility of a confession. You could argue that such effects were a relevant circumstance in the same way that the defendant's mental or emotional state was a factor to be considered. An example is *McGovern* (1990), where the accused's pregnancy should have been taken into account in determining her vulnerability.

Confessions and third parties including co-defendants

This issue may arise in two possible situations. A defendant may want to exclude an admissible confession by a third party which inculpates him. He may on the other hand want to adduce an excluded confession as exculpatory evidence. See Fig 3.2.

Defendant (D1) implicated by a third party, either a co-defendant (D2) or a non-defendant (ND)

A confession in a criminal trial is only evidence against the person who made it. The definition in s82(1) PACE enshrines this common law rule. In *R v Spinks* (1982) the Court of Appeal addressed the situation where in the trial of S for attempting to impede the prosecution of F, the trial judge had given the jury the clear impression they could use F's confession as evidence against S. F's conviction was quashed. The court referred to 'the universal rule which excludes out of court admissions being used to provide evidence against a co-accused, whether indicted jointly or separately'. D1's out of court confession cannot be evidence against D2. In civil cases the Civil Evidence Act 1995 provides that out of court admissions may be evidence in the case generally so civil and criminal evidence law is different on this point. Note of course that D1's oral testimony at the criminal trial may be evidence against D2 (a cut-throat defence).

The House of Lords in *R v Hayter* (2005) made what Glover (2015, p380) refers to as '[a] disturbing and, it is submitted, incorrect inroad into the common law exclusionary rule'. If D1 confesses pre-trial and implicates D2 this remains evidence only against D1 unless the jury are satisfied that D1 is guilty. In that instance they may use that finding of guilt as evidence of the guilt of D2 (and/or other defendants). The House here drew on s74 PACE making what Glover (p467) argued was a radical extension of the application of the section. This provides that the previous conviction of a third party may be admissible, if relevant, in a subsequent separate trial as evidence that the previous offence was committed. After *Hayter*, s74(1) could now be used in the same proceedings. In *Hayter* Lord Steyn stated (para 23) that *Spinks* 'would be decided differently' after the enactment of s74(1). In *Persad v Trinidad and Tobago* (2007) the Privy Council did not follow *Hayter*.

How do the safeguards operate?

✱✱✱✱✱✱✱✱✱✱

Defendant (D1) exonerated by a confession by a third party, either a co-defendant (D2) or a non-defendant (ND)

It may be the case that a defendant (D1) may want to make use of the confession of a co-accused in situations where that confession was excluded either by the judge or by a tactical decision by the prosecution. Before 2005, when s76 PACE was amended to include s76A, the leading authority was the House of Lords decision in *R v Myers* (1998), where the two accused were on trial for murder. The trial judge had allowed D1 to cross examine Myers (D2) on her confession which was not adduced by the prosecution because of possible breaches of the Codes of Practice. D2 appealed against conviction and the House of Lords held that D1 had been entitled to make use of her confession. The situation was distinguished from that in *R v Blastland* (1985), where the confession of a non-accused third party was held to be not admissible. In *Myers* the House held that a defendant must be allowed to cross examine a co-defendant in relation to an out of court confession and there was no discretion to exclude it. Arguably it follows that cross examination of the interviewing officer would be allowed if D2 did not testify.

Myers has now been overtaken by s76A PACE, which was introduced in 2005. The test for the admissibility on behalf of D1 of an excluded confession made by D2 is in the same terms as that when tendered by the prosecution except that the standard of proof is on the balance of probabilities. In *R v Sliogeris* (2015) the Court of Appeal addressed the question whether a statement by D4 that identified D1 (the appellant) as responsible for the offence of murder could be relied upon by D3 under s76A. The court held that D1's statement was not a confession and so should not have been admitted under s76A but it was admissible under s114(1) CJA 2003 (see further Chapter 6).

Hartshorne (2004) argues that s76A PACE, following the amendments in the Criminal Justice Act 2003, is unsatisfactory since it allows a co-defendant's confession to be excluded, notwithstanding that it may be true. The author suggests an amendment which, it is argued, would make the provision compliant with Art 6 ECHR.

Revision tip

In assessment questions on s76A you need to consider how the judge should direct the jury on the evidential worth of a confession by D2, inadmissible for the prosecution, admitted for the defence of D1 under s76A. In *R v Sliogeris* (2015) the Court of Appeal made it clear, albeit as obiter, that it should only be evidence in favour of D1. It stated (para 37):

> In the circumstances we do not have to resolve the further ground of appeal, which essentially raises the question whether, once evidence of a confession by a defendant is properly admitted in favour of a co-defendant, it can in principle thereafter be used against all defendants and not merely the maker of the statement. In the light of the purpose behind the provision, there is a cogent case for saying that it should not be treated as evidence in the case generally but only in favour of a co-defendant. That would require the judge to direct the jury that it should not treat that statement as evidence against a co-defendant (other than the party making the confession) but that the jury may treat it as evidence in favour of the co-defendant who has successfully applied for it to be admitted. However, we leave that issue to be decided on another occasion.

Figure 3.2 Defendant (D1) exonerated by a confession by a third party, either a co-defendant (D2) or a non-defendant (ND)

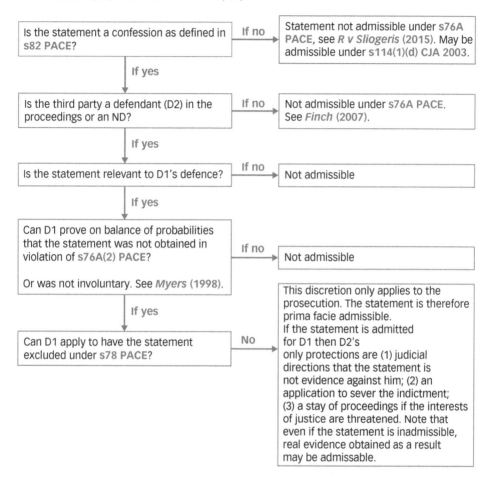

Silence

Silence as evidence (i) common law

The right to silence is an aspect of the privilege against self-incrimination whereby a suspect who is being interrogated by a state official is not forced to respond to questions. The principle is thus applied to protect the individual from the power of the state. It was and remains the case that at common law, where two individuals are on 'even terms', silence in the face of an accusation of guilt may amount to an admission and is thus admissible as evidence of guilt. *Parkes v R* (1976) illustrates the point. Section 34(5) CJPOA preserves this common law rule. Section s82 PACE defines a confession as a statement 'whether made in words or otherwise'. In *R v Osborne* (2005) the Court of Appeal gave guidance as to the factors to be taken into consideration by a judge when deciding whether to admit in evidence a prejudicial statement made in the defendant's presence and to which the defendant, by his conduct, was said to have acquiesced.

R v Osborne (2005)

FACTS: O, who had killed an Asian man, pleaded self-defence. Two days after the killing a woman had asked O, who was with a friend, why he had hit the victim. The friend had replied that they did not like Asian people. O had said nothing but had walked off.

HELD: The trial judge had correctly admitted that incident. The Court of Appeal set out guidelines (para 19): 'Where the defence challenged the prosecution's intention to put before the jury evidence of a defendant's reaction, or lack of reaction, to a statement made in his presence, three questions arise: (1) could a jury properly directed conclude that the defendant adopted the statement in question? If so, (2) is that matter of sufficient relevance to justify its introduction in evidence? If so, (3) would the admission of the evidence have such an adverse effect on the fairness of the proceedings that the judge ought not to admit it?'

Silence as evidence (ii) statute

The CJPOA 1994 (as amended) has made considerable inroads into what was the common law principle of the right to silence. In essence, under certain conditions, a suspect's failure to respond to police questions may be used as supportive evidence of guilt. The key sections are ss34, 36, and 37.

Section 34 CJPOA covers the effect of the accused's failure to mention facts when questioned or charged by a constable or other persons charged with investigating offences. Before such failure may be used as evidence the preconditions shown in Fig 3.3 should apply.

Note the particularly complex question of how the courts have approached legal advice as an explanation for the suspect's silence: see the cases cited in Fig 3.3 and the 'Key Debates'.

Other key sections of the CJPOA are ss36 and 37. These deal with specific circumstances and failure to give an account. The police interview under these two sections may form part of the primary case against the defendant even if he does not give an explanation at trial. Section 36 covers failure to account for objects, substances, or marks, and s37 with the suspect's failure to account for his presence in a particular place. Like s34, these only apply if the suspect who is at an authorised place of detention has had an opportunity to consult a solicitor.

Revision tip

In answering questions on the evidential value of silence at the police station it is not enough to be familiar with the complex wording of the statute. You need also to have at your fingertips the growing body of interpretive case law, particularly on s34. An important case on the meaning of responding to police questions is *R v Knight* (2004), which establishes that a prepared written statement given to police at interview, and from which he did not depart at trial, meant that s34 did not apply.

What is meant by a 'fact relied on for his defence'?

There is considerable case law on what amounts to a 'fact' given at trial under s34 CJPOA. Consider the following scenario: A and B are charged with conspiracy to murder. A gave a 'no comment' interview to police and did not testify. At trial, B gave an innocent explanation of the whereabouts of both himself and A, and in his submission A's counsel adopted that explanation. Is the counsel's submission a 'fact' relied upon by the accused but not given earlier? In other words, does a *defendant* risk an adverse inference under s34 as well as s35 if he does not give evidence but his counsel introduces a fact in his defence? The answer is yes: see the House of Lords decision *R v Webber* (2004). In that case, the defendant did not give evidence but his counsel put facts to prosecution witnesses which the defendant had not referred to at the police interview. The House of Lords held that s34 applied.

The House of Lords' judgment in *Webber* addresses a number of questions of interpretation of s34.

R v Webber (2004)

FACTS: W, A, and L were on trial for conspiracy to murder. W made no comment when interviewed by police and did not testify. His counsel put suggestions to A concerning the behaviour of the victim and also relied on parts of A's testimony in his submission. The judge gave a s34 direction and W was convicted. He appealed.

HELD: the House addressed two questions: (i) can s34 apply where the matters which the defendant failed to mention when interviewed are matters put to, but not accepted by, prosecution witnesses or (ii) matters of which evidence is given by a co-defendant which the defendant, in the submissions made by his counsel, adopts? They answered in the affirmative. The House criticised the decision in *R v Mountford* (1999), where the Court of Appeal had held that s34 did not apply where the fact that the defendant had failed to mention at interview, at trial constituted his entire defence. The judgment also made it clear that the section does not apply where the 'fact relied on' is accepted by the prosecution as true. It follows that the section does not apply if the matter is agreed by defence and prosecution to be true. The House observed that (para 28) 'rarely if ever could a section 34 direction be appropriate on failure to mention an admittedly true fact at interview.' See also *R v Chivers* (2011).

Silence as evidence (iii) ECHR

A number of Strasbourg cases have covered the complex question of whether s34 complies with the provisions of Art 6 ECHR. As you will be aware, the right to silence is not specifically referred to in Art 6 but its importance as a fundamental, if not an absolute, principle was made clear in *Murray (John) v UK* (1996). The court, going further than the UK statute, stated that a conviction should not be based solely or mainly on inferences of guilt from silence. The judgment also stressed the importance of access to legal advice. The case led to an amendment of the statute to provide that the silence provisions would only apply if the suspect had access to legal advice.

Again, in *Condron v UK* (2001) the court stressed that s34 was compatible with the ECHR and that it was not a violation of the Convention to permit inferences to be drawn if the accused claimed he had remained silent on legal advice. However, the court indicated the crucial importance of carefully worded judicial directions to the jury on the permissibility of drawing inferences from silence.

Responding to *Condron v UK*, the Court of Appeal held in *R v Betts and Hall* (2001) that the jury should be permitted to draw an adverse inference if they believed the defendant had not genuinely relied on legal advice. However, in *R v Howell* (2003) it held that reliance on legal advice had to be reasonable as well as genuine to avoid an adverse inference being drawn. This position was followed in *R v Knight* (2003), *R v Beckles* (2005), and *R v Hoare* (2004).

Choo (2015, p136), while expressing disappointment that the ruling in *R v Betts and Hall* was not followed, points out that 'The existence of good reason for legal advice to remain silent would support a defendant's argument that his or her reliance on the advice was reasonable'. But he adds that 'by revealing the reason for the advice, however, the accused may well be waiving legal professional privilege'. (See further on this in Chapter 11). Choo adds, that 'This state of affairs was not regarded as problematic by the European Court in *Strasbourg v UK*'. Note that in *R v Bowden* (1999) it was held that where a defendant claims legal advice he has waived his legal professional privilege.

✅ *Looking for extra marks?*

First class evidence students are open to the proposition that there is often no one answer to a question. By reading widely you will arm yourself with scholarly references to back up your appreciation of differing perceptions of the law. University students are encouraged to be critical but such criticism carries more weight if it is also supported by authorities.

To give one example, opinions differ on the decision in *Mountford*. As the account on p53 shows, the House of Lords in *Webber* was critical of the approach taken by the Court of Appeal in that case. Glover (2015, p407), however, contrasts *Mountford* favourably with the decision in *R v Daly* (2002). In that case s34 was held to be engaged when the defendant's entire defence was that he admitted theft but not robbery. A pre-trial plea on this was rejected by the prosecution and the defendant had not made a separate admission of theft.

Figure 3.3 Inferences of guilt and s34 CJPOA

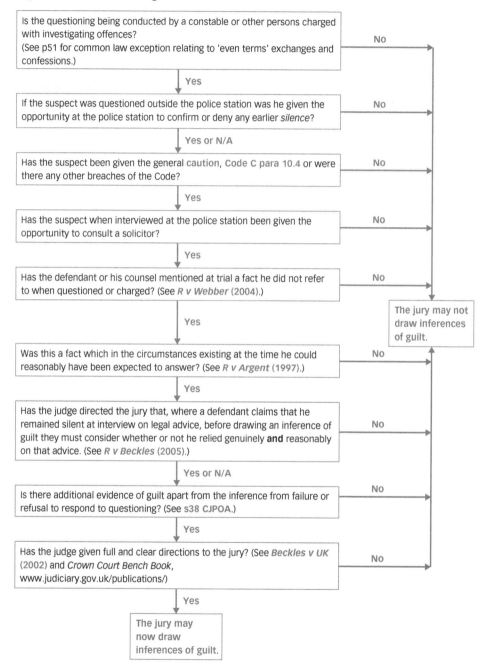

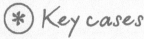

Case	Facts	Principle and comment
	Confessions: definition	
R v Hasan [2005] 2 AC 467	H was charged with aggravated burglary. In an 'off-the-record' statement to police not carried out under caution or, tape-recorded, he claimed duress. There were inconsistencies between this statement and his evidence at trial. The Court of Appeal held that the off-the-record statement was a confession and fell to be excluded under **s76(2)(b)** since when it was sought to admit it at trial it was **inculpatory**.	The House of Lords reversed the Court of Appeal. To fulfil the definition of an out of court confession, the statement must be wholly or partly adverse to the maker at the time it was made so **s76(2)(b)** did not apply. Lord Steyn stated that **ss76, 78, and 82(1)** 'are designed to provide in a coherent and comprehensive way for the just disposal of all decisions about statements made by accused persons to the police'.
R v Sharp [1988] 1 WLR 7	S was spotted running away from the site of a burglary. He admitted being near the scene of the crime but gave an exculpatory reason to the police for this.	His statement was 'mixed', ie both inculpatory and exculpatory, and was admissible as a whole as evidence going to the truth of its contents.
	Confessions: inadmissibility and exclusion	
R v Barry (1991) 95 Cr App R 384	B was charged with conspiracy to steal. He was anxious to obtain bail because he had custody of his young son. In interviews held in breach of **Code C para 16.8** he offered assistance in return for bail. In a later recorded interview where he had not been offered legal advice, he confessed. He argued that the confession had been induced by the offer of bail. The Court of Appeal held the trial judge had erred in admitting the confession. The conviction was overturned.	The courts set out the steps which should be taken when a defendant alleges that his confession was unreliable within **s76(2)(b) PACE**. First, identify the thing said or done, which requires the trial judge to take into account everything said or done by the police. Second, ask whether what was said or done was likely in the circumstances to render unreliable a confession made in consequence. The test is objective, taking into account all the circumstances. The last step is to ask whether the prosecution have proved beyond reasonable doubt that the confession was not obtained in consequence of the thing said or done, which is a question of fact to be approached in a common sense way.

Case	Facts	Principle and comment
R v Fulling [1987] QB 426	F confessed after being told by police that her lover's mistress was in the next cell. She claimed her distress had been caused by police oppression which led to her confession. The Court of Appeal rejected her submission.	Oppression in s76(2)(a) PACE must be given its ordinary dictionary meaning, which connotes 'detestable wickedness'. Ordinarily, oppression would entail impropriety on the part of the interrogator. Contrast with *R v Paris; R v Abdullahi; R v Miller* (1994), where bullying questioning, even with a solicitor present, was held to amount to oppression and the confession should be excluded.
R v Goldenberg (1989) 88 Cr App R 285	G, who was a heroin addict, gave admissions to police about his supplier. At trial he argued that he had confessed in order to get more drugs. The trial judge had correctly admitted the confession.	The test set out in s76(2)(b) required that things said or done were extraneous to the maker of the confession.
R v Harvey [1988] Crim LR 241	The police, acting without evidence of bad faith, had made H aware of her lover's confession to a murder. H, who was psychopathic and of low intelligence subsequently also confessed. H's confession should have been excluded.	There is no need for police impropriety for s76(2)(b) to apply.
R v Kirk [2000] 1 WLR 567	K was arrested and questioned about an incident in which an elderly woman had had her bag snatched. She had fallen and subsequently died from her injuries. K was not initially told about her death and did not seek legal advice. He wanted to retract his confession admitting the theft. His convictions for robbery and manslaughter were overturned.	Code C para 10.3 requires that the person who is arrested must be informed at the time or as soon as reasonably practicable that they are under arrest and the grounds for their arrest. See also Art 5(2) ECHR, which provides that 'Everyone who is arrested shall be informed promptly, in a language that he understands, of the reasons for his arrest and of any charge against him'.
R v Mason [1988] 1 WLR 139	M was suspected of involvement in an arson attack. Police pretended to both him and his solicitor that his fingerprints had been found at the scene. His subsequent confession should have been excluded because of the police deceit.	Deliberate and serious malpractice on the part of the police may lead to a confession being excluded under s78.

Key cases

✳✳✳✳✳✳✳✳✳

Case	Facts	Principle and comment
R v Spens [1991] 1 WLR 624	S was charged, along with others, with insider dealing. They had made adverse statements to inspectors appointed by the Trade and Industry Secretary which were admitted at trial. It was claimed that they ought to have been excluded under **s76(2)(a)** since it was not explained to them that they could be used in evidence at trial under the **Companies Act 1985**. It was held that the questioning was not oppressive since S was intelligent and sophisticated.	The particular characteristics and mental state of the accused are relevant in considering whether the confession was a result of oppression.
R v Walsh (1989) 91 Cr App R 161	Breaches of the Code and statute which occurred during interview included denial of a solicitor and failure to record the interview or give the suspect a chance to check it.	Serious and significant breaches of the statute and the Code may lead to exclusion of a confession under **s78 PACE** in the absence of bad faith on the part of the police.
Confessions and third parties		
R v Hayter [2005] 1 WLR 605	There were two other co-defendants, B and R, as well as H, to a charge of murder. The prosecution case was that B wanted to arrange the murder of her husband and H recruited R as contract killer. At trial R's confession was admitted.	The rule that a confession is only evidence against the person who made it (see **s76(1)**) does not mean that where there are co-defendants, the jury cannot use one defendant's confession in establishing his guilt and use that finding of guilt in deciding the guilt of the co-defendant.
Silence and the common law		
Parkes v R [1976] 1 WLR 1251 (PC)	P was confronted by the mother of a woman bleeding from stab wounds. She asked P, who was holding a knife, why he had stabbed her daughter. P made no reply but when the mother tried to get hold of him, he tried to stab her. The PC held that the jury had been entitled to take into account P's silence and his reaction as evidence of guilt.	At common law where the parties are on even terms, silence in the face of an accusation may amount to a confession. See also *R v Collins* (2004), which involved the evidential status of the defendant's failure to contradict a lie told by an accomplice. The Court of Appeal held that in this instance the silence did not amount to adoption of the lie, but in principle if the parties were on 'even terms' an 'important lie' which was not contradicted may lead to the drawing of an adverse inference.

Case	Facts	Principle and comment
	Silence of the accused at pre-trial questioning by police etc	
R v Argent (1997) 2 Cr App R 27	The defendant gave no comment in interviews but at trial claimed he had left the scene before the crime occurred.	The reference to 'fact' in s34(a) and (b) means a fact that the accused could reasonably be expected to mention in the circumstances. The judge should direct that the personal characteristics and circumstances of the accused should be taken into account.
Condron v UK (2001) 31 EHRR 1	Two drug addicts were advised by their solicitor, who considered they were suffering withdrawal symptoms, not to answer police questions. The judge did not direct the jury that they could only draw adverse inferences if they were satisfied that their silence could only sensibly be attributed to their having no explanation which would stand up to scrutiny.	**Section 34** did not violate **Art 6 ECHR**. Legal advice to remain silent under questioning did not, in itself, mean that the jury could not draw an inference of guilt but the judge must direct the jury on how to assess the effect of this legal advice.
R v Hoare [2005] 1 WLR 1804	H manufactured illegal drugs as a by-product of his glassware company. On legal advice he failed to respond to police questions and at trial claimed he believed the drugs were for cancer research.	The judge must direct the jury to consider whether, regardless of legal advice genuinely given and genuinely accepted, an accused has remained silent not because of that advice but because he had no, or no satisfactory, explanation to give.
R v Knight [2004] 1 WLR 340	K was charged with indecent assault on a child. At the start of a police interview his solicitor gave a written statement and K failed to answer further questions. His evidence at trial was consistent with the content of the statement.	Adverse inferences could not be drawn when a pre-trial written statement was comprehensive and new material was not raised at trial

 Key debates

Topic	Is the test for allowing inferences to be drawn from silence on legal advice too harsh?
Author	B Malik
Viewpoint	Reviews the differing approaches of the Court of Appeal in *R v Betts and Hall* (2001) and *R v Howell* (2003). In the latter the court held that genuine reliance on legal advice, as accepted in *Betts and Hall*, was not sufficient: it had also to be reasonable. Suggests that consequently the suspect is having to 'second guess' the jury and calculate whether it will believe that reliance on legal advice was the true reason for his or her silence.
Source	'Silence on Legal Advice: Clarity but Not Justice? *R v Beckles*' (2005) 9/3 *E&P* 211

Topic	Importance of availability of legal advice for suspect at police interview
Author	I Dennis
Viewpoint	*Cadder* (2010) will have a clear impact on English law. It is likely to lead to exclusion of a confession in the overwhelming number of cases where a suspect makes a confession after requesting legal advice in vain.
Source	'Legal Advice in Police Stations: 25 Years On' [2011] *Crim LR* 1

 Exam questions

Essay question

Is the current law on drawing inferences from silence a violation of the right to a fair trial?

🜨 Online Resource Centre

To see an outline answer to this question visit www.oup.com/lawrevision/

Problem question

Dorrit, Tim, and Nell are accused of murdering Pip. Dorrit is confronted by Pip's friend David when he is discovered with the body. David accuses him of having killed Pip and Dorrit makes no reply. Dorrit is arrested, cautioned, and taken to the police station. Meanwhile David tells Nell that if she tells him what happened he will not tell anybody. Nell confesses to having killed Pip. She is also arrested, cautioned, and taken to the police station. There she is offered access to a solicitor but declines it on the grounds that she cannot afford it. She is pregnant, has a low IQ, and is in a highly emotional state. She tells the investigating officer she did poison Pip and that Dorrit had nothing to do with it. She also tells him that the poison is in her kitchen. At a later interview where she is given access to a solicitor she repeats the confession and also exonerates Dorrit. The police find poison in Nell's kitchen. Tim gives a 'no comment' interview to police. He had refused the offer of legal advice. All three defendants plead not guilty. Tim elects not to testify. At the trial Dorrit claims that Pip had talked about killing herself. Tim's barrister adopts this assertion as part of his argument in Tim's defence.

Advise on evidence.

See the Outline Answers section in the end matter for help with this question.

Concentrate Q&As

For more questions and answers on evidence, see the *Concentrate Q&A: Evidence* by Maureen Spencer and John Spencer.

Go to the end of this book to view **sample pages**.

#4

Improperly obtained evidence other than confessions

- There is no rule of law requiring the exclusion of evidence simply because it has been improperly, illegally, or unfairly obtained.
- There is a judicial discretion to exclude such prosecution evidence under both common law and statute and the key test is whether the pre-trial action threatens the fairness of the trial.
- Section 78 Police and Criminal Evidence Act 1984 (PACE) applies to the exclusion of non-confession as well as confession evidence on which the prosecution proposes to rely.
- The most common areas of exclusion, other than confession evidence, fall into two: first, undercover police activity involving traps or entrapment and second, obtaining evidence by acting improperly or unlawfully, including trespass or breach or evasion of legislation such as PACE and the Codes of Practice.
- The court may elect to stay the prosecution rather than exercise discretion to exclude evidence if the continuation of the prosecution would be an affront to the public conscience.
- The Court of Appeal will interfere with a trial judge's exercise of his discretion to exclude evidence only for unreasonableness by the *Wednesbury* test but the appellate court will review the grounds for stay of prosecution more robustly.
- The common law discretion, retained in s82(3) PACE, may still be employed, in particular if the evidence has already been admitted at trial, to guide judicial directions to the jury.
- The relationship between the common law and s78 PACE has not been clearly set out in case law but it is arguable that the latter allows a more extensive discretion.
- The European Court of Human Rights (ECtHR) has held that s78 enshrines the relevant principles of Art 6 European Convention on Human Rights (ECHR).

Chapter overview

Improperly obtained prosecution evidence

```
                    ┌─────────────────────────────┐
                    │ Evidence likely to be admissible │
                    └─────────────────────────────┘
```

If no   If yes   If no

Was there evidence of entrapment where the incitement caused the offence?

Was the improperly obtained evidence
- Highly cogent
  OR
- Obtained without violating legal professional privilege?

Was there a breach of PACE and other legislation, whether in the course of a covert operation or not, which undermined the integrity of the criminal process?

If yes   If no   If yes

Stay of prosecution may be ordered, see R v Looseley (2001)

Evidence likely to be excluded under s78 PACE

Note also s82 PACE – Common law discretion

Evidence likely to be excluded under s78 PACE

Note also s82 PACE – Common law discretion

Related areas

In Chapter 3 we examined how confession evidence tendered by the prosecution may be excluded by the exercise of judicial discretion under s78 PACE. In this chapter we examine how prosecution evidence other than confession evidence, which might be considered relevant, may be excluded because of flaws in the way it was obtained. Of course the improper activity may also involve obtaining a confession along with other evidence, eg where police use undercover agents or listening devices to obtain a suspect's admission. We consider specifically the exclusionary discretion contained within s78 PACE. Common law and statutory exclusionary discretion may also be exercised in relation to other areas of evidence, in particular character evidence (see Chapter 5) and hearsay evidence (see Chapter 6) and identification evidence (see Chapter 8).

The assessment: key points

The question of improperly or illegally obtained evidence is prompting much debate. Current concerns stretch from the propriety of undercover police activities to the admissibility of evidence obtained by torture. It is an area that is likely, therefore, to appear in assessments either in the form of an essay where you would review the ethical and human rights issues or a problem on the likelihood of the admissibility of evidence at trial. You need to be clear also on the conditions in which a stay of prosecution as an alternative to exclusion of evidence might be ordered.

Key features and principles

Trials have a factual and a moral dimension. It is vital that the right person is convicted and the innocent acquitted. It is also crucial that the outcome is arrived at in a way which satisfies standards of propriety and integrity, and that evidence is not tainted by being collected in a morally dubious way or is so prejudicial that it clouds the fact finder's judgement. In this chapter we will be looking exclusively at criminal trials since the same requirement of moral probity is not so crucial in civil law. The question posed in this chapter is why should apparently relevant evidence be excluded from criminal trials?

Historically, English law has been reluctant to exclude evidence, other than confession evidence, on the grounds that there was some impropriety in the way it was obtained. The exception for confession evidence was based on the acknowledgement that obtaining a confession improperly may involve subverting the will of the suspect in some way. Two subsequent changes to the law have impacted on this area. First, s78 PACE allows the discretionary exclusion of prosecution evidence. Second, the Human Rights Act has led to a more jurisprudential approach in this area, although the House of Lords has concluded that the requirements of Art 6 ECHR are compatible with the pre-existing s78 (see *R v Looseley; A-G's Reference* (No 3 of 2000) (2001)).

The general rule and the common law background

The traditional rule of English law is that the impropriety of the method by which evidence is obtained is irrelevant to its admissibility. There were exceptions, however, for confession evidence and evidence which undermined the defendant's privilege against self-incrimination. The view of the English courts (as opposed to those of the United States and other jurisdictions) has traditionally been that if evidence is relevant to issues in the trial, it is admissible no matter how obtained. *R v Sang* (1980) is the leading case before PACE.

R v Sang [1980]

FACTS: S was charged with conspiracy to issue forged bank notes. He sought to exclude evidence obtained, he claimed, due to the activities of an **agent provocateur** while he was in prison. The trial judge refused the application and he pleaded guilty.

HELD: The House of Lords acknowledged that there was a general discretion to exclude evidence on the grounds that its prejudicial effect exceeded its probative value. There was also discretion to exclude evidence obtained after the commission of the offence if it had been obtained unfairly or by trickery in violation of the privilege against self-incrimination. There was no defence of **entrapment** known to English law.

Developing a principled approach: s78 PACE

Academic commentators have debated whether it is possible to derive from the case law a coherent set of principles which the courts apply in excluding improperly obtained evidence. The common law test for exclusion is whether the probative value of the evidence is less than its prejudicial effect. Following *Sang*, save in the case of evidence akin to a confession obtained after the commission of the offence, there was no discretion to exclude evidence on the grounds that it was improperly or unfairly obtained. PACE marked a departure from that narrow stance.

Section 78(1) PACE subsequently gave a discretionary power to judges and magistrates to exclude evidence on which the prosecution proposes to rely if it appears that 'having regard to all the circumstances, including the circumstances in which the evidence was obtained, the admission of the evidence would have such an adverse effect on the fairness of the proceedings that the court ought not to admit it'. The statute also preserves the common law discretion (see s78(2)).

As you read the case law and in particular the apparent retreat from *Sang* in the post-PACE cases keep in mind the various criteria which have been put forward to justify exclusion of improperly obtained evidence (see Fig 4.1). You will be able to find *dicta* in the cases to justify each of the somewhat overlapping list of reasons for exclusion but it is arguable that there is no overall coherent judicial stance. The debate ranges between those who argue that if relevant evidence exists it defies common sense not to admit it, to others who protest

Key features and principles
✳✳✳✳✳✳✳✳✳✳

Figure 4.1 Matrix of exclusion criteria

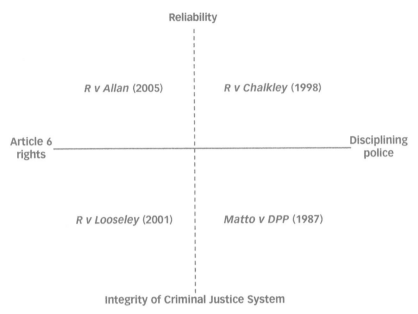

that the moral authority of the verdict may be undermined if the court admits apparently reliable evidence that has been obtained wrongly in some way.

Reliability and fair process considerations

An early decision under PACE in the Divisional Court seemed to herald a disciplinary approach to exclusion of evidence under s78 PACE. In *Matto v DPP* (1987) the court held that the police had acted in bad faith and beyond their powers in trespassing in order to obtain a breath specimen from a suspect. Subsequent cases have shown that it is difficult to derive clear principles for exclusion. Thus, in *R v Khan* (1997), even though the police had committed trespass and criminal damage in planting a listening device on premises used by a suspect, the House of Lords held that the evidence should not be excluded. The Strasbourg court held that there had been no violation of Art 6 but there had been a violation of Art 8 (*Khan v UK* (2001)).

Post-HRA 1998

A more jurisprudential approach appears to have followed the implementation of the Human Rights Act. Evidence obtained by torture in any jurisdiction is indisputably inadmissible. In a landmark decision, the House of Lords, reversing the Court of Appeal, has ruled that evidence obtained by torture abroad is not admissible in English courts, *A v Secretary of State for the Home Department (No 2) (2006).* The appeal was granted on the basis of the common law prohibition on torture, on Arts 3 and 6 ECHR, and on general principles of public international law. The case of course raises far wider issues than those of the admissibility of evidence. As Lord Bingham (at para 51) put it:

> It trivialises the issue before the House to treat it as an argument about the law of evidence. The issue is one of constitutional principle, whether evidence obtained by torturing another human being may be admitted to proceedings in a British court, irrespective of where, or by whom, or on whose authority the torture was inflicted. To that question I would give a very clear negative answer.

This is a welcome decision but commentators (eg Keane and McKeown (2016, p62)) point out that the absolute exclusionary rule does not stretch to inhuman or degrading treatment.

Revision tip

The common law discretion has largely been overtaken by s78 PACE, but you will gain credit in a question on improperly obtained evidence for citing cases where judges have drawn on it. A good example is *R v Stagg (Colin)* (1994). Ognall J relied on the common law as well as s78 to exclude evidence obtained by an undercover policewoman and then subsequently stayed the prosecution.

The following table (Table 4.1) gives a picture of the contrasting approaches taken by the courts to the acceptance of improperly or illegally obtained evidence under the common law and PACE.

Table 4.1 Contrasting judicial approaches to excluding improperly obtained evidence

Cases tending to show a more restrictive approach, eg emphasis on reliability of the evidence, crime control, deference to investigative authorities	Cases tending to show a more robust approach, eg emphasis on human rights, due process, criticism of authorities
R v Leatham (1861)	*Matto v DPP* (1987)
R v Sang (1980)	*Teixeira de Castro v Portugal* (1998)
Williams and O'Hare v DPP (1993)	*R v Looseley; A-G's Ref (No 3 of 2000)* (2001)
R v Chalkley (1998)	*Allan v UK* (2002)
R v Khan (1997)	*R v Grant* (2005)
Nottingham City Council v Amin (2001)	*A v Sec State Home Department (No 2)* (2005)
R v Button (2005) *Warren v A-G for Jersey* (2012)	*R v Moon* (2004)

Revision tip

It is important when structuring an argument in an essay that you are able to show differing approaches of the courts, illustrated in Table 4.1, before you come to your own assessment. Confession cases apart, the instances of stay of prosecution or exclusion of evidence are not common. *R v Moon* (2004) is one such example. In that case the Court of Appeal held that there should have been a stay where the defendant needed much persuasion by an undercover officer to supply a small quantity of heroin. There was no evidence to show she had previously been involved in supplying drugs.

PACE and unfairly obtained evidence

Discretionary exclusion under PACE

The following points should be noted:

- the judge has to consider fairness to the proceedings in considering whether to exercise discretion to exclude evidence tendered by the prosecution: consideration must be given to fairness to the prosecution as well as fairness to the defendant;
- it is not sufficient for exclusion that the admission of the evidence will have some adverse effect, it must have such an adverse effect that the fairness of the proceedings is at risk;
- fairness to the proceedings means proceedings in court;
- the Court of Appeal will interfere with a trial judge's exercise of his discretion to exclude evidence under s78 PACE only for unreasonableness by the *Wednesbury* test; and
- breach of the Codes of Practice or a provision of the statute may help to get the evidence excluded (most cases on the exclusion of confessions are decided under this section).

Several cases have shown that the reliability of the evidence is a key factor in determining admissibility. In *R v Chalkley* (1998) the Court of Appeal took a very narrow view of s78 and considered that it did not enlarge the common law. The trial judge had admitted evidence of secret tape recordings obtained in breach of PACE and the civil law of trespass and in violation of Art 8 ECHR. Auld LJ in the Court of Appeal held that 'save in the case of admissions and confessions and generally as to evidence obtained from the accused after the commission of the offence there is no discretion to exclude evidence unless its quality was or might have been affected by the way in which it was obtained'. The tape recordings were highly probative of guilt and not affected by the improper police activity.

On the other hand in *Allan v UK* (2002) there had been direct psychological pressure applied to the defendant and the evidence should have been excluded. The police coached an informant to question A, who was on remand, in a prison cell about his involvement in a murder. The conversation was recorded and admitted at trial. The Court of Appeal subsequently accepted the Strasbourg court's analysis (*Allan v UK* (2002)) that the evidence should not have been admitted and quashed the conviction. Hooper J stated (*R v Allan* (2005) at para 122) that, 'Allowing an agent of the state to interrogate a suspect in the circumstances of this case bypasses any necessary protections developed over the last twenty years.' The Strasbourg court did not consider, however, that admission of secret recordings of conversations between Allan and a friend who visited him in prison and between Allan and another fellow prisoner conflicted with Art 6(1).

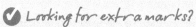

Looking for extra marks?

The examiners will be impressed if you demonstrate that you are aware of some exceptions to the general reluctance of the courts to exclude evidence in these circumstances. One contentious area is intercept evidence. Under s17 Regulation of Investigatory Powers Act 2000 the admission of evidence of an 'intercepted communication' is not permitted if it might reveal the existence or absence of a warrant. The purpose is to protect the secrecy of such surveillance operations. See *R v P* (2001). Note that in that case Lord Hobhouse stated that it was not within the power of the criminal court at trial to provide a remedy for a breach of Art 8.

Entrapment

An identifiable group of 'non-confession' cases involving possibly improperly obtained evidence falls into the category of 'entrapment', or cases involving an agent provocateur.

Teixeira de Castro v Portugal (1999)

FACTS: Two plain-clothes police officers had asked a known petty drug trafficker to obtain heroin. He mentioned the name of the applicant who eventually obtained packets of the drug for the undercover officers. The applicant was arrested, charged, and convicted. He claimed breaches of **Arts 3, 6, and 8.** He claimed that the officers had engaged in immoral conduct since he had supplied the drug solely at the officers' request. They had not been carrying out drug trafficking searches to a court order.

HELD: The ECtHR held that there was a violation of **Art 6** and it was not necessary to consider violations of **Arts 3 and 8**. The officers had instigated and incited the offence and there was nothing to suggest that but for their intervention it would not have been committed. The applicant had been denied the right to a fair trial.

Williams and O'Hare v DPP (1993)

FACTS: The police had set a trap in an area plagued by car theft. They parked a van filled with cigarette cartons with its door open. Two young men helped themselves and were arrested, charged, and convicted.

HELD: The convictions were upheld since the police had acted lawfully and there was no incitement.

In *R v Looseley* (2001) (see p70) the House appeared to endorse the position in Williams in that although the police must act in good faith it is not always essential to have grounds for suspecting a specific individual. Note that in *Ramanauskas v Lithuania* (2010) the officer was held by the Strasbourg court to have acted improperly when he was prompted to act undercover on what were only rumours of the malpractice of a state prosecutor.

The question of entrapment was reviewed exhaustively in *R v Smurthwaite* (1994). The Court of Appeal conceded that evidence could be excluded if it had the necessary adverse effect on the fairness of the proceedings. This demonstrates a pragmatic rather than a principled approach. The questions to ask were:

- was the officer acting as an agent provocateur in that he was enticing the defendant to commit an offence he would not otherwise have committed?
- what was the nature of the entrapment—was it evidence of admission to a completed offence, or did it consist of the actual commission of an offence?
- how active or passive was the officer's role? and
- is there an unassailable record of what occurred or is it strongly corroborated?

R v Shannon (2001)

FACTS: The defendant was convicted of supplying drugs to a journalist posing as an Arab sheikh, part of a stratagem to obtain evidence of drug offences against him. The judge refused an application to exclude the evidence as unfairly obtained.

HELD: The Court of Appeal held that the appeal against conviction be dismissed. There was no general rule requiring a court on grounds of fundamental fairness not to entertain a prosecution in all cases of incitement or instigation by an agent provocateur regardless of whether the trial as a whole could be fair in the procedural sense. The judge found correctly in that the evidence fell short of establishing actual incitement or instigation of the offences and in any event the admission of the evidence would not have an adverse effect on the procedural fairness of the trial. The Court of Appeal were referred to *Teixeira de Castro v Portugal* (1999) and held that the end result of that case, couched as it was in terms of incitement and causation, was not necessarily at odds with English law. It considered that the approach of the Strasbourg court was not inconsistent with the approach in *R v Smurthwaite* (1994), namely that the evidence would be open to exclusion only if the incitement had caused the offence.

The case illustrated the specific issue of entrapment by non-state actors, specifically journalists. See also *Admissibility Decision Shannon v UK* (2004) in the ECtHR. The application was refused on the facts but the court considered that it was in principle possible for the activity of a non-state agent to render proceedings unfair under Art 6 ECHR.

Stay of prosecution or exclusion of evidence?

The courts have the option of staying a prosecution rather than just excluding evidence at trial in cases involving improperly obtained evidence, and have adopted the former in relation to entrapment cases (see also p75). The prosecution may also be abandoned if the only evidence was that which was excluded under s78 PACE. In *R v Looseley; A-G's Reference (No 3 of 2000)* (2001) (conjoined appeals) the House of Lords held that the court must in such cases balance the need to uphold the rule of law by convicting and punishing those who committed crimes with the need to prevent law enforcement agencies acting in a way which offended ordinary notions of fairness. The House distinguished between entrapment which might lead to exclusion of evidence and entrapment which will lead to a stay of prosecution. There is not one simple test. The court must ask the central question, which is whether the actions of the police were so seriously improper as to bring the administration of justice into disrepute. If there has been an abuse of state power, then the appropriate remedy is a stay of the indictment, rather than exclusion of the evidence under s78 PACE. In *Looseley* the appeal was dismissed since the undercover officer did no more than present himself as an ordinary customer to an active drug dealer and there was nothing in the officer's conduct which constituted incitement. For further discussion on the test for stay of prosecution, see *Warren v Att-Gen for Jersey* (2012).

Concerning the conjoined appeal, *A-G's Reference (No 3 of 2000)*, the trial judge had been entitled to stay the proceedings on the ground that the officers had instigated the offence by offering inducements which would not ordinarily be associated with the commission of that offence. The House stated that the principle to be applied was that it would be unfair and an abuse of process if a person had been lured, incited, or pressurised into committing a crime which he would not otherwise have committed but that it would not be objectionable if the law enforcement officer, behaving as an ordinary member of the public, gave the person an exceptional opportunity to commit a crime and that person freely took advantage of the opportunity. The judgment demonstrated strong judicial recognition of the dangers of excessive police behaviour in cases of entrapment and the need for the courts to protect citizens.

Revision Tip

The decision in *Looseley* has been welcomed widely but your essays on this area would be improved if you were aware of some of the academic criticism. A wide-ranging article by Hyland and Walker (2014) provides a sceptical view. They point out (p577) that '*Looseley* represents a stronger structuring of due process and does begin to move away from a trial focus towards attention to the conduct of the police. But the judgment remains very limited as a basis for the regulation of covert policing. It still reflects a lobby in favour of police effectiveness by rejecting assertions that entrapment is a defence in English law or that police officers must conduct themselves in an entirely passive manner.'

The test

Following *Looseley* the focus of the court's approach must be on an objective assessment of the conduct of the police rather than the predisposition of the defendant. Thus, for example, the defendant's criminal record is unlikely to be relevant. Lord Nicholls specifically recognised (at para 16, p2067) that *R v Sang* (1980) had been 'overtaken' by statute and case law. Lord Hoffmann (at para 36, p2071) stressed the importance of the 'protection of the integrity of the criminal justice system'. Their Lordships considered that their judgment was compatible with *Teixeira de Castro v Portugal* (1999). It did not follow from *Teixeira* that taking any active steps, such as offering to buy drugs, necessarily amounts to 'incitement'. By contrast with *Teixeira*, in *Looseley* the undercover operation was compliant with the then Code of Practice on Undercover Operations, so the judgment did not address the need to reform the regulation of police undercover activity. Among the factors to be considered are the following:

- the nature of the offence,
- the factual basis for the police carrying out the operation,
- the degree and extent of the police inducement.

The former test of whether the offender was predisposed to commit such an offence was not appropriate.

Lord Nicholls of Birkenhead stated (para 23): '[A] useful guide is to consider whether the police did no more than present the defendant with an unexceptional opportunity to commit a crime. I emphasise the word unexceptional.'

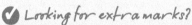 **Looking for extra marks?**

A frequent criticism of the law on undercover policing is that insufficient attention is given to violations of Art 8 ECHR. This issue has come to the fore with the revelations about police secretly targeting political actvists and in some cases forming sexual liaisons with women members. These activities led to miscarriages of justice, such as the prosecutions of 26 members of an environmental group who were charged with conspiracy to commit aggravated trespass as a result of the activities of K, a serving police officer. Of the 26, six denied being part of a conspiracy and were due to be charged. The prosecution offered no evidence when a material non-disclosure was uncovered. K had secretly recorded meetings of the group which revealed he had exceeded his authorisation. The earlier trial of 20 of the group had not had access to the recordings and they had been convicted. The DPP invited them to appeal. See *R v Barkshire* (2011).

R v Barkshire (2011)

FACTS: The appellants had admitted being part of a conspiracy to commit aggravated trespass. The appellants had justified their activities by the defence of necessity caused by global warming. They were convicted. They now claimed K had gone beyond his authority and that his status had not been revealed to the defence. K had purported enthusiastically to be a supporter of the beliefs of the group.

HELD: The appeals were allowed.

The case has led to a governmental review of the safeguards which ought to be in place when undercover officers infiltrate such legitimate organisations.

Breach of PACE or other legislation, codes, etc

Thus, the 'entrapment' cases form one group of cases possibly involving illegal or improper incitement by state and non-state actors. A second group of 'non-confession' cases involves breaches of PACE, other legislation, or Codes of Practice and Protocols. A number of these cases involve covert surveillance. The ECtHR has held that evidence so obtained is not necessarily to be excluded.

Khan v UK (2001)

FACTS: The applicant had been convicted of involvement in importing heroin. The evidence against him came from an electronic listening device installed by police in a private house he visited. The police had allegedly committed criminal damage in planting the device. K claimed violations of **Arts 6 and 8**.

HELD: The court held that the evidence had been obtained in violation of **Art 8** but it had not been unlawful in the sense of being contrary to domestic criminal law. The authenticity of the recordings was not in question; only their admissibility. Since the domestic courts could exercise discretion whether or not to admit such evidence and had concluded its admission would not affect the fairness of the trial, there was no breach of **Art 6**. The court found a breach of **Arts 8 and 12** since there was no legal basis and thus no redress for the invasion of privacy.

Overwhelming cogency of evidence

On occasion, police evidence obtained unlawfully is so cogent that to refuse to admit it affronts justice. An example is the admissibility of unlawfully retained **DNA** specimens.

A-G's Reference (No 3 of 1999) (2001)

FACTS: In two cases, one involving murder and one rape, the Crown had put forward as part of its case DNA evidence collected during other investigations which had both led to the defendants being acquitted. Under the then current wording of **s64(1) PACE** a sample taken from a suspect during the investigation of an offence must be destroyed if that person is 'cleared' of the offence and according to **s64(3B)** such sample 'shall not be used in evidence against that person . . . or for the purposes of any investigation of an offence'.

HELD: The Court of Appeal declared that **s64** was mandatory and such evidence was inadmissible. At the request of the Attorney General it referred a question for the opinion of the House of Lords as to whether in such circumstances a judge had a discretion to admit the relevant evidence notwithstanding the terms of **s64(3B)**. The House of Lords reversed the Court of Appeal decision. Whereas **s64(3B)** made express prohibition against the use of a DNA sample which should have been destroyed, **s64(3B)(b)**, in prohibiting the use of an unlawfully retained sample for the purposes of any investigation, did not amount to a mandatory exclusion of evidence obtained as a result of a failure to comply with the prohibition. It should be read along with **s78**, which left the question of its admissibility to the discretion of the trial judge. A decision by a judge in the exercise of his discretion not to exclude such evidence would not be in breach of **Art 8 or 6 ECHR**. The information obtained as a result of the failure to destroy the DNA sample ought not to have been rendered inadmissible.

(Subsequently, the law has been changed so that it is lawful for the police to keep DNA specimens of those who are arrested but not charged.)

Revision tip

Khan v UK (2001) demonstrates that the Strasbourg court is likely to find a breach of **Art 8** if covert surveillance is carried out outside of legislative provisions. Bear in mind that it is always open to Parliament to give the police extensive additional powers so their scope for acting illegally is narrowed. Thus, the undercover operation undertaken by the police in *R v Khan* (1997) ➡

⟶ would now be authorised under Pt III of the Police Act 1997 or Pt II of the Regulation of Investigatory Powers Act 2000 (RIPA). Note that in *R v Khan* (2013) the Court of Appeal held that the trial judge had been correct not to exclude a secret recording of the appellants.

Police surveillance, national security, and legal professional privilege

The courts appear to take a trenchant stance on protecting legal professional privilege and the trial may be stayed or evidence excluded even where the fairness of the trial may not be affected. In *R v Grant* (2005) police had secretly and without authorisation recorded the conversation (see p76) of a suspect and his solicitor. This amounted to a breach of legal professional privilege and the trial was stayed. However, this contrasts with the Court of Appeal's decision in *R v Button* (2005) involving a secret recording of a suspect in his cell. There was breach of Art 8 but it was not unfair to admit the evidence. The court rejected the appellants' argument that it would be unlawful not to exclude evidence obtained in breach of Art 8, stating 'This is a startling proposition and one which we are pleased and relieved to be able to reject'.

Disapproval of the decision in *Grant* was expressed by the Privy Council in *Warren v A-G of Jersey* (2011), a case involving illegal surveillance in a vehicle from another jurisdiction where a stay was not ordered. Lord Dyson stated that a stay was appropriate in cases of abduction of a witness and entrapment but not in illicitly intercepting privileged conversations. Another case illustrating the court's reluctance to exclude evidence for police breaches and avoidance of the surveillance regulations in RIPA is *R v Khan* (2013). There the unlawful use of a listening device was beyond the authorisation given under RIPA and the breach was less serious than that in *Warren*. The court stated there had been no bad faith. There was a breach of Art 8 but no remedy could be ordered.

The House of Lords has now held that the police, in cases involving national security, may bug a solicitor client interview if authorised under the stringent provisions of RIPA, see *Re McE* (2009). RIPA thus overrode legal professional privilege (see Chapter 11). In a powerful dissenting judgment Lord Phillips identified a distinction between legal professional privilege and the statutory right of a detained person to consult privately with a solicitor. He stated (at para 26), 'I would interpret the statutory right to consult a lawyer privately as one that confers on the detainee an absolute right to privacy that precludes covert surveillance in any circumstances.'

Of course, *Re McE* does not mean that evidence obtained in such circumstances will be admissible at trial, but it marks a significant step in legitimising what had been previously perceived as unauthorised police activity.

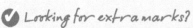 **Looking for extra marks?**

You should demonstrate that you understand the difference between impropriety carried out by non-state actors as opposed to those who represent state power. In *Council for the Regulation of Health Professionals v GMC* (2007) Goldring J stated that where there had been 'sufficiently gross misconduct by the non-state agent it would be an abuse of the court's process and a breach of Article 6 for the state to rely on the resulting evidence'. See also *Shannon* (2001) (p70).

① Conclusion

Roberts and Zuckerman (2010) review the rationales for exclusion of improperly obtained evidence and observe that it is short-sighted not to take account of the fact that the evidence exists as then 'our knowledge of the world has changed forever and moral evaluation must take account of the realities of the situation' (p183). They call for a development of 'principles of attribution specifying the circumstances in which the state is properly answerable for the activities of its servants and agents' (p189). They argue that 'an inflexible rule, either of exclusion or of admissibility, is bound to be inadequate' (p190). Recent case law does suggest that English courts are now engaging with this moral dimension and have moved beyond the view that reliability is the only criterion for admissibility in relation to improperly obtained evidence. The approach evidenced in *Chalkley* (1998) that evidence suggesting factual guilt was sufficient may be short-lived.

In particular, it does seem that the law on entrapment has thus moved away from *Sang* (1980). Entrapment is still not a defence but a more robust approach to exclusion or stay of prosecution is now taken, recognising that fair trial rights extend to pre-trial proceedings, including police investigations. The issues are complex policy ones. The investigative authorities, particularly the police will argue that their hands should not be tied by technicalities, especially given the threat from organised crime and hardened offenders. Civil libertarians will argue that it is vital that the integrity of the criminal justice process is upheld by high standards.

It is clear that on occasion, albeit unusually, the courts will exclude such evidence or stay a prosecution because, however compelling it might be, the integrity of the criminal process might otherwise be at risk. This is particularly so in cases of entrapment and far less so, torture cases aside, in other situations where the evidence is reliable. It is expected that the jurisprudence from Strasbourg applied under the **Human Rights Act** will lead to more careful delineation of the principles on which the courts should approach such cases. The tension is between concentrating too much on the reliability of the evidence to the detriment of considerations of fairness. It is notable of course that s78 **PACE** refers to 'fairness of the proceedings' and not just to the defendant. Finally, of course, it is always open to Parliament to authorise extended police operations by statute and legitimise formerly improper or unlawful police actions.

It is generally agreed that the judicial exclusionary discretion is based on a pragmatic rather than a principled approach. Commentators have remarked on the position of other jurisdictions where in particular there is a more active stance on exclusion, particularly if there is a violation of a constitutional right. Examples are the United States' case *Mapp v Ohio* (1961) and s24(2) **Canadian Charter of Rights and Freedoms**, which provides:

> Where . . . a court concludes that evidence was obtained in a manner that infringed or denied any rights or freedoms guaranteed by this Charter, the evidence shall be excluded if it is established that, having regard to all the circumstances, the admission of it in the proceedings would bring the administration of justice into disrepute.

Note also the provisions of the **Rome Statute of the International Criminal Court** on improperly obtained evidence. **Article 69(7)** reads:

Key cases

Evidence obtained by means of a violation of this Statute or internationally recognised human rights shall not be admissible if:

(a) The violation casts substantial doubt on the reliability of the evidence; or

(b) The admission of the evidence would be antithetical to and would seriously damage the integrity of the proceedings.

Warren v A-G for Jersey (2011)

FACTS: The police obtained evidence from an unauthorised listening device by measures which included misleading authorities in other jurisdictions. The judge refused to stay the proceedings and admitted the evidence at the trial of the appellant for drug dealing and manslaughter.

HELD: The Privy Council upheld the trial judge's rulings. Although the police had acted improperly, there were circumstances such as the seriousness of the charges which should be taken into account.

The Privy Council made a strongly worded criticism of the police malpractice.

The case illustrates the difficulty the courts have in imposing sanctions against abuse of surveillance powers including those involving breaches of **RIPA**.

 Key cases

Case	Facts	Principle and comment
A v Secretary of State for the Home Department (No 2) (2006) 2 AC 221	The Special Immigration Appeals Commission (SIAC) and the Court of Appeal had held that evidence obtained by torture abroad was admissible for the purpose of deciding whether a person was a terrorist and a threat to national security.	The exclusion of evidence obtained by torture, including outside the jurisdiction, is a principle of the common law.
Khan v UK (2001) 31 EHRR 1016	Police planted a covert listening device to a property frequented by a suspected drug dealer. There was no statutory authority for their action. The evidence from the recordings founded the conviction. The House of Lords rejected the argument that there was a violation of **Art 8 ECHR**.	There had been a violation of **Art 8** but not **Art 6**. The admissibility of evidence was primarily a matter for the domestic court and this had properly applied the law. The question was whether the proceedings as a whole were fair.

Case	Facts	Principle and comment
Nottingham City Council v Amin [2001] 1 WLR 1071	Plain clothes officers hired a taxi without a licence. The magistrate had excluded the evidence on the grounds of entrapment and violation of **Art 6**.	Evidence should be admitted. D would have behaved in the same way if others had offered the opportunity.
R v Chalkley and Jeffries (1998) 2 Cr App R 79	A covert listening device had been planted and police had unlawfully entered the appellant's home to replace batteries.	The evidence should not be excluded. The evidence was authentic, probative, and relevant. The quality of the evidence had not been affected by the police action.
R v Looseley; A-G's Ref (No 3 of 2000) [2001] UKHL 53	An undercover police officer arranged with the defendant to exchange heroin for money. The defendant was charged with supplying or being concerned in supplying to another a class A controlled drug, contrary to **s4 Misuse of Drugs Act 1971**. The trial judge refused a preliminary request to exclude evidence or stay proceedings. In the second case, two undercover police officers were introduced to the accused as a potential buyer of contraband cigarettes. They sold him cigarettes and asked if he could get them heroin. He did so and was charged with supplying heroin. The trial judge stayed the proceedings on the ground that the police had incited the commission of the offence and that otherwise the accused would be denied his right to a fair hearing under **Art 6(1) ECHR**.	Appeal in the first case dismissed and in the second case the trial judge was held to have acted correctly. The proper approach is to ask did the police do more than present the defendant with an unexceptional opportunity to commit a crime. It would be unfair to offer inducements and entice a person into actions he would not normally have taken. The proper approach is stay of proceedings but evidence may be excluded if trial has commenced. In one case, that of a known drug dealer, the conviction was upheld but in the other it had been properly stayed as an abuse of process in that there had been the encouragement of an uncharacteristic offence.
R v Sang [1980] AC 402	The defendants were convicted of conspiracy to issue forged banknotes. It was argued that evidence had been obtained by the activities of an agent provocateur.	Entrapment was not a defence. There was no common law discretion to exclude relevant evidence, other than confession evidence or evidence obtained after the commission of the offence, because it was improperly obtained.

Key debates

✳✳✳✳✳✳✳✳✳

Case	Facts	Principle and comment
R v Smurthwaite (1994) 98 Cr App R 437	An undercover police officer posed as contract killer and secretly recorded conversations with the defendant. The defendant had said he wanted to hire someone to kill his wife. Trial judge refused to exclude evidence in trial for solicitation to murder.	The Court of Appeal reviewed the factors to be considered in exercising judicial discretion to exclude evidence obtained by entrapment. There was no defence of entrapment but s78 PACE could in principle be applied to exclude such evidence on grounds of unfairness to the proceedings.

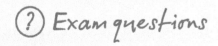

⑨⑨ Key debates

Topic	Should the discretion under s78 PACE be structured and should there be a presumption of exclusion?
Authors	D Ormerod and D Birch
Viewpoint	The authors set out the arguments for and against a statutory adoption of a more structured approach to exclusion of evidence. One risk of a structured approach is that it might be resisted by the judiciary and signal a return to the common law discretion.
Source	'Evolution of the Discretionary Exclusion of Evidence' [2004] *Crim LR* 138

Topic	Legal values and discretionary exclusion of evidence
Author	A Ashworth
Viewpoint	Puts the theoretical argument for the principle that those who enforce the law should obey it and if government officials have played a part in creating an offence the trial should be stopped.
Source	'Testing Fidelity to Legal Values: Official Involvement and Criminal Justice' (2000) 63 *MLR* 633

⑦ Exam questions

Essay question

'Section 78 of the Police and Criminal Evidence Act 1984 empowers the court to exclude prosecution evidence if its admission "would have such an adverse effect on the fairness of the proceedings that the court ought not to admit it". However, so far there has been little inclination to elucidate the principles which should govern the exercise of this discretion' (Zuckerman (1989, p352)).

Explain, with reasons, whether Zuckerman's comment is still valid today in relation to the discretionary exclusion of improperly obtained evidence other than confessions.

Online Resource Centre

To see an outline answer to this question visit www.oup.com/lawrevision/

Problem question

The police are concerned about a spate of thefts from houses and shops on the Stafford Cripps Estate. The offenders have not been caught. Inspector Tamara, acting undercover, engages a group of women in conversation at the school gates when they are collecting their children. She admires the earrings they are wearing. Janet, one of the mothers, agrees to get a pair of earrings for Tamara. They arrange to meet the next day and the earrings are exchanged for money. They turn out to have been stolen from a jewellery shop on the estate. Janet is arrested for dealing in stolen goods.

Advise on evidence.

See the Outline Answers section in the end matter for help with this question.

Concentrate Q&As

For more questions and answers on evidence, see the *Concentrate Q&A: Evidence* by Maureen Spencer and John Spencer.

Go to the end of this book to view **sample pages**.

#5
Character evidence

- Two legal processes are at stake in discussing character evidence: whether the evidence is admissible or not, and if it is admissible, what is its evidential worth.

- Character is found in two spheres, namely good character and bad character.

- The admissibility and evidential worth of good character is governed by the common law.

- Good character, defined as general reputation, or lack of criminal record, may be evidence of lack of guilt (propensity) and of trustworthiness as a witness (credit). The leading case is *R v Hunter* (2015).

- Bad character evidence, if admitted, may be evidence of either **propensity**, or **credibility**, or both.

- Under the common law there was a presumption that bad character evidence of defendants was not admissible, the exceptions to this were (i) the '**similar fact**' common law principle and (ii) the statutory provisions relating to cross examination of the witness who chose to testify under s1(3) Criminal Evidence Act (CEA) 1898.

- Bad character evidence of both defendants and non-defendant witnesses is now defined by statute, s98 Criminal Justice Act (CJA) 2003.

- The admissibility of bad character evidence of non-defendants is determined by s100 CJA 2003, which adopts a more restrictive approach to admissibility in contrast to the common law position and in line with the more protective attitude to victims.

- The admissibility of bad character evidence of defendants is governed by s101(1) CJA 2003.

- Bad character of the defendant may now be admissible whether he testifies or not, in contrast to the former position where, under the common law, bad character evidence was admitted for the non-testifying defendant only under the similar fact rule or if a witness gave good character evidence. Under the CEA 1898 imputations made against a prosecution witness where the defendant did not testify did *not* trigger the admissibility of his bad character evidence.

Chapter overview

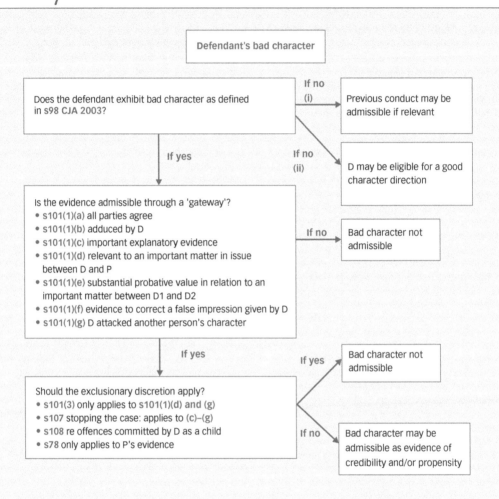

Defendant's bad character

Does the defendant exhibit bad character as defined in s98 CJA 2003?

If no (i) → Previous conduct may be admissible if relevant

If yes

If no (ii) → D may be eligible for a good character direction

Is the evidence admissible through a 'gateway'?
- s101(1)(a) all parties agree
- s101(1)(b) adduced by D
- s101(1)(c) important explanatory evidence
- s101(1)(d) relevant to an important matter in issue between D and P
- s101(1)(e) substantial probative value in relation to an important matter between D1 and D2
- s101(1)(f) evidence to correct a false impression given by D
- s101(1)(g) D attacked another person's character

If no → Bad character not admissible

If yes

Should the exclusionary discretion apply?
- s101(3) only applies to s101(1)(d) and (g)
- s107 stopping the case: applies to (c)–(g)
- s108 re offences committed by D as a child
- s78 only applies to P's evidence

If yes → Bad character not admissible

If no → Bad character may be admissible as evidence of credibility and/or propensity

Non-defendant's bad character

Does the non-defendant exhibit bad character as defined in s98?

If yes

Is it important explanatory evidence s100(1)(a)?
Or does it have substantial probative value in relation to a matter which is in issue and is of substantial importance in the context of the case as a whole, s100(1)(b)? Or do all parties agree to its admission, s100(1)(c)?

If yes

Evidence may be admissible as evidence of credibility provided the court gives leave. If both parties agree the evidence is admissible without leave

Defendant's good character

Does the defendant have good character (*R v Hunter* (2015))

If yes

May be entitled to good character direction on credibility and propensity even if D2 has bad character (*R v Vye* (1993); *R v Aziz* (1996); *R v Hunter* (2015))

Related areas

Character evidence may be considered alongside that on confessions since the defendant may choose to challenge the admissibility of his confession by attacking the behaviour of the police, for example, at interview. This may lay him open to having his criminal record revealed. Since previous bad behaviour may involve testimony from witnesses making out of court statements the law on hearsay may also play a part. Finally, Chapter 8 in relation to sexual history evidence of complainants in rape trials needs to be read in conjunction with this chapter since you may need to discuss whether the prior sexual behaviour of the alleged victim is covered by ss98 and 100 CJA 2003.

The assessment: key points

This chapter explains that character evidence falls into three main areas, namely bad character of the defendant, good character of the defendant, and bad character of a non-defendant witness. It concludes with a short note on the good character of non-defendant witnesses.

The law relating to each is quite different. There are frequently two questions to address in any assessment, first whether the character evidence is admissible at trial and second, if it is, what is it admissible for, ie what is its evidential worth? The law relating to the bad character of the defendant is the most difficult and forms the bulk of this chapter. It is covered by a very complex statute, CJA 2003, and a growing body of case law. You should be very careful that you understand the statutory provisions and treat the cases as examples of its operation. The cases should not be seen as exact precedents since each situation turns on its own facts. In many instances the cases are conjoined appeals covering many first instance trials. They will be referred to here for the most part by the first named case.

Admissibility

Bad character evidence comprises a controversial series of provisions where the old common law exclusionary rule that the defendant's previous convictions should not be disclosed to the court has in many ways been turned on its head. There is now, in effect, a presumption that a criminal record should be admitted but in order to achieve admissibility the provisions of the statute should be scrupulously followed. This again is an area where it does help to have at least outline knowledge of the history of the law. Some of the cases on bad character that are cited in the judgments under CJA 2003 were determined under the common law or the CEA 1898. The Supreme Court in *R v Platt* (2016) expressed its disapproval of this practice (see p86).

Evidential worth

You need to clarify in your mind the sometimes obscure distinction between relevance to propensity (lack of guilt) and relevance to credit (trustworthiness). The criminal justice system (apart from the Law Commission) and the legal profession, with little evidence from psychological research, have long maintained that both good and bad character, if admitted, may be predictors of behaviour in either or both of the following two ways:

- they may indicate that the defendant is either less or more likely to have committed the offence; and

- that he or she is more or less likely to be telling the truth as a witness.

Revision tip

It is sound practice, particularly in preparation for essay questions, to read the consultation papers and reports produced by the Law Commission, which provide helpful guides to the principles and public policy considerations underlying this area of law. Thus, in its Consultation Paper, No 141, produced in 1996, it referred to the light that psychological research had thrown on this area. It pointed out (paras 6.16–6.17) that there was no sound psychological research confirming a link between criminal record and lack of truthfulness as a witness. In 2001 the Law Commission published its Final Report, *Evidence of Bad Character in Criminal Proceedings* (Law Com No 273) (http://www.lawcom.gov.uk/wp-content/uploads/2015/03/lc273_Evidence_of_Bad_Character_in_Criminal_Proceedings_Report.pdf). It is a good exercise to contrast its proposals with the shape of the final statute, which arguably has taken a more prosecutorial approach. There is also a large body of scholarship, in particular work by Redmayne (see pA6), analysing the type of reasoning that is engaged when the fact-finder learns of the defendant's previous convictions.

Key features and principles

Rationale and evolution of the law on character

This area is one of the most controversial in the law of evidence. To what extent should a defendant have a 'clean slate' when facing trial? It helps to have some overview of the history, particularly of the provisions on bad character. There are two strands to this, one under the common law and one under statute.

Statute pre-2003

Until 1898 the defendant was not allowed to testify, so was protected from being questioned about any previous convictions, unlike other witnesses who were not so protected. However, if evidence was given on his behalf of his good character the prosecution was allowed under the common law to admit any bad character. The CEA 1898 brought about a compromise whereby if the defendant chose to testify, he was shielded from questions in cross examination about any bad character unless he

- claimed to be of good character,

- impugned a prosecution witness or a dead victim (a 1994 amendment to the 1898 Act), or

- made an attack on a co-defendant.

Key features and principles

If he did any of these he lost his 'shield'. Note that the section only applied to the testifying defendant. The evidence, if admitted, was only evidence for lack of credibility.

Common law pre-2003

The common law strand of cases on bad character related to what was known as 'similar fact'. The starting point was the exclusionary rule that previous bad character was not admissible to show guilt. The exception was that if the previous behaviour was so relevant that it shed more probative light than prejudice on the instant charge, it was admitted.

Gradually, the case law demonstrated a lowering of the threshold of admissibility in 'similar fact' cases. The rule on admissibility applied whether the defendant testified or not, and the evidence, if admitted, was evidence of guilt.

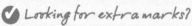

Looking for extra marks?

The above historical account has been included because it is important that evidence students understand how the law in this area has evolved. However, you need to make clear in writing essays or answering problem questions on this subject that s99 CJA 2003 abolished the common law rules on admissibility of bad character save in relation to reputation. The Supreme Court in *R v Platt* (2016) commented on this (paras 23–29). It stated, 'Those editing the textbooks might well consider that the time has come for a substantial revision to remove the old law where it has been replaced by the code set out in the CJA 2003.' *R v Randall* (2004), decided under the earlier law, had been wrongly cited in relation to the application of s101(1)(e). The court cited the observation in *R v Chopra* (2007) that the 2003 Act represented a 'sea-change' in the law.

Reform: Criminal Justice Act 2003

The complexities of the law in this area and the pressure to secure more convictions led to a review of the legislation. The Law Commission published two reports in which they identified the dangers of too readily admitting the defendant's bad character. The jury might give it too much weight and thus fall into a 'reasoning prejudice' or they might fall into 'moral prejudice' by not looking at the evidence carefully since they had formed a prejudicial view of the defendant on the basis of his record. The highly prejudicial effect of admitting defendants' previous convictions before both juries and magistrates has been identified in research by Lloyd Bostock (1973, 2006) and the risk, therefore, is that too ready an admissibility of bad character evidence may lead to miscarriages of justice.

In the event, the government legislated in the CJA 2003 to admit character evidence more readily than the Law Commission had recommended. The concept of a 'shield' for the defendant, which lay behind the CEA 1898, was replaced by that of 'gateways' (see Table 5.1) of admissibility indicating that there is a presumption the bad character evidence will be admitted. As Keane and McKeown (2016, p510) point out, this approach is 'radically different' from that under the earlier law. Now 'It is not one of inadmissibility subject to exceptions but of admissibility if certain criteria are met.'

Section 99 CJA 2003 abolishes the common law rules on admissibility (but not on other aspects of character, eg definition of good character or judicial directions to the jury on the evidential worth of character). It also repeals s1(3) CEA 1898.

Bad character

Section 98 CJA 2003 describes bad character for 'persons', that is for both defendants and non-defendants (whether they appear as witnesses or not) as evidence of, or a disposition towards, misconduct on his part, other than evidence which—

(a) has to do with the alleged facts of the offence with which the defendant is charged, or

(b) is evidence of misconduct in connection with the investigation or prosecution of that offence.

Relevant behaviour (not forming 'bad character')

If the behaviour falls within s98(a) or (b) it may be admissible if it is relevant. In addition there may be prior behaviour which is arguably not 'evidence of, or a disposition towards, misconduct' and which is potentially admissible.

As far as non-defendants are concerned, bad character can only be admitted if it satisfies s100. As far as defendants are concerned, to be admitted bad character has to satisfy one of the s101 'gateways'. Before considering more fully the definition of 'misconduct' and the 'gateways' of admissibility it is important to realise that there are three sorts of prior behaviour for which the only test of admissibility is relevance. Taking each in turn:

Relevance test (1): The alleged facts of the case

In *R v Edwards (Stewart) and Rowlands* (2006) the discovery of a cartridge buried in the defendant's garden was admissible under s98(a) and not as evidence of bad character through s101.

Relevance test (2): Evidence of misconduct in connection with the investigation or prosecution of that offence

This might include, for example, evidence of witness intimidation after the alleged commission of the offence admissible under s98(b).

Relevance test (3): Other relevant behaviour (not listed in s98)

Here, the earlier tests in the 'similar fact' cases may be helpful in understanding admissibility under the common law. The evidence will need to be more probative than prejudicial. Behaviour here may be neither criminal nor morally reprehensible. Cases involve relevant behaviour which is not necessarily misconduct. This might include, for example, a relationship with a much younger female. See *R v Manister (sub nom Weir)* (2006).

Bad character

✱✱✱✱✱✱✱✱✱✱

Previous convictions and other 'reprehensible behaviour'

The interpretive section to s98, s112, defines misconduct as 'the commission of an offence or other reprehensible behaviour'. The term 'reprehensible behaviour' has not featured in other statutes and its vagueness in meaning has been the subject of academic and judicial debate. In *R v Mitchell* (2016) the Supreme Court admitted 'non-conviction' bad character evidence of the propensity to use knives to threaten despite the absence of convictions. The defendant was on trial for stabbing her partner to death.

Bad character certainly includes, but is not limited to, previous convictions. The Explanatory Notes which accompanied the Act gave a broad definition of 'bad character' as including 'evidence such as previous convictions as well as evidence on charges being tried concurrently and evidence relating to offences for which [the accused] has been charged, where the charge is not prosecuted, or for which [the accused] was subsequently acquitted'. Bad character evidence may be sourced by the defendants: see *R v Lewis* (2014) on appearance in YouTube videos suggesting gang membership (see p100). On the other hand, in *R v Osbourne* (2007) using aggressive words was held not necessarily to be reprehensible.

Revision tip

In answering a problem question you may be given the age of the defendant when a previous offence was committed. Section 108(2) provides that convictions committed while the defendant was under 14 years old are not admitted in trials where the defendant is over 21 years. The exception is if offences allegedly committed at the current trial and also when the defendant was under 14 years are only triable on indictment and the court considers that 'the interests of justice require the evidence to be admissible'.

Relationship between common law and s98 CJA

The conjoined five appeals in *R v Weir* (2006) will give you a good overview of the relationship between the common law test of relevance and the requirements of the CJA in relation to the definition of character.

***R v Weir* (2006)**

FACTS:

(1) W had been convicted of sexual assault by touching a girl under the age of 13 and appealed against the decision to allow the Crown to adduce evidence that W had been cautioned for taking an indecent photograph of a child. W submitted that the evidence of the caution should not have been admitted because the offence in respect of which the caution was administered was not, for the purposes of s103(2)(b), an offence of the same category as the one with which he was charged.

---

(2) S had been convicted of rape. The Crown had been permitted to call evidence about S's previous inappropriate but not criminal sexual behaviour from three witnesses under **s101(1) of the 2003 Act**. S submitted that the bad character evidence should not have been admitted under **s101(1)(d)** because none of it was relevant to any important matter in issue between S and the Crown, and before the implementation of the **2003 Act** it would only have been admitted if it satisfied the requirements of similar fact evidence.

(3) Y had been convicted of assault occasioning actual bodily harm and assault with intent to resist arrest. Y's girlfriend, a defence witness, admitted that she had been cautioned for possession of cocaine but the prosecution did not cross examine further on this. The judge ruled that the caution had substantial probative value to her credibility, which was an important issue in the case and was therefore admissible under **s100(1)(b)**, but in his summing-up directed the jury to disregard the evidence. Y submitted that the judge had erred both in holding that the evidence of the caution was admissible, because **s100(1)** did not cover issues of credibility.

(4) M submitted that the bad character evidence of his relationship with a 16-year-old should not have been admitted.

(5) H (two appellants who did not testify) had been convicted of violent disorder after a running fight between two groups of young men. A co-defendant had claimed that H were known to the police from previous incidents. The judge ruled that the evidence in issue could not amount to bad character but was admissible at common law because of its relevance.

HELD:

(1) A defendant's propensity to commit offences of the kind with which he was charged could be proved in ways other than by evidence that he had been convicted of an offence of the same description or an offence of the same category under the **Criminal Justice Act 2003 Order 2004**. W's appeal was dismissed.

(2) The previous similar fact test, which balanced probative value against prejudicial effect, was obsolete. The bad character evidence in the case of S satisfied the requirements of **s101(1)(d)**. S not only denied rape but any improper behaviour. The evidence was plainly relevant to the credibility of the complainant and S. It was also relevant to the issue of propensity to untruthfulness. The evidence was also admissible under **s101(1)(f)** and **s101(1)(g)**. S's appeal failed.

(3) **Section 100(1)** covered matters of credibility. The judge had erred in concluding that the evidence of the caution had substantial probative value in relation to the witness's credibility and the evidence of the caution was inadmissible under **s100**. However, in the light of the very strong warning given by the judge when summing-up, Y's convictions were not unsafe.

(4) The judge had been wrong to hold that the previous sexual relationship between M and a 16-year-old girl was evidence of bad character under **s98 of the 2003 Act**. However, the evidence was admissible at common law because it was relevant to the issue of whether M had a sexual interest in the complainant, which he denied. M's appeal based on bad character failed.

(5) The evidence that H were known to the police from previous incidents could only be relevant if it might show that either appellant had a propensity to violent conduct and therefore bear on the co-defendant's case of self-defence. To show such a propensity it had to amount to reprehensible behaviour, misconduct, and, therefore, bad character under the **2003 Act**. The evidence did not show such behaviour and was not admissible whether adduced by the co-defendant or the Crown. H's convictions were unsafe.

Bad character

✳✳✳✳✳✳✳✳✳✳✳

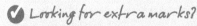 *Looking for extra marks?*

You will impress the examiner if you connect the material in each of the specific areas with the general principles you have learnt and which are outlined in Chapter 1. Thus, for example, you will be aware that the question of the nature of prior bad character could be seen as a 'collateral fact' and the courts will not want to spend too much time on arguments about what amounts to 'reprehensible behaviour'. In *R v McKenzie* (2008) the Court of Appeal was critical of time being taken up on collateral matters which could add to the length of the trial. However, on the facts of this case the definition did allow the Crown to adduce evidence of prior bad driving (where there was no conviction) under s101(1)(d) in order to prove aggressive and impatient driving.

Evidence of the defendant's bad character (as defined in s98 CJA 2003) is only admissible if one of the gateways in s101(1) applies. Subsections (c)–(g) have an accompanying explanatory section (ss102–106), which is also given in Table 5.1.

Note the differing descriptors of the test for admissibility between the sections. Under s112 'an important matter' means 'a matter of substantial importance in the context of the case as a whole'. This appears to blur the distinction between 'relevant to an important matter' and 'substantial probative value in relation to an important matter in issue'.

Note also that 'probative value' and 'relevant' are to be read in accordance with s109:

(1) the relevance or probative value of evidence is a reference to its relevance or probative value on the assumption that it is true.

(2) In assessing the relevance or probative value of an item of evidence . . . a court need not assume that the evidence is true if it appears, on the basis of any material before the court (including any evidence it decides to hear on the matter) that no court or jury could reasonably find it to be true.

The gateways

Taking each gateway in turn, their scope and examples of case law will be reviewed:

First gateway: section 101(1)(a)

All the parties agree:

This is not a controversial provision and it may occur if the defendant thinks tactically it is best to pre-empt the prosecution admitting the bad character evidence or it might be necessary in establishing an alibi. Note that under this head any co-defendants would have to also agree.

Second gateway: section 101(1)(b)

Elicited in examination or cross examination:

Again this might be a tactical decision by the defendant. The risk for the defendant in both these instances is that the evidence may then be used by the prosecution to demonstrate lack of credibility and propensity. In other words he may control its admissibility but not its evidential use (see further 'Third gateway' (p91)).

Table 5.1 The gateways and explanatory statutory sections

Gateway	Provision
s101(1)(a)	All the parties agree
s101(1)(b)	Evidence is adduced by defendant, or given in examination or cross examination
s101(1)(c)	It is important explanatory evidence. See also s102
s101(1)(d)	It is relevant to an important matter in issue between the defendant and the prosecution. See also s103
s101(1)(e)	It has substantial probative value in relation to an important matter in issue between the defendant and a co-defendant. See also s104
s101(1)(f)	It is evidence to correct a false impression given by the defendant. See also s105
s101(1)(g)	The defendant makes an attack on another person's character. See also s106

Third gateway: sections 101(1)(c) and 102

Important explanatory evidence:

Evidence under this gateway will be admitted if, without it, the court would find it 'impossible or difficult properly to understand other evidence in the case, and its value for understanding the case as whole is substantial'. It is not admissible if the purpose of admitting it is to contradict rather than explain or help the jury understand the other evidence in the case. The provision overlaps to some extent with evidence which is part of the offence as provided for in s98(a). There was provision under the common law for what was known as background evidence and here the overlap is with s101(1)(d). The section, however, is limited in scope and the case law suggests that it should not be used to circumvent the requirements of s101(1)(d), where there is statutory discretion to exclude admissible evidence under s102(3) and (4) and s103(3).

Revision tip

It is important you are clear on the somewhat overlapping sections ss98(a), 101(c) and 101(d), and are aware of the case law illustrating how they have been applied. In *R v Sullivan* (2015) the appellant was convicted of cultivation of cannabis between the period of 1 December 2012 and 21 February 2013. The trial judge had admitted evidence of text messages under s98(a) suggesting cultivation of cannabis between March and November 2012. He directed the jury with the words 'A matter entirely for you, as you read through those, what it is you make of it'. The Court of Appeal quashed the conviction on the grounds that the evidence was wrongly admitted since the appropriate section was s101(1)(d), which required a differently worded direction. Similarly, in *R v Davis* (2008) evidence from a former girlfriend of 20 years ago was not admissible under s101(1)(c) since it had no substantial value for understanding the case as a whole. It would have been appropriate to consider admissibility under the more stringent requirements of s101(1)(d).

Fourth gateway: sections 101(1)(d) and 103

It is relevant to an important matter in issue between the defendant and the prosecution:
Here, the amount of case law indicates the complexity of the provision, which is the successor to the old 'similar fact' rule. Section 103(1) provides that matters in issue between the defendant and the prosecution include:

(a) the question whether the defendant has a propensity to commit offences of the kind with which he is charged, except where his having such a propensity makes it no more likely that he is guilty of the offence;

(b) the question whether the defendant has a propensity to be untruthful, except where it is not suggested that the defendant's case is untruthful in any respect.

Section 112(1) defines an 'important matter' as 'a matter of substantial importance in the context of the case as a whole'. Section 103 contains a number of conditions concerning this evidence. They explain similarities between offences as:

• offences are of the same description if the indictment would in each case be written in the same terms. Offences are of the same category if they belong to the same category of offences prescribed in the order made by the Secretary of State for the purpose of this section;

• offences may be excluded 'by reason of the length of time since conviction or for any other reason, that it would be unjust for it to apply in this case'. (Note the overlapping exclusionary discretion under s101(3) and (4)); and

• only the prosecution may adduce evidence under this gateway.

Propensity to commit offences of the same kind

Under the common law, propensity or disposition evidence was circumstantial evidence of guilt. Propensity is not defined in the CJA 2003. There are three main differences between the common law and statute:

• The common law position of a rule of exclusion subject to an inclusionary discretion is reversed. The Court of Appeal in *R v Weir* (2006) stated that s101(1)(d) 'completely reverses the pre-existing general rule . . . if the evidence of a defendant's bad character is relevant to an important issue between the prosecution and the defence . . . then, unless there is an application to exclude the evidence, it is admissible . . . The pre-existing one-stage test which balanced probative value against prejudicial effect is obsolete.' The balancing act is performed when an application is made under s101(3) and the judge must consider whether 'the admission of the evidence would have such an adverse effect on the fairness of the proceedings that the court ought not to admit it'.

- The Court of Appeal will not readily reverse the exercise of judicial discretion to admit evidence (*R v Tully* (2006) is one of the small number of cases where the Court of Appeal has held that character evidence was wrongly admitted at trial. A general propensity to obtain property belonging to another should not have been admitted to prove propensity in a case where the defendant was charged with the robbery of a taxi driver. Factually, the cases were quite different).

- The courts are aware of Parliament's intention to increase the instances of admissibility of bad character. In *R v Edwards (Stewart)* (2006) it stated that it 'was apparent that Parliament intended that evidence of bad character would be put before juries more frequently than had previously been the case'.

You cannot treat the cases necessarily as binding precedents since they turn on their specific fact situations. However, the following case does set out general guidelines. The account below is an attempt to derive some principles on admissibility in relation to propensity to commit the offence from a selection of the leading cases.

In *R v Hanson* (2005) (one of three conjoined appeals) the appellant had allegedly stolen money from a bedroom above a public house. He had been drinking in the pub and according to the prosecution was the only person who had had the opportunity to enter the bedroom. His previous convictions for dishonesty offences were admitted to suggest propensity. Some offences such as handling stolen goods were not evidence of propensity but the burglary offences were. See Fig 5.1.

Revision tip

Your examiners will be impressed if you show you understand the need to connect hearsay and character evidence where necessary. Thus, in *R v Kang* (2013) the court held that when determining the admissibility of evidence of the accused's bad character under s101(1)(f) it may be necessary to consider if the hearsay rules are engaged. K appealed against his conviction for rape on the grounds that the trial judge had wrongly allowed the prosecution to adduce an interview with X, a minor. K had been cautioned for sexual activity with X. The parties had agreed the caution's admissibility. It was held that the manner of the cross examination was calculated to introduce inadmissible hearsay evidence. The conviction was, however, safe.

Glover (2015, p191) suggests that the use of the word 'include' in relation to 'propensity' in s103(1) indicates the wide scope of this section. Thus, he points out, evidence of identity rather than propensity was at issue in *R v Richardson* (2014), where a previous conviction for assaulting a traffic warden was admissible to identify the defendant in another unprovoked violent attack in the same area.

Propensity for untruthfulness

One of the complications of the statute is that it draws a distinction between propensity for untruthfulness and lack of credibility.

Bad character

✳✳✳✳✳✳✳✳✳✳

Figure 5.1 Test for admissibility under s101(1)(d): *R v Hanson* (2005)

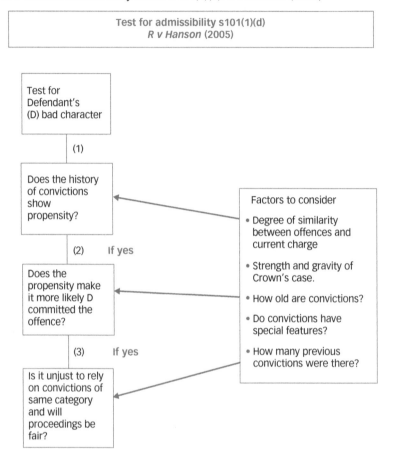

The Explanatory Note which accompanied the Act explained:

> Section 103(1)(b) makes it clear that evidence relating to whether the defendant has a propensity to be untruthful (in other words, is not to be regarded as a credible witness) can be admitted. This is intended to enable the admission of a limited range of evidence such as convictions for perjury or other offences involving deception . . . as opposed to the wider range of evidence that will be admissible where the defendant puts his character in issue by, for example, attacking the character of another person.

The definition of untruthfulness has caused some problems. In *R v Hanson* (2005) (at p3174) the Court of Appeal stated that a propensity to be untruthful is not the same as a propensity to be dishonest. Perjury aside, the question is not so much the nature of the previous offences but whether the facts surrounding them demonstrate a propensity to be untruthful such as a not guilty plea when the defendant is convicted. See also *R v Campbell* (2007) and Table 5.2.

R v Campbell (2007)

FACTS: The defendant was charged with false imprisonment and assault against a woman with whom he had a sexual relationship. The prosecution was permitted to adduce evidence of recent crimes of violence against girlfriends since they showed propensity under **s101(1)(d)**. He had pleaded guilty to those offences. On appeal the defendant argued that the judge should not have directed the jury that the previous convictions were relevant to credibility as well as propensity.

HELD: The courts had in the past drawn a distinction between propensity to offend and credibility. The distinction was usually unrealistic and it would be comparatively rare in the case of a defendant who had pleaded not guilty for there not to be some element that the prosecution suggested was untruthful.
   However, the question of whether a defendant had a propensity for being untruthful would not normally be capable of being described as an *important* matter in issue between the defendant and the prosecution. Whether or not a defendant was telling the truth was likely to depend simply on whether or not he committed the offence. The jury should focus on that question.

Table 5.2 Statutory references to propensity to be untruthful

Gateways to admissibility of bad character	Who can use the section?	Approach of court to admissibility of evidence of credibility	
Section	Defence/Prosecution	Restricted	Broad
s101(1)(d) s103(1)(b) **Propensity to be untruthful included**	Prosecution	*R v Hanson* (2005) *R v Campbell* (2007)	*R v Belogun* (2008) *R v N* (2014)
s101(1)(g) **No reference to propensity to be untruthful**	Prosecution		*R v Singh* (2006)
s101(1)(e) **Propensity to be untruthful included**	Defence		*R v Lawson* (2007)
s100(1)(b) **No reference to propensity to be untruthful**	Defence/Prosecution	*R v South* (2011)	*R v Stephenson* (2006) *R v Brewster* (2011)

Bad character
✳✳✳✳✳✳✳✳✳✳

In *R v N* (2014) the accused was charged with historic child abuse, which he denied. His propensity for untruthfulness, including lying about his Army record, was admissible under s101(1)(d). *R v Campbell* (2007) was not followed.

Fifth gateway: sections 101(1)(e) and 104

It has substantial probative value in relation to an important matter in issue between the defendant and a co-defendant:

The dilemma for legislators and courts under this section is balancing the rights of defendants with those of co-defendants who might be running what is known as 'cut-throat' defences, each blaming the other. The current provision is a broader version of one contained in the CEA 1898 and some of the earlier case law is cited in recent judgments. The new statute explicitly states it is only to be used by co-defendants, thus the prosecution cannot apply to have evidence adduced.

The 2003 Act also requires that the evidence under this section has 'substantial probative value', whereas s101(1)(d) refers to 'relevant to an important matter', which means, according to s112, 'a matter of substantial importance in the context of the case as a whole'. Another distinctive feature of s101(1)(e) is that the discretion to exclude does not cover this section, nor of course does s78 PACE, which only applies to prosecution evidence. According to s104(1), 'Evidence which is relevant to the question whether the defendant has a propensity to be untruthful is admissible under s101(1)(e) only if the nature or conduct of his defence is such as to undermine the co-defendant's defence.' The court may of course decide to hold separate trials, in which case the defendants will not be co-defendants.

The differing approaches the courts may take to s101(1)(d) and (e) in relation to admissibility of evidence on 'propensity to be untruthful' are illustrated by the case of *R v Lawson* (2007). In that case D1 was allowed to adduce evidence of D2's conviction for wounding as evidence of credibility, not going to the issue. The court stated that 'it was wholly rational that the degree of caution which is applied to a Crown application against a defendant who is on trial when considering relevance or discretion should not be applied when what is at stake is a defendant's right to deploy material to defend himself against a criminal charge'. It was for the judge to decide whether D2's bad character had substantial probative value in relation to his credibility and the appeal courts would only interfere with this on grounds of *Wednesbury* unreasonableness. As Mirfield (2009) argues, the restrictive approach set out in *Campbell* in relation to s101(1)(d) if applied to s101(1)(e) would be in contradiction to the traditional policy of allowing a defendant to use all relevant evidence in his defence.

In *R v Phillips* (2012) the Court of Appeal set out the principles governing the operation of this section and the high threshold of admissibility, in part, because there was no exclusionary discretion. The underlying assumption was that if the statutory test of enhanced probative value upon a matter of substantial importance was met, the scope for unfairness was removed. In this case evidence was wrongly excluded but the conviction was safe. Of course it is very difficult to ensure fairness for both defendants in such a situation. See also *R v Platt* (2016) (p86).

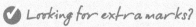 **Looking for extra marks?**

The examiners will be impressed if you show an awareness of the many different ways propensity can be demonstrated. One area where the current case law is complex is that of the cross-admissibility of character evidence on other counts in the indictment. See *R v Freeman and Crawford* (2008). Similarly, in *R v Mitchell* (2016) the Supreme Court held that evidence of propensity could be established by considering the items of evidence cumulatively. The outline answer to the problem question at the end of the chapter guides you through this difficult area.

Sixth gateway: sections 101(1)(f) and 105

Evidence to correct a false impression given by the defendant:

Section 105(1)(a) refers to the defendant 'making an express or implied assertion which is apt to give the court or jury a false or misleading impression about the defendant'. The impression may be given by conduct such as appearance or dress (s105(4) and (5)) and can be given by the defendant in pre-trial interviews or at the time of being charged or at trial. It can also be given by his witness. However, under s105(3) the defendant will not be responsible for making the assertion if he withdraws it or otherwise actively dissociates himself from it (see *R v Renda* (2006)).

In this area the cases cannot be seen as providing clear definitions of what is meant by a 'false impression' since as the Court of Appeal noted in *R v Weir* (2006) at para 43 it is 'fact specific'. Evidence in rebuttal must go 'no further than is necessary to correct the false impression' (s105(6)). The courts must also be careful to distinguish situations where the accused is doing no more than denying the offence. Thus, in *D, P and U* (see p99) in the claim by the defendant that his relationship with his niece was that of an ordinary close uncle was a mere denial and evidence of his alleged sexual interest in young children was not admissible under s101(1)(f) although might have been admissible under (d). In *R v Ovba* (2015) the defendant was charged with dangerous driving and assault. In cross examination she had made an 'implied assertion' that 'she was not the sort of person that would do something like this, either because she is a nice friendly person, or because she herself has been the victim of violence. The Court of Appeal considered that this was 'far too unspecific and insubstantial to support the introduction of bad character under section 101(1)(f)'.

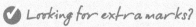 **Looking for extra marks?**

If you are having to make an assessment of the ways the 2003 Act helped the defence or prosecution, an example from s105(6) could suggest that it is not entirely pro-prosecution. You could refer here to the abolition of the common law rule on the indivisibility of character (s105(6)). In *R v Winfield* (1939) a defendant who claimed to be of high moral standing sexually, lost his shield and faced having his offences for dishonesty adduced. This pro-prosecutorial advantage is not available under CJA 2003.

Bad character

✳✳✳✳✳✳✳✳✳✳

Seventh gateway: sections 101(1)(g) and 106

The defendant has made an attack on another person's character:
The differences with the former law are:

- an attack on anybody dead or alive may trigger the section,
- this may be made by a non-testifying defendant, and
- this may be made pre-trial, see s106(1)(c).

Note that 'attacking another person's character' is broadly defined. It includes evidence of committing an offence as well as evidence that the person 'has behaved, or is disposed to behave, in a reprehensible way' (s106(2)).

An example of what is meant by an 'attack' short of an allegation of a crime is *R v Renda* (2006), where the allegation was one of loose sexual morals on the part of the victim.

Section 101(1)(g)

R v Singh (James Paul) (2007) gives guidance on the application of this section:

- the purpose of the gateway 'is to enable the jury to know from what sort of source allegations against a witness (especially a complainant but not only a complainant) have come',
- the gateway does not depend upon evidence demonstrating propensity to offend as charged or propensity to be untruthful,
- evidence may be relevant to credibility while not showing a 'track record for untruthfulness'; non-dishonesty offences may be evidence of lack of credibility,
- once admitted under (g) bad character evidence goes to credibility,
- evidence is admissible even if the attack is a necessary part of the accused's defence,
- the court will only interfere with the judge's discretion to exclude under s101(3) or s78 PACE on grounds of *Wednesbury* unreasonableness.

The courts take a broad view of the sort of convictions admissible under this section. In *R v Clarke* (2011) the accused, who was charged with sexual offences against his stepdaughters, testified that they had colluded to make false claims against him. His convictions for vehicle theft, robbery, and firearms offences were rightly admitted even though some were 20 years old.

Revision tip

Read the legal journals to keep up to date with the law as they often give a succinct summary of the main issues. In the commentary on *Clarke*, Roberts (2011, p642) observed that 'The court's judgment . . . further entrenches the rather indiscriminate approach that has been taken to the reception of bad character evidence through gateway (g).' The court stated, 'all convictions were potentially relevant to assist the jury to assess the character of the accused, but it was not generally necessary for the detailed facts about the nature and circumstances of those convictions to be put before the jury'.

Evidential worth of bad character evidence and the gateways

It is a matter of some controversy how far the gateway through which bad character is admitted determines its evidential worth. The standard textbooks seem to have some difference of emphasis. In *R v Highton* (2005) the defendant's previous convictions had been admitted under s101(1)(g). However, the judge was held by the Court of Appeal to have correctly given a direction on propensity. The defendant's previous convictions for violence and dishonesty were relevant to his current charge of kidnapping, robbery, and theft. In other words once the evidence has been admitted through a gateway it is open to the jury to consider it with regard to any issue that is relevant. The conjoined appeals, *R v D, P and U* (2012) shed further light on the issue.

R v D, P and U (2012)

FACTS: The defendants were charged with committing sexual offences with children. The judge had permitted bad character evidence to be admitted which consisted of child pornography and Internet searches. The gateways were **(d)**, **(f)**, and **(g)**. They were convicted and appealed on the grounds that this evidence was wrongly admitted.

HELD: Once bad character has been admitted under one gateway it can be considered by the jury in any way that is legitimately relevant, following *R v Highton*, but the specific gateway is important. The decision as to the relevant gateway or gateways will normally be of great help in identifying the issues to which it is relevant. As *Highton* itself makes clear, it is not law that once bad character evidence is admitted, having by definition passed at least one gateway, it can thereupon be used by the jury in any way the jury chooses. On the contrary, it may be used on any issue to which it is legitimately relevant but not otherwise.

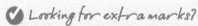 ✓ *Looking for extra marks?*

In assessing the impact of the statute this section provides a good example of how the final legislation departed from the more liberal approach of the Law Commission proposals. This relates to what is known as the 'no stymie rule' evidenced by the case of *Selvey v DPP* (1970), whereby the defendant lost his shield even where the imputation was a necessary part of his defence, here that the alleged victim was a male prostitute. The Law Commission had proposed that imputations should not include evidence to do with the alleged facts of the defence. This was not accepted in the legislation. In *R v Lamaletie* (2008) the Court of Appeal considered that the defence of self-defence did not prevent the triggering of s101(1)(g) by the defendant's allegation at interview that another person had behaved 'in a reprehensible way' as specified in s106 CJA 2003.

Safeguards: exclusionary discretion

Section 101(3) and (4) also include an exclusionary discretion which only applies to s101(1)(d) or (g), namely that 'The court must not admit evidence under [these subsections] if, on application by the defendant to exclude it, it appears to the court that the admission of the evidence would have such an adverse effect on the fairness of the proceedings that the court ought not to admit it. On an application to exclude evidence the court must have regard to

Bad character

✳✳✳✳✳✳✳✳✳✳

the length of time between the matters to which that evidence relates and the matters which form the subject of the offence charged.'

Fairness to the proceedings includes fairness to the prosecution.

R v Lewis (2014)

FACTS: Seven defendants were charged with serious offences of public disorder arising out of riots in Birmingham in 2011. At trial, among the issues for the jury were, whether the group had acted with a common purpose and whether any of the appellants had been at the scene inadvertently or innocently. In order to establish gang association the Crown adduced bad character evidence comprising videos featuring five of the appellants. The videos were said to suggest that those appearing in them were members of, or were associated with, criminal or street gangs. The defendants appealed against conviction.

HELD: The appeals were dismissed. It was well established that evidence of membership of, or association with, a criminal gang could be admissible under **s101(1)(d) CJA 2003**. The videos were relevant to the issues before the jury and it was fair to the proceedings to admit them. The fact that the evidence of bad character was not 'essential' to the prosecution case was not grounds for exclusion under **s101(3)**. It was important to remember that an assessment of the fairness of the trial had to involve a consideration of fairness not only to the defence, but also to the prosecution. Fairness to the prosecution was sometimes insufficiently considered. It was well established that evidence of membership of, or association with, a criminal gang could be admissible under **s101(1)(d) CJA 2003**. The appeals were dismissed.

It is quite a good exercise to review the ways the CJA 2003 sets out protective measures and compare how they apply to defendants and non-defendants. See Table 5.3.

Table 5.3 Safeguards and admissibility of bad character evidence

Safeguard	Explanation
Leave of court	Leave of court required for admissibility of bad character of non-defendant but not for defendant.
Discretion to exclude under **s101(3) and (4) CJA 2003**.	Applies to **s101(1)(d) and (g) CJA 2003**.
s78 PACE and common law discretion.	No clear authority on its application to **s101(1)(a)** to (c) and (f). May apply to **s101(1)(f) CJA 2003** (see *R v Highton* (2005)). Only covers prosecution evidence so cannot apply to **s101(1)(e) CJA 2003**.
s110 CJA 2003	Judge must give ruling in open court on decision on admissibility of bad character evidence or application of **s107**. Applies to defendants and non-defendants.
Stopping the case where evidence is 'contaminated' under **s107 CJA 2003**. The term is defined in **s107(5) CJA 2003** as 'false or misleading' evidence including that resulting from collusion between the witness and others.	Applies to **s101(1)(c) to (g) CJA 2003**. See *R v C* (2006).

Admissibility and evidential worth of bad character of non-defendant

Section 100 provides for the admissibility of bad character evidence of the non-defendant. There are a number of safeguards against the too ready admission of such evidence and the test appears to be higher than that set out for defendants in s100:

- its admissibility needs the leave of the court, s100(1)(c), unless all the parties agree; the criteria for giving leave are set out;

- it must be either important explanatory evidence, s100(1)(a), or have substantial probative value in relation to a matter which (i) is a matter in issue in the proceedings and (ii) is of substantial importance in the context of the case as a whole, s100(1)(b).

A broad view of credibility has been taken. In *R v Stephenson* (2006) the Court of Appeal stressed the right of a defendant to defend himself against a criminal charge. The test of admissibility was whether the evidence of the previous convictions or bad behaviour was sufficiently persuasive to be worthy of consideration by a fair minded tribunal upon the issue of the creditworthiness of the witness. Thus, a complainant's convictions for non-fraudulent dishonesty had substantial probative value under s100(1)(b). The judge, relying on *R v Hanson* (2005), had been wrong to refuse leave to cross examine her in a sexual abuse case on her previous offences of dishonesty not involving deception, nor a plea of not guilty (although it could not be said that the conviction was unsafe).

Similarly, in *R v Brewster* (2011) the Court of Appeal held that the trial judge had wrongly refused leave for the complainant in a case of kidnapping to be cross examined on her previous convictions, which included shoplifting and manslaughter. It was not only convictions for making false statements which were admissible under the section. Convictions, in order to qualify for admission on the question of creditworthiness, did not have to demonstrate a tendency to dishonesty or untruthfulness. Moreover, the manslaughter conviction was directly relevant to the witness's credibility since the events surrounding the conviction showed a propensity to similar behaviour to that alleged by the defendants. However, there are some inconsistencies in the case law. In *R v South* (2011) the Court of Appeal adopted a narrow approach to the question of admissibility. The judge had been wrong to allow evidence of a defence witness's convictions for dishonesty without considering whether they involved truthfulness or a guilty plea.

Revision tip

Students should be aware of the particular question of complainants in sexual cases and connect the application of s41 Youth Justice and Criminal Evidence Act 1999 covering previous sexual behaviour of the witness (see p165) with s100 CJA 2003. An example of allegations by the defendant of non-sexual reprehensible behaviour on the part of the alleged victim is *R v Hussain* (2015), where the judge had wrongly disallowed questions on her previous convictions. The ➡

→ Court of Appeal stated, 'We are persuaded that, having correctly ruled that the complainant's general creditworthiness was central to the case, the judge should also have ruled that the convictions were so numerous, varied and recent that they were of substantial probative value upon the issue of whether her accusation against the appellant was worthy of belief. It was for the jury to judge whether in the particular factual context of the present case her general bad character was of any assistance to them in resolving who was telling the truth.'

Note that s74 PACE is relevant to the bad character of a non-defendant witness. It provides that the fact that a person other than the accused has been convicted of an offence is admissible to prove the commission of the offence. The test of relevance of course applies and this might arise in the case of a former co-defendant of the accused. Munday (2013, p35) suggests that, 'The simple fact is that s74 can all too easily jeopardise a defendant's entitlement to a fair trial.' He points out that the non-defendant's conviction may implicate the defendant in earlier proceedings without the need to call the former as a witness. Section 78 PACE, however, may allow the exclusion of such evidence tendered by the prosecution. See also discussion on p49.

Definition, admissibility, and evidential worth of good character

Section 118(1) CJA 2003 preserves the common law rule whereby 'in criminal proceedings evidence of a person's reputation is admissible for the purpose of proving his good or bad character'. Good character is defined by the leading cases: see *R v Rowton* (1865) and *R v Redgrave* (1982) in the 'Key cases'. The strict rule is that only evidence of general reputation is admitted but in practice the rule is often not observed and good character is held to be synonymous with no criminal record. Good character is relevant to both credit and propensity, see *R v Vye* (1993). In *R v Aziz* (1996) the House of Lords gave further guidance on the importance of a good character direction. Three defendants were charged with conspiracy to evade VAT payments. Two had no previous convictions but admitted separate acts of dishonesty at trial and were not given the propensity limb of the good character direction. The House stated that failure to give a good character direction could mean the conviction being overturned on appeal but that the judge had a residual discretion to refuse to give one if it was 'an insult to common sense'. In this case the convictions were overturned. The Court of Appeal has made a comprehensive review of the law relating to good character of the defendant in *R v Hunter* (2015), five conjoined appeals. Table 5.4 explains the categories of good character. The appropriate judicial direction depends on whether there is one defendant or more than one. This is explained in Table 5.5 and Fig 5.2.

Considering the position where there is more than one defendant, the court set out the propositions to be derived from *Vye* and *Aziz*. This is summarised in Fig. 5.2.

Table 5.4 Categories of good character, see *R v Hunter* (2015)

Category of good character	Definition	Judicial directions
(i) Absolute good character	Accused has no previous convictions or cautions recorded and no reprehensible conduct alleged, admitted, or proven.	Accused entitled to directions on two limbs: credibility and propensity.
(ii) Effective good character	Accused has previous convictions or cautions which are old, minor, and have no relevance to the charge.	Judge must make a judgement whether accused is of effective good character and if so must give directions on both limbs.

Table 5.5 Judicial directions on good character where there is one defendant, see *R v Hunter* (2015)

Defendant	Judicial directions
Previous convictions, not in same category as charge, adduced by D under **s101(1)(b) CJA 2003**.	Discretion whether to give modified direction on good character.
Misconduct, not amounting to convictions, adduced by D under **s101(1)(b)**.	Judge has 'open text' discretion (see *R v Aziz* (1996)).
Prosecution adduce evidence of D's misconduct not including convictions.	Judge obliged to give bad character direction but may in addition give modified good character direction.
Prosecution adduce D's convictions.	Good character direction would be absurd (see *R v Aziz*).
D pleads guilty to one or more charges on the indictment, but not guilty to others. D has no previous convictions.	D should not be treated as being of good character (see *R v Challenger* (1994)).
D appeals failure to give good character directions.	No fixed rule that absence of directions is fatal. Court should adopt approach in *R v Renda* (2006). If directions are given should be both limbs if relevant, see *R v Singh* (2006).

Figure 5.2 Judicial directions on good character, more than one defendant (see *R v Hunter* (2015), see also *R v Vye* (1993); *R v Aziz* (1996))

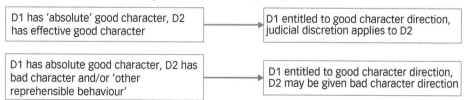

Conclusion

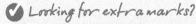

Looking for extra marks?

Good character evidence of the defendant is covered by the common law and there is considerable case law on this. An area that has been given relatively scant attention is the good character of the prosecution witness, but there now is a developing line of authority on good character evidence of complainants in sexual cases. Thus, in *R v Tobin* (2003), where a defendant alleged that the complainant had initiated sexual activity in thanks for a lift, the Court of Appeal held that the trial judge had been right to allow a complainant's mother to give evidence of her good character. The article by Crinion (2010) gives helpful guidance through this developing area.

① Conclusion

In a critical concluding comment on the complex provisions of the CJA 2003, Choo (2015, p279) sees a worrying tendency on the part of the Court of Appeal to leave too much freedom to trial judges in admitting character evidence. He writes: '[I]t is arguable that the current approach of the Court of Appeal may not protect defendants sufficiently and that gateway (d), at least, should be the subject of a thorough and authoritative consideration by the UK Supreme Court.'

✱ Key cases

Case	Facts	Principle and comment
R v Hanson [2005] 1 WLR 3169	The appellant had been convicted on circumstantial evidence of the theft of cash from a public house where he had been drinking. His previous convictions for dishonesty included offences for handling stolen goods and aggravated taking and driving away a vehicle. They were admitted as evidence of propensity to commit offences of the kind charged. His appeal failed.	The court set out guidelines for the admissibility of propensity evidence. Merely establishing the offences were of the same description or the same category (according to Home Office prescriptions) was not sufficient. The court should ask if the history of convictions established propensity to commit offences of the kind charged and if yes, whether such propensity made it more likely that the defendant had committed the offence. Finally, it should consider if it would be unjust to rely on the convictions and if admitting the evidence would have such an adverse effect on the fairness of the proceedings that it ought not to be admitted.
R v Phillips [2012] 1 Cr App R 25	In a trial for defrauding the Revenue the applicant was not permitted to adduce evidence of his co-defendant's bad character. The Court of Appeal held the evidence was wrongly excluded but the conviction was safe.	The threshold for admissibility under s101(1)(e) was much higher than under the CEA 1898. If applied correctly the risk of unfairness was lessened.

Case	Facts	Principle and comment
R v Renda [2006] 1 WLR 2948	R was convicted of attempted robbery. He had claimed that he had been injured while serving in the British Army and that he worked regularly as a security guard. Both were false claims. The Court of Appeal held he was rightly cross examined under s101(1)(f) on his 'reprehensible behaviour', which included a violent attack not leading to a conviction.	The decision may be contrasted with that in *R v Weir* (2006), where the court referred to s105(6) in that the accused should only be cross examined on previous bad character necessary to correct the false impression he had given. In general, the Court of Appeal will defer to what it referred to (at p2950) as the trial judge's 'feel for the case'.
R v Rowton (1865) Le and Ca 520	A teacher charged with indecently assaulting a pupil called a number of character witnesses to attest that he had a good general reputation in the community. The prosecution's evidence of a contrary individual opinion was not admissible since evidence of character should be that of general reputation, not isolated acts.	This case is still authority for the definition of good character, which is governed by the common law. The principle in many ways reflects nineteenth century society with its more static population. It was, however, confirmed in the case of *R v Redgrave* (1982), where a defendant charged with importuning for immoral purposes was not permitted to produce good character evidence that he had a loving heterosexual relationship.
R v Singh (James Paul) [2007] EWCA Crim 2140	S was convicted of robbery. He had made an attack on a prosecution witness claiming he took drugs and had lied in his evidence. S's previous convictions were admitted under s101(1)(g). The appeal was dismissed.	In reviewing the exercise of the discretion to exclude under this section, the court referred to the continuation of the practice which had been evidenced under the old law. The fact that an attack on a witness was necessary in the case the accused chose to make, was not a reason to refuse to allow the jury to assess the reliability of the defendant by seeing 'the full nature of the source from which the allegation comes'.
R v Vye [1993] 3 All ER 241	A man with no criminal record was convicted of rape. His defence was consent. The Court of Appeal held that the judge had been wrong not to direct that his good character was relevant to both his lack of guilt or propensity and his credibility.	It set out general guidelines on the correct judicial directions. If the defendant does not testify but makes an exculpatory statement to the police then a direction on credibility should still be given. If he neither testifies nor makes an out of court exculpatory statement then only the direction on propensity should be given. A defendant with good character is entitled to a good character direction even if tried with a defendant with a record. Failure to give such a direction could lead to the conviction being overturned.

Key debates

✱✱✱✱✱✱✱✱

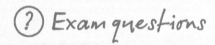 Key debates

Topic	Effect on lay magistrates of hearing about a defendant's character
Author	S Lloyd-Bostock
Viewpoint	Research suggests the potentially prejudicial nature of being informed of previous convictions, particularly if they were serious and similar to the current charge. Magistrates were drawing on preconceived notions rather than examining from scratch. However, 'guessed at' previous convictions did not appear to have a prejudicial effect and evidence of 'good character' was not in itself very influential.
Source	'The Effect on Lay Magistrates of Hearing that the Defendant is of "Good Character" Being Left to Speculate, or Hearing that He Has a Previous Conviction' [2006] *Crim LR* 189

Topic	Propensity evidence
Author	M Redmayne
Viewpoint	The article examines one of the most controversial aspects of the CJA, namely the increased opportunity it afforded for the admissibility of evidence of previous offences. In particular the distinction between propensity and cases of 'coincidence' is examined but, since there is an overlap between the two modes of reasoning, it would be better to dispense with the coincidence terminology. The author concludes that, although over-estimating propensity is a risk, it is a welcome development that in the majority of cases the courts are being open and honest about the fact that previous convictions are evidence of propensity to commit crime.
Source	'Recognising Propensity' [2011] *Crim LR* 117

 Exam questions

Essay question

Has the concept of the indivisibility of character evidence survived the CJA 2003?

> ⓦ Online Resource Centre
>
> To see an outline answer to this question visit www.oup.com/lawrevision/

Problem question

Swann, a driving instructor, is charged with three separate counts on the same indictment. The first charge is of sexually assaulting his 6-year-old stepdaughter Jane, the second is for rape of one of his driving pupils, Alice (who is 19 years old), and the third is for indecently exposing himself in the local park. He pleads not guilty to all of these offences.

Advise the prosecution on the application of the cross-admissibility of the character evidence on each of these counts.

See the Outline Answers section in the end matter for help with this question.

Concentrate Q&As

For more questions and answers on evidence, see the *Concentrate Q&A: Evidence* by Maureen Spencer and John Spencer.

Go to the end of this book to view sample pages.

#6
Hearsay evidence

- The rule against hearsay originated under the common law. It provides that a statement made out of court may not be tendered in evidence as proof of its contents.

- The rule applies to out of court statements of witnesses who are testifying as well as of those who are not called as witnesses.

- Statements include oral and written statements and gestures; documents are anything in which information of any description is recorded.

- The rule applies equally to defence and prosecution.

- Different rules apply in civil and criminal cases.

- In criminal proceedings the rule still exists but with a large number of statutory and common law exceptions.

- In criminal proceedings hearsay is admissible (i) if any of the statutory provisions in the Criminal Justice Act (CJA) 2003 allow it, or (ii) under the common law provisions preserved under CJA 2003, or (iii) if all the parties agree, or (iv) under the statutory discretion conferred on the court, namely that it is satisfied it is in the interests of justice for it to be admissible.

- In criminal law no new exceptions can be made under the common law.

- In civil proceedings the rule has been abolished by statute, Civil Evidence Act (CEA) 1995.

- The law distinguishes between first-hand and multiple hearsay.

Chapter overview

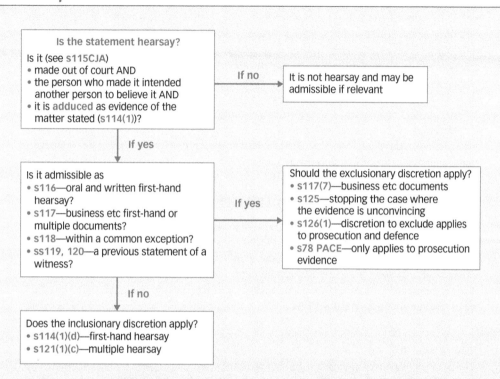

Is the statement hearsay?

Is it (see s115CJA)
- made out of court AND
- the person who made it intended another person to believe it AND
- it is adduced as evidence of the matter stated (s114(1))?

If no → It is not hearsay and may be admissible if relevant

If yes ↓

Is it admissible as
- s116—oral and written first-hand hearsay?
- s117—business etc first-hand or multiple documents?
- s118—within a common exception?
- ss119, 120—a previous statement of a witness?

If yes → Should the exclusionary discretion apply?
- s117(7)—business etc documents
- s125—stopping the case where the evidence is unconvincing
- s126(1)—discretion to exclude applies to prosecution and defence
- s78 PACE—only applies to prosecution evidence

If no ↓

Does the inclusionary discretion apply?
- s114(1)(d)—first-hand hearsay
- s121(1)(c)—multiple hearsay

Admissibility of first-hand and multiple hearsay

First-hand	Multiple
May be admissible under s116, 117, 118, or 114(1)(d)	May be admissible under s117 (if in a document), or s119, 120, or 121(1)(c)

Related areas

The question of hearsay evidence is closely related to additional protections for victims dealt with in Chapters 7 and 8. Hearsay evidence may be tendered by a witness who is reluctant, unwilling, or too frightened to testify, so there is considerable overlap between this chapter and Chapter 7, see particularly the section on anonymous witnesses.

Arguably, the biggest exception to the rule against hearsay, and one which aids the prosecution, is confession evidence. There is, therefore, considerable overlap between this chapter and Chapter 3.

The CJA 2003, in creating a number of new statutory exceptions to the rule against hearsay, has connected this area with that of examination and cross examination more closely, particularly on the question of the new status of previous consistent and inconsistent statements and identification evidence (see Chapter 8).

The assessment: key points

This is another area where it does help to have at least an outline knowledge of the history of this notoriously complex rule. The CJA 2003 has codified the law but you will see that the common law exceptions can still apply. It is important that you go through a logical sequence of questions. First, see if the statement is hearsay or not, then if it is, whether any of the exceptions to the rule of exclusion apply and, if they do not, finally, if it may be admitted by the new inclusionary discretion.

Revision tip

Do not forget that evidence in order to be admitted must first of all be relevant. You must make it clear to the examiners that you understand this as the starting point for all evidence. In *R v T* (2006) a woman alleged she had been indecently assaulted by her father and her uncle. Her father had subsequently died and a confession by the father had been improperly adduced under s116 CJA 2003 at the uncle's trial. It had no relevance.

Key features and principles

Rationale and evolution of the exclusionary rule

The rule against hearsay is one of the great exclusionary rules of evidence. The reasons for the rule are derived both from efficiency and from principle. From the point of view of the most effective evidence, out of court statements which cannot be tested on cross examination risk introducing mistake, false recollections, ambiguity, and insincerity (see *R v Teper* (1952) and Tribe (1974)). On the question of principle there are two aspects to the exclusion. First, such statements have not been made on oath in open court. Second, and more controversially, it has been argued that the rule against hearsay protects what in the US constitution is known as the 'right to confrontation', the right to confront one's accuser. The latter's existence, however, has never been fully acknowledged in English common law and it should be noted that Art 6 European Convention on Human Rights (ECHR) refers to the right of defendants to examine or *have examined* witnesses called against them.

Abolition of the rule against hearsay in civil proceedings

The relatively uncomplicated law relating to hearsay in civil proceedings will not be covered in great depth in this chapter. Later, in Table 6.1, are the key provisions taken from the CEA 1995.

Problems with the common law rules

Criminal Justice Act 1988 (CJA 1988) admitted first-hand documentary hearsay where the maker was not available to give evidence and there was an acceptable reason for not calling him. Admitted multiple documentary hearsay if it was created in the course of trade, business, etc (see now s117 CJA 2003).

Law Commission: Law Commission Report No 245 (Cm 3670, 1997), *Evidence in Criminal Proceedings, Hearsay and Related Topics*, recommended the rule against hearsay should be retained but the number of exceptions increased. It also recommended an inclusionary discretion to 'allow for the admission of reliable hearsay which could not otherwise be admitted

Table 6.1 Overview of the Civil Evidence Act 1995 provisions

Section	Provision
s1(1)	Evidence in civil proceedings shall not be excluded on the ground that it is hearsay. This applies to first-hand as well as multiple hearsay.
s2	Sets out notice provision for admission of hearsay but failure to comply does not in itself mean statement is inadmissible.
s3	Power to call witnesses for cross examination on hearsay provisions.
s4	Sets out factors to consider in weighing hearsay statements.
ss5–6	Sets out rules on assessing the competence and credibility of the person who made the statement and whether there had been previous inconsistent statements.
s70	Provisions relating to common law rules.
ss8–9	Status of copies of documents and proof of records of a business or public authority.

particularly to prevent a conviction which that evidence would render unsafe' (para 8.133). The Report cited instances where evidence that might be helpful to the defence had been excluded as the sort of situations envisaged. One such case was *R v Sparks* (1964). However, the Report made it clear that any such discretion would be available to defence and prosecution as a 'safety valve to be used in very limited circumstances' (para 8.143).

CJA 2003: This Act introduced new exceptions for first-hand oral hearsay. Certain common law exceptions were preserved. The Act extended the acceptable reasons for non-appearance of a witness including fear of financial loss.

Definition of hearsay in criminal proceedings

The definition

The CJA 2003 defines hearsay as follows:

- s115(2) and (3): '(2) A statement is any representation of fact or opinion, made by a person by whatever means; and it includes a representation made in a sketch, photofit, or other pictorial format. (3) A matter stated is one to which this Chapter applies if (and only if) the purpose, or one of the purposes, of the person making the statement appears to the court to have been—(a) to cause another person to believe the matter, or (b) to cause another person to act or a machine to operate on the basis that the matter is as stated.'

It follows from this definition that implied assertions are not covered by the rule against hearsay. This reverses the decision in *R v Kearley* (1992) that the evidence of the callers to the defendant requesting drugs was inadmissible hearsay.

The statutory definition (1): express or implied assertion?

Recognising an implied assertion still causes problems. Particular difficulties have been caused by the status of text messages. In some cases stored phone text messages asking for a supply of drugs from which the Crown sought to draw inferences of drug dealing on the part of the recipient of the messages were held to be hearsay but admissible under s114(1)(d): see *R v Leonard* (2009). *R v Twist* (2011), a conjoined appeal of four cases, addressed how to approach the problem of the definition of hearsay. Hughes LJ (at para 17) set out the test:

(i) Identify what relevant fact (matter) it is sought to prove.

(ii) Ask whether it was one of the purposes (not necessarily the only or dominant purpose) of the maker of the communication that the recipient, or any other person, should believe *that matter* or act upon it as true? If yes, it is hearsay.

The following table (Table 6.2), which gives the outcome of the appeals in *Twist*, will help you understand how the courts have interpreted the new definition of hearsay.

Table 6.2 Admissible non-hearsay statements

Admissible, non-hearsay statements *R v Twist; R v Boothman; R v Tomlinson and Kelly; R v L* [2011] EWCA Crim 1143	
Statements	**Comment**
1 T 24 text messages sent to T containing requests for supply of drugs.	Messages not hearsay since they did *not* contain a statement that T was a supplier of drugs. They were admissible because relevant to the issue whether there was an existing relationship of buyer and seller between senders and T.
2 B Text messages to B which were orders for drugs or comments on past supplies.	(as above)
3 T & K Message on T's phone: 'Need dat gun [sic] today so can sell it and give you lot da tenner back. Does laws [sic] still want it?' There was evidence sender was known to T & K.	The issue was whether T & K were in possession of a gun, the charge being robbery at gunpoint. Statement was admissible non-hearsay since it was not one of the purposes of the sender to cause anyone to believe he had a gun.
4 L 47 messages sent by L (aged 15) to girlfriend (aged 15) after the incident which was the basis for the charge of rape. He denied intercourse took place and claimed the messages were apologies for another matter not, as the Crown contended, for the rape.	Messages not hearsay since L's purpose in sending them was not to cause complainant to believe she had been raped. Alternatively they were statements against interest and were admissible under **ss114(1)(b) and 118**.

Keane and McKeown (2016, p 317) points out that the analysis in *Twist* is problematic. Citing *R v Teper* (1952) as an example, he writes, 'It would surely be correct to treat as hearsay, a statement with an implied representation where it appeared that the purpose of the maker was to cause someone to believe that what was impliedly represented was true, or to act on it as if it was true.'

Examples of the arguably inconsistent approach of the courts include two judgments which appear to have departed from the reasoning in *Twist*. *R v Bucknor* (2010) concerned the admissibility of gang-related videos on YouTube and other social network sites. This prosecution evidence was held, obiter, to be hearsay. They were arguably admissible under s114 but the judge had not given the correct direction in considering this. Glover (2015, p 263) comments, '[I]n view of the decision in *Twist*, this decision must be wrong.' In *R v Lam Hai Vo* (2013) a text message to N, the alleged accomplice of L, was admitted. It read 'Want to meet you this evening. I intend to ask Uncle Lam to take me as last time.' It was relevant because

L denied he knew N. The court, while upholding the safety of the conviction, held that this was inadmissible hearsay.

Revision tip

Before the passing of the CJA 2003 evidence students would have spent much effort in assessments, trying to decide if a statement was hearsay or not. Although a logical chain of reasoning must still be followed you should let the examiner know that you are aware that this definitional exercise has now changed. A useful case is *R v Isichei* (2006). In that case the disputed evidence was that of identification, referring to an alleged assailant by name. The judge ruled that the evidence was admissible as non-hearsay under s115(3) since the name had not been said for the purpose of causing a person to believe the matter stated. Alternatively, it was admissible under s114(1(d). The Court of Appeal held that even if the application of s115(3) was in doubt, the statement was admissible under s114(1)(d) as 'part of the story of a common sense series of events'. Thus, s114(1)(d) may apply to non-hearsay statements.

The statutory definition (2): first-hand or multiple hearsay?

If the statement is indeed hearsay, the next question to ask is whether it is first-hand or not. First-hand oral hearsay takes this form: A testifies what B told him. Multiple hearsay takes this form: A testifies what B told him C had said. Written hearsay, or a statement in a document, is first-hand if the author has endorsed it in some way. Thus, if A writes down what B has said to him and B signs it, then the statement can be tendered under s116 as first-hand hearsay as long as B, the 'relevant person' has a reason not to appear, is identifiable, and would have been a competent witness.

Current rules on hearsay exceptions in criminal cases
Oral or written first-hand hearsay

This form of hearsay evidence is admissible under s116 if the statutory conditions apply. Under s116(2) the acceptable reasons for not calling the witness are that the witness is

- dead;
- unfit to be a witness because of bodily or mental condition;
- outside the United Kingdom and it is not reasonably practicable to secure his attendance;
- not to be found although such steps as is reasonably practicable to take to find him have been taken; or
- is not giving or not continuing to give oral evidence in the proceedings through fear, either at all or in connection with the subject matter of the statement and the court gives leave for the statement to be given in evidence. Note that fear is to be widely construed and includes fear of the death or injury of another person or of financial loss.

One question is whether the broad interpretation of 'fear' is open to abuse. There is a safeguard in that the court has to give leave to allow such a statement. In addition, there is somewhat of an acknowledgement of the 'equality of arms principle' in that the statement is not restricted to investigating officers, thus opening up the possibility of admitting defence evidence under this head.

In *R v Boulton* (2007) the Court of Appeal again considered the sort of evidence required to establish fear for the purposes of s116(2)(e). The facts of the offence, although not sufficient reasons, could constitute the conditions in which to evaluate the evidence. It was not relevant that fear was not the only reason for not testifying if fear was a significant ingredient.

Oral multiple hearsay

This is only admissible if the parties agree, or under s121(1)(c)—see later under inclusionary discretion.

Written business documents, first-hand and multiple

The statutory business etc document exception has a long history. It is obviously the case that such documents, by definition in a permanent form, will not suffer in the same way as personal, oral, or written documents from false recollections, mistake, ambiguity, and insincerity. Their authenticity is more assured. The conditions for admitting such documents are set out in s117. The wording is complex. Figure 6.1 gives an illustration of how this section operates.

Evidence is admissible under s117 if conditions apply. The conditions are as follows:

- person supplying the information was acting in the course of trade etc, *and/or*
- may reasonably be supposed to have had personal knowledge of the matters dealt with, *and*
- each person through whom information passes was acting in the course of trade etc.

Figure 6.1 An illustration of multiple hearsay and s117 CJA 2003

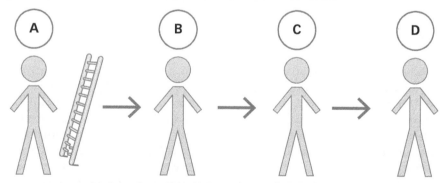

A – a worker has an accident with a broken ladder and reports this to B
B – the trade union health and safety representative reports this to C
C – the factory Health and Safety Officer reports this to D
D – the general manager of the factory

Definition of hearsay in criminal proceedings
✳✳✳✳✳✳✳✳✳✳✳

Note that the court has a discretion to refuse to admit a document even if conditions apply, s117(6) and (7).

Maher v DPP (2006) 170 JP 441

FACTS: The case involved a driver, M, who had left the scene of an accident in a car park but who was traced in the following way. An onlooker (O) who saw the crash left a copy of M's number plate on the bonnet of the stationary car that M had damaged. The driver of the damaged car (V) passed it to the police (P) whose record was admitted at trial under **s117**. M was convicted and appealed. The Divisional Court considered whether the statement was admissible under **s117** and held it was not.

HELD: **Section 117** did not apply since there had been a break in the line of persons in authority. The police log was a document prepared for the purpose of criminal proceedings but the statutory criteria were not fulfilled since, although the person who gave the information could not reasonably be expected to have a recollection of the number (see **s117(5)(b)**) the chain of business etc documents had been broken. This was a case of multiple hearsay, which is only admissible under **s121(a)** if **s117, 119, or 120** were fulfilled. **Section 121(b)** did not apply since the parties did not agree. That left **s121(c)**, 'the court is satisfied that the value of the evidence in question, taking into account how reliable the statement appears to be, is so high that the interests of justice require the later statement to be admissible for that purpose.' The court considered that the trial judge should have considered this section as well as **s114(1)(d)**. However, since the trial judge did not express any concerns about the statement's reliability under **s117**, the statement could be considered to be properly admitted.
  Table 6.3 illustrates this case.

Table 6.3 See *Maher v DPP* (2006)

O passes the note to V who passes it to P

O fulfils **s117(2)(b)**—supplied information and may reasonably be supposed to have had personal knowledge of the matters dealt with.

V does NOT fulfil **s117(2)(a)** since the document was not created or received by a person in the course of a trade etc. The chain was therefore broken (even though P is acting in the course of a trade etc, **s117**).

Documents prepared for criminal proceedings

Admissible under s117 if conditions apply. Conditions: in addition to those stated above and earlier there must be one of the statutory reasons for not calling the witness or the additional reason that 'the maker cannot reasonably be expected to have any recollection of the matters dealt with in the statement'. *Kamuhuza* (2008) shows the approach of the courts to the admissibility of documents generated by the police. In that case the court considered the admissibility of an analysis of fingerprints left by the defendant at the scene of the crime some five years before the trial. The prosecution had not traced the police forensic expert. The court held that s116 was not the appropriate section since it could not be realistically assumed that a public servant in that post could not be traced. Section 117(5)(b) applied since the document was prepared for the purpose of criminal proceedings, and the maker could not reasonably be expected to remember the contents of the document.

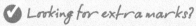
✔ Looking for extra marks?

Be aware that you may be posed some knotty definitional problems on hearsay. One such is whether absence of a record (eg a name missing on a register) is hearsay. The common law view was that it was direct evidence and not hearsay, as in *R v Shone* (1982). But note s115(3) CJA, which suggests that if it was the purpose of the person who made the record to cause a person to believe the content of the register then it may be hearsay. Arguably, it would fall anyhow into the category of business records. For a more recent example of real evidence, see *DPP v Leigh (2010)*. Evidence of the absence of an entry in a police record of responses to requests for information of the name of a driver under s172 Road Traffic Act 1988 was not hearsay evidence because it was not relied on for the purpose of establishing the veracity of any matter stated therein.

Common law exceptions

The CJA 2003 specifically preserves some but not all of the common law exceptions. Their admissibility is not subject to the rather complex statutory provisions and the common law does not make a distinction between oral and written statements. See Table 6.4.

Revision tip

Assessment questions are likely to refer to *res gestae*.

You must ensure you understand that not all the common law exceptions are preserved. Thus, for example, if you have a question that includes a dying declaration (one of the common law exceptions which is not preserved), you will need to apply the *res gestae* exception, which is preserved, or the inclusionary discretion under s114(1)(d). On this, see *R v Lawson* (1998).

There is limited case law under s118 but note *Walker (Levi Soloman)* (2007), where the Court of Appeal preferred to apply the statutory discretion to a statement where arguably the case was one of common enterprise. The case involved a statement by a third party as to what a co-defendant had said which the trial judge had admitted against both defendants.

✔ Looking for extra marks?

One difficult question is under what conditions evidence of motive is admissible as an exception to the rule against hearsay. The common law exception for statement of intention is preserved (s118(1)4(c)). Your answer to a question on this area must make it clear that the case law is unclear as to whether the court is able to infer from the statement that the intention was carried out. This is an instance where a detailed knowledge of the judgments will increase your marks.

In *Mohgal* (1977) the Court of Appeal (obiter) was of the view that a tape recording by the accused's mistress six months earlier was admissible to suggest she had carried out the murder. On the other hand, some doubt was thrown on this in *Blastland* (1985), and see also *R v Thomson* (1912), where a statement by the victim that she had intended to carry out an abortion on herself was not admissible in a trial of her alleged murderer. Support for statements of intention as evidence of subsequent action is found in the more recent case of *R v Valentine* (1996), where the earlier statement of intention by an alleged rapist was admissible as relevant to his *mens rea*. See also *R v Callender* (1998), where a defendant was refused permission to submit a statement he had made two weeks before his arrest for carrying explosives. He had wanted to put in the statement to support his claim he intended to carry only false explosives.

Common law exceptions

****

Table 6.4 Common law exceptions preserved in s118 CJA 2003

Exception	Comment
Records containing public information: **s118(1) para 1**	Much of the evidence under this head would be admissible also under **s117**.
Reputation as to character: **s118(1) para 2**	See **R v Rowton (1865)**.
Reputation or family tradition: **s118(1) para 3**	This refers to evidence of pedigree, the existence of a marriage, the existence of a public or general right, or the identity of any person or thing.
Res gestae (i) Excited utterances: **s118(1) para 4(a)**	The leading case on excited utterances prompted by an event is **R v Andrews (1987)**. This set out a test for admissibility of the statement replacing the earlier test, which had concentrated on closeness in time between the utterance and the event. The new test rested on discounting the possibility of mistake or concoction. In **R v Callender (1998)** the Court of Appeal proposed that the same test applied to all aspects of the *res gestae* exception.
Res gestae (ii) Statements accompanying an act: **s118(1) para 4(b)**	A good example of this exception is **R v McCay (1990)**. The police officer at a trial arising from an assault in a public house was allowed to state which number the witness had given identifying the defendant at a pre-trial identification parade. See further Chapter 8 on identification evidence.
Res gestae (iii) Statements related to the maker's physical sensation or a mental state (such as intention or emotion): **s118(1) para 4(c)**	In **R v Gilfoyle (1996)** the defence said that the victim had committed suicide and the prosecution that she had been murdered by her husband. She had left suicide notes. The Court of Appeal held that statements by the wife to her friends that G had asked her to write the notes to help with a course he was taking were admissible as evidence of her non-suicidal state of mind. They were not evidence as to the cause of her state of mind. They would also have been admissible under the **Andrews** test.
Confessions or mixed statements: **s118(1) para 5**	See Chapter 3.
Admissions by agents: **s118(1) para 6**	Such vicarious admissions are rarely admissible in criminal proceedings.
Statements made in furtherance of common purpose: **s118(1) para 7**	A statement made by one party to a conspiracy is admissible against any other party to the conspiracy as evidence of its truth if it demonstrates that the conspiracy is in operation. In **R v Hulme (2005)** the court properly admitted text messages sent between alleged IRA terrorists.
Expert evidence: **s118(1) para 8**	See Chapter 9.

Questions on the safeguards under CJA 2003

How is the inclusionary discretion exercised?

Hearsay is only admissible as stated in s114(1) CJA 2003:

* if any provisions in the statute make it admissible,
* if any preserved common law provisions in s118 CJA 2003 make it admissible,
* if all the parties agree, or
* if the court is satisfied that it is in the interests of justice for it to be admissible.

Section 114(2) sets out considerations the court should bear in mind before exercising the inclusionary discretion, namely that it is in the interests of justice to admit an otherwise inadmissible statement. These are:

* probative value,
* the extent of other evidence,
* how important it is in the context of the case as a whole,
* circumstances in which it was made,
* reliability of maker of the statement,
* reliability of the evidence in the statement,
* if oral evidence on this can be given and if not why,
* difficulty in challenging the statement, and
* the extent to which such difficulty would prejudice the party.

Note also the inclusionary discretion for multiple hearsay in s121(1)(c) cited in *Maher* (see p116). See also *R v Walker* (2007), where the court stated that s121(1)(c) imposes a higher standard than s114. Keane and McKeown (2016, p347) comments, 'Thus if reliance is placed on a hearsay statement to prove "an earlier hearsay statement" admissible under s114(1)(d) and s114(2), s121(1)(c) is an additional test to be met.' Table 6.5 illustrates how the inclusionary discretion is applied.

Do the courts apply the inclusionary discretion in s114(1)(d) to defence and prosecution submissions?

Munday (2015, p 388) comments: 'Interestingly, what emerges in the reported case law is that s114(1)(d) appears to afford assistance to the prosecution more frequently than it does the defence.' However, Glover (2015, p290) observes that in the light of the landmark series of cases in the Strasbourg court, *Al-Khawaja and Tahery v UK* (2009–11), 'it is possible to discern a distinct tempering of the courts' readiness to admit hearsay concerned with

Questions on the safeguards under CJA 2003

✶✶✶✶✶✶✶✶✶✶

Table 6.5 Cases under s114 CJA 2003

Case	Principle
R v Xhabri (2005)	Section may be relied upon even if evidence is inadmissible by another section.
R v Finch (2007)	Trial judge's ruling will only be reversed on grounds of **Wednesbury** unreasonableness.
R v Y (2008)	The section was not limited to hearsay assisting the defence. The court did, however, stress the general unreliability of hearsay, and the need to consider the factors set out in **s114(2)** extremely thoroughly. Since the trial judge had in consequence of his preliminary ruling not considered these at all, the case was sent back for the resumption of the trial.
R v L (2009)	A wife made a statement to police who had not advised her that she was not compellable to give evidence against her husband in his trial for alleged rape of their 19-year-old daughter. She declined to testify. The statement was admissible under **s114(1)(d)**. Section 80 **PACE** did not preclude a witness from giving evidence of a voluntary statement made in the past by the defendant's wife. Whether it was just in such instances to admit the statement depended on the specific facts.
R v Z (2009)	The defendant was charged with a series of historical sexual offences. The prosecution was allowed to adduce a statement of a witness who was unwiling to testify. Appeal against conviction was allowed. **Section 114(1)(d)** should be 'cautiously applied, since otherwise the conditions laid down by Parliament in s116 would be circumvented'.
R v CT (2011)	Hearsay evidence of complainant in a trial for assault was improperly admitted since she should have been called as a witness.
R v Burton (2011)	Appropriate to apply **s114(1)(d)** since it was not right to call the alleged victim who was a child. It was an exceptional case.

the relationship between ss114(1)(d) and 116 of the Criminal Justice Act 2003.' The following cases demonstrate that the inclusionary discretion is available in law for all types of hearsay, first-hand or multiple, and on application by any party to a criminal trial and also that it was relevant, in applying 'the interests of justice' test whether the applicant was the defence or the prosecution. It is clear that confessions may be admitted under CJA and PACE and that if admissible under the CJA the grounds of exclusion under s76(2) PACE do not apply. Glover (2015, p291), citing such cases as *R v Z* (2009), considers that the Court of Appeal has become 'less inclusionary' in its application of s114(1)(d).

R v McLean (2007)

FACTS: M, P, and H were charged with the murder of C on the basis of joint enterprise. M and P each blamed the other. H was silent at interview and did not give evidence. While on remand he told officers that P had stabbed C. M applied for this statement to be admitted at trial under **s114(1)(d)**.

HELD: Out of court statements made by one defendant against another were admissible under **s114(1)(d)**. The judge had erred in applying the historical rule on hearsay. The convictions were quashed and a retrial ordered.

R v Y (2008)

FACTS: The prosecution claimed Y had attacked V and called for X to stab V. X did so and caused fatal wounds to V. X pleaded guilty and Y was separately charged. Before X's arrest he was said to have told his girlfriend that he killed V and that Y had been the other assailant. The Crown applied to adduce the girlfriend's statement. The Crown conceded that without the statement it did not have a prima facie case. The judge ruled that **s114(1)(d)** had no application to a statement contained in a confession and refused to consider the Crown's submission on its merits. The Crown submitted, on appeal, that **s114(1)(d)** allowed the admission of hearsay material which was contained in a confession by another person and that **s118(1) para 5** (preserving any rule of law relating to the admissibility of confessions or mixed statements) did not apply. The Court of Appeal called this the 'section 114/118 issue'.

HELD: Allowing the Crown's appeal, that **s114(1)(d)** was available in law for all types of hearsay, including confessions, and on application by any party to a criminal trial. In the case of an out of court statement contained in, or associated with, a confession, **s118(1) para 5** did not exclude the application of **s114(1)(d)**. The court should ensure that it was in the interests of justice that the jury should rely on the statement without seeing its maker. It is not the effect of **s114(1)(d)** that out of court statements, whether by co-accused or anyone else, are routinely to be admitted.

Keane and McKeown (2016, p335) observe, citing *R v Marsh* (2008), that '[t]he test to be applied to a defendant on a serious criminal charge will often be less exacting than that which would apply to the prosecution but the interests of justice are synonymous not with the interests of the defendant but with the public interest in arriving at the right conclusion in the case'. In *Marsh* the appellant was charged with conspiracy to import cocaine. His defence was he thought the drug was cannabis. He appealed unsuccessfully against the exclusion under s114(1)(d) of a witness statement by a serving prisoner, Bennett. This claimed that a fellow prisoner, Rosier, had confessed to Bennett he had 'set up' Marsh over the drug transaction. The Court of Appeal upheld the judge's decision, in part because of the lack of means to judge the veracity of Bennett's statement. There had been no attempt to call Rosier.

R v Finch (2007)

FACTS: F wanted to adduce the statement of his former co-accused, R, which exonerated him of the offence. R pleaded guilty to the offence. His statement was inadmissible under **s76A PACE** because he was no longer 'an accused person'.

> **HELD**: There was a distinction between a witness who was unavailable and one who was unwilling. R could have been compelled to give evidence. Where a confession was not admissible under **PACE** because a person who had pleaded guilty to an offence was no longer 'an accused person' the confession may be admissible under **s114(1)(d)**. However, (at para 24) 'It is not, in short, the law that every reluctant witness's evidence automatically can be put before the jury under s114 of the 2003 Act.'

✅ Looking for extra marks?

It follows from the case law above and earlier that confessions may be available under the CJA when they are inadmissible under **PACE** (see also *R v Thakrar* (2010)). This outcome is the subject of much academic discussion and you may well be asked in an essay question to evaluate the current position in relation to fairness to the defence. Glover (2015, p353) points out that confessions are subject to mandatory or discretionary exclusion in certain cases under **ss76(2) and 78 PACE**. They doubt whether the conditions of admissibility under **s114(2)** adequately deal with the issue of voluntariness and fairness of confessions. They suggest that *R v Y* is wrongly decided. On the other hand you could argue that the opening up of the possibility of the admissibility of third party confessions may be helpful to the defendant and note that that oral or written third party confessions may be admissible under **s116(2) CJA**. Thus, a case such as *R v Blastland* (1985) might be decided differently today.

What is the relationship between s116 and s114?

The power to admit evidence under s114(1)(d) in the interests of justice should not be used to circumvent the conditions laid down in s116. However, there may be situations where the reason a witness cannot be called to testify falls outside the five listed reasons in s116(2). In such a case the statement may be admissible under s114(1)(d).

R v Warnick (2013)

FACTS: G was attacked by two men who fled the scene in a car. An eyewitness, X, gave the police the registration number of the car, which, at the time of the attack, had been leased to W. G identified W as his assailant and the driver of the getaway car. X did not give evidence at the trial, claiming to be afraid. The judge refused the prosecution's application to give X's evidence under **s116(2)(e)** on the grounds that the conditions of the subsection were not satisfied and it was unclear whether X remained in fear. He allowed it to be admitted under **s114(1)(d)**.

HELD: X's hearsay statement should not have been admitted under **s114(1)(d)**. The judge had used the subsection to circumvent the conditions under **s116**. He had not satisfied **s114(2)(g)**, which required the court to have regard to whether oral evidence could have been given. However, the conviction was safe despite the judge's error.

Are anonymous statements admissible under s114?

It was held in *R v Mayers* (2008) and approved in *R v Horncastle* (2010) that the prosecution may not adduce anonymous hearsay statements.

Note that the application of the comprehensive inclusionary discretion in s114(2) is made more complex in that there is another inclusionary statutory provision:

Section 121(1)(c): the court may admit multiple hearsay that is not otherwise admissible under the section if it 'is satisfied that the value of the evidence in question, taking into account how reliable the statements appear to be, is so high that the interests of justice require the later statement to be admissible for that purpose.' The case of *R v Thakrar* and a helpful commentary by Ormerod shed light on the use of this section.

R v Thakrar (2010)

FACTS: Two men were tried for the killing of three male occupants in a house. D1 had fled to Cyprus before arrest and D2 was arrested prior to boarding a flight there. Both pleaded not guilty. The prosecution wished to adduce evidence from three witnesses detailing their conversations with D1 on his arrival in Cyprus. The statements were made to a Northern Cypriot police officer and contained admissions by D1 of his and D2's involvement in the murders. The witnesses were unwilling to come to the trial in the UK and no video link could be used. The defendants challenged the admissibility of the statements, which were multiple hearsay.

HELD: The judge was correct to hold that the statements were admissible in the interests of justice under s121(1)(c). There was no doubt about the safety of the convictions and there was strong additional evidence to support the hearsay statements.

Ormerod (2011, p402–403) points out several anomalies in this judgment.

(i)   The judge has regard to the factors in s114(2) of the 2003 Act in determining admissibility under s116(2)(c), although '[t]echnically that is unnecessary'. He adds, however, that since 'the use of the hearsay rule is under such close scrutiny in ECHR terms, reliance on these factors can only reduce the risk of unfair trials and encourage consistency in decision-making. Of course this does not respect the legislative scheme, but that is a different matter'. He points out that in any case the statements were not admissible under s116 since they were multiple hearsay.

(ii) In the statement, admissible under s121(1)(c), one defendant, D1, incriminated the other, D2. Ormerod adds, 'Cases under the 2003 Act have not dealt with the issue directly but the court has implicitly acknowledged the possibility of admissibility of D1's confession as against D2.' He suggests that the courts ought to specifically address the common law rule that D1's confession is not evidence against D2. See *R v McLean* (2007) (p121).

(iii) The judgment does not address the question of whether the statement by D1, even if admissible under s76 PACE, would be admissible against D2.

R v Musone (2007) also involved the admissibility of multiple hearsay. Here a statement identifying M as his killer told by a dying prisoner, Reid, to a fellow prisoner who passed the information to a prison officer, Patterson. The judge ruled that Patterson's evidence should be admitted in evidence, pursuant to s114(1)(d) and s121(1)(c). M's appeal against conviction failed since Patterson's statement was rightly admitted.

How is the exclusionary discretion exercised?

There are two specific sections dealing with exclusion of evidence, namely s125(1) (see p125) and s126(1). The latter is written in narrow terms, 'taking account of the danger that to admit the evidence would result in undue waste of time'. Note that the section applies to defence and prosecution evidence, unlike s78 PACE, which only applies to prosecution evidence. Emson (2010, p412) notes: 'Whatever the precise scope of s126(1), as a matter of practical reality few trial judges are likely to feel confident about excluding defence evidence, even if the provision empowers them to do so, for the simple reason that the evidence might well be true.'

In addition s116(4) gives the court a power to exclude evidence if the witness is not appearing through 'fear' and s117(6) and (7) give the court power to exclude otherwise admissible business and other documents.

In practice, the courts have applied s126(1) more widely than its terms suggest. In *Cole and Keet* (2006) the court was of the view that even if the conditions of admissibility were satisfied, here the relevant section being s114(1)(d), there would still be a need to consider the general discretion under s126(1) and on occasion s78 PACE. See also *R v Gyima* (2007), where the judgment does not make it clear whether the evidence of a video-recording made by a foreign witness before going back home was admitted under s114(1)(d) or s116(2)(c) or not excluded under the exclusionary discretions including s126(1).

What protection is afforded when the statements are prepared for criminal proceedings?

Section 117(4) covering the admissibility of statements prepared for criminal proceedings contains similar provisions to those in the CJA 1988. The reason for the additional safeguards is the need to avoid purely paper trials. Thus, 'the person who supplied the information contained in the document (the relevant person)' should be called to give oral testimony unless one of the acceptable reasons for not calling him applies. Note also that the case of *R v Kamuhuza* (2008) suggests that first-hand documentary statements made by the police, and presumably this would include an endorsed witness statement, could in principle be admissible under s116 (the successor to s23 CJA 1988) if there is a statutory reason for not calling the witness.

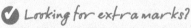 ✅ Looking for extra marks?

You should make it clear to the examiners that you are aware that the courts are not willing to allow witnesses to give evidence by the hearsay provisions if the reason the witness cannot be brought to court is prosecution mistakes. In *R v Adams* (2007) the Court of Appeal rejected any suggestion of a distinction between being unable to find and being unable to contact a witness. It emphasised the unsatisfactory procedure adapted by the prosecution in this case to alert witnesses to the need to attend to testify at trial. Thus, s116(2)(d) did not apply.

How does the court treat the question of the witness's credibility?

Section 124 provides that evidence which would have been admissible as relevant were he to have testified is also admissible in his absence. The person against whom the hearsay statement is admitted may seek to use evidence to discredit the maker of the statement or to show he has contradicted himself. The admissibility of the absent witness's bad character is governed by s100(1)(b) CJA 2003 (see p101). Thus, in *R v Harvey* (2014), the Court of Appeal held that this section applied to witnesses who were absent through fear.

How is the power to stop the case exercised?

Section 125(1) is an important safeguard in that the court has the power to stop the case under the following conditions:

- case is wholly or partly based on hearsay,
- such evidence is so unconvincing that a conviction would be unsafe,
- the case is a trial on indictment before a jury.

Section 125(1) was considered in *R v Joyce* (2005). The disputed evidence in the trial of appellants, who were convicted of possessing a firearm with intent to cause fear of violence, was identification evidence which was retracted by witnesses who then claimed they had been mistaken. Their testimony at trial was not consistent with their earlier statements (for further details on s119, which applied here, see Chapter 8). The court compared the test under s125(1) to that in *Galbraith* (1981), which applies to identification evidence. The court considered that it was not believable that all three witnesses were indeed mistaken and refused to apply s125(1).

What safeguard is there as to the capacity of the absent witness?

Under s116(1) it is required that the witness whose hearsay evidence is being used is competent and compellable to give evidence and that he is identified to the court's satisfaction. There has also to be an acceptable reason for the absence.

Are there rules of court setting out additional procedures?

These may be made under s132. It is noticeable that such rules are well established in the case of hearsay in civil proceedings.

Hearsay evidence and ECHR

Article 6(3)(d) ECHR provides that everyone charged with a criminal offence has the right to examine or have examined witnesses against him. Thus, the right to confront a witness personally is not absolute since 'have examined' may include a pre-trial examination by an advocate. In some cases the court has upheld that this section has been violated by the non-appearance of a witness as in, for example, *Kostovski v Netherlands* (1990), where the out of court statements were either the only evidence or an important part of the evidence. On the other hand there was no violation in *Doorson v Netherlands* (1996). In this case, frightened witnesses in a trial involving large-scale drug dealing were cross examined in a pre-trial hearing without the presence of the defendant.

The hearsay provisions in the CJA 1988 had been held by the English and Strasbourg courts to be compliant with the ECHR in that there were in place safeguards such as the exclusionary discretion. Doubts were cast, however, on this argument by the Strasbourg court's subsequent decision in *Al-Khawaja and Tahery v UK* (2009). In Al-Khawaja's case a witness statement had been admitted under the now repealed s23 CJA 1988, which allowed a written statement to be admitted if the witness was dead and the court considered it was in the interests of justice to admit it. In Tahery's case the witness statement was admitted under s116(2)(e), which allows a statement to be admitted where the witness does not attend to give oral evidence through fear. The court held that allowing a witness statement to be admitted as evidence where the witness is not available for cross examination, and that evidence is the 'sole or decisive' basis for convicting the accused, is a violation of the right to a fair trial under Art 6(1) and (3)(d). In *R v Horncastle* (2009) the Supreme Court refused to adopt this reasoning.

In the event, the Grand Chamber in *Al Khawaja and Tahery v UK* (2011) did not uphold the 'sole or decisive test' as an inflexible rule. There should be regard to the relevant provisions of national law. As Dennis (2012, p376) in his commentary on the judgment wrote, 'Its effect is to allow English courts to continue to apply the Criminal Justice Act 2003 and the Coroners and Justice Act 2009 in a fact-sensitive way, without the anxiety that hearsay or anonymous evidence would necessarily have to be excluded once it reached a certain level of importance.' He adds (p377), 'This is not to say that Strasbourg has given English hearsay law an unrestricted blessing . . . Strong procedural safeguards will be required and there must be sufficient counterbalancing factors in place, including measures that permit a fair and proper assessment of the reliability of the evidence.' There will have to be strong procedural safeguards including a very strong reason not to call the witness.

Reconciling *Horncastle* and *Tahery*

R v Riat (2013)

FACTS: The case involved several conjoined appeals. R, a teacher, had committed sexual offences against a 13-year-old pupil who had died before the trial; in D's case an elderly householder had

---

died before D's trial for robbery and theft at his property was concluded but a video-recorded interview had been made; W was charged with assault occasioning actual bodily harm and the complainant and two witnesses feared giving evidence at trial; C's case concerned the statement of a 3-year-old victim of a sexual assault where there had been no assessment of her ability to be interviewed under Achieving Best Practice conditions; B's case concerned the conviction of sexual activity by a psychiatric nurse with a person with a mental disorder.

HELD: Appeals allowed in part.

(i) The common law prohibition on the admission of hearsay evidence remained the default rule. The law was as stated in the CJA 2003 and courts generally needed to look no further than the Act and *Horncastle*. Neither the CJA nor *Horncastle* permitted hearsay evidence to be automatically admissible as if it were first-hand evidence.

(ii) It was clear from s116 of the Act that a reason for resorting to second-hand evidence had to be shown, eg a witness's illness or death. Where a witness was in fear of giving evidence, s116(4)(c) required consideration of special measures. Even if hearsay evidence was prima facie admissible, it had not to be simply 'nodded through'; it could still be ruled inadmissible under s126 of the Act or under s78 PACE (paras 19–25). The evidence could also be stopped under s125 of the 2003 Act.

(iii) In R's case, statements from the deceased had been rightly admitted because they were strongly supported by other evidence and did not stand as untestable allegations. In D's case the interview had been properly admitted. In W's case it had been unfair to admit the statements because the fear gateway had not been established. In C's case, the statement of a 3-year-old victim of a sexual assault had been properly admitted since her statement did not stand alone, and her very strong reaction to examination or enquiry was a powerful reason, at her age, not to trouble her further. In B's case the victim's statements were properly admitted under the s116(2)(b) gateway to support other evidence.

Revision tip

You will put yourself in a strong position if you read the very recent case law as part of your revision. Bear in mind that examiners may draw on the scenarios in these cases for questions. The above account has indicated that *Riat* is the leading case on the application of *Horncastle*. However, the law in this area is fast evolving. The subsequent case of *R v Shabir* (2012) addressed the use of the term 'demonstrably reliable', the meaning of which had been at issue in *Riat* and in *R v Ibrahim* (2012). In this case, Aikens LJ did not use that phrase, preferring (at para 107) 'potentially safely reliable'. In *R v Harvey* (2014) the Court of Appeal gave further attention to the interpretation of 'sole or decisive'. Here, the evidence of the absent witnesses was very important but since there was other corroborative evidence it was not decisive.

Note also that this controversy could be pertinent in discussing in an essay question the general matter of corroboration, which the Law Commission had held unnecessary in the case of hearsay. They had confidence in the safeguard of s125.

Conclusion

✱✱✱✱✱✱✱✱✱

In *Seton v UK (2016)* and *Simon Price v UK (2016)* the Strasbourg court held that the admissibility of hearsay evidence had not violated **Art 6**. In *Seton* the evidence was a telephone recording of an absent prosecution witness. In *Price* the absent witness was a customs broker whose statement supported the prosecution case about the destination of illegal drugs. The witness declined to testify despite offers of special measures such as giving evidence via a video-link.

 ① Conclusion

Commentators differ as to whether the changes detailed in this chapter have been an improvement. They certainly appear to have generated a flexible approach, but one which arguably makes the law more complex and uncertain. The mixture of detailed rule-based provisions with open textured discretion has overall created a certain amount of tension in its operation.

 ✱ Key cases

Case	Facts	Principle and comment
R v Andrews [1987] AC 281	The victim of a robbery and stabbing was able to tell police at the scene who his assailants had been. He died before the trial. The statement to the police was held by the House of Lords to be hearsay but admissible under the *res gestae* exception, the test for which was redefined.	The House here was marginalising the element of contemporaneity which had previously been the feature of the *res gestae* test. The statement to the police had of course been made some time after the stabbing.
R v Blastland [1985] 3 WLR 345	B was convicted of murder and appealed on the grounds that evidence should have been allowed that a third party, M, had spoken to others that a boy had been murdered before it was public knowledge. M was not called as a witness.	The House of Lords, taking a very narrow view of relevance, held that the evidence was irrelevant and hearsay. It was inadmissible and the conviction was upheld. Arguably, such evidence could be admissible under s116 or s114.
R v C [2006] EWCA Crim 197	At the defendants' trial for fraud, the prosecution was proposing to adduce a witness statement made by a resident of South Africa, who was related to one of the defendants. The witness was not willing to attend trial. The judge admitted the witness	The court here indicated the scope of the exclusionary discretion even where the evidence was admissible under the statutory provisions. It also indicated the use of s78 for prosecution hearsay evidence.

Case	Facts	Principle and comment
	statement under **s116(2)(c) CJA 2003** and refused to exercise his discretion to exclude it under **s78 PACE**. The court held that the expression 'reasonably practicable' in **s116(2)(c)** had to be judged on the basis of the steps taken or not taken, by the party seeking to adduce the witness's evidence. There had been insufficient explanation of the reasons for the witness's refusal to attend, or to give evidence by video-link. The defendant's appeal at the interlocutory stage was allowed.	
R v Cole and Keet [2007] EWCA Crim 1924	Keet was accused of having grossly overcharged an old woman for house repairs. By the time the case came to trial the householder had become demented and could not give evidence in person. The admission of her witness statement was contested. In Cole's case, the body of a woman who had committed suicide showed other injuries which were said to have been caused by the defendant. Before her death, the victim had told other people that the defendant had attacked her. The issue on appeal was whether their hearsay evidence could be used. The court held that there was no absolute rule that evidence of a statement could not be adduced unless a defendant had an opportunity to examine a witness.	In considering whether hearsay evidence should be admitted in a criminal trial, the only role of **Art 6 ECHR** was to determine whether the admission of the evidence was compatible with a fair trial. Hearsay evidence was not precluded by **Art 6** even where it was the sole or decisive evidence against a defendant.
R v Horncastle [2009] UKSC 14	The case concerned four conjoined appeals, in all of which the convictions were based on the hearsay evidence of identifiable witnesses who did not testify. In the cases of H and B the witness had died and in the cases of M and C the witness was absent through fear. The defence argued that, following *Al-Khawaja and Tahery v UK* (2009), the convictions based solely or decisively on the evidence of absent witnesses were a violation of **Art 6(3)(d) ECHR**.	The Supreme Court rejected the reasoning in *Al-Khawaja and Tahery v UK* (2009) and upheld the convictions. The **Human Rights Act 1998** does not require English courts to apply the decisive or sole rule in relation to hearsay. The clash between the Supreme Court and the Strasbourg court in part arises from the fact that hearsay is more broadly defined in English law. The Strasbourg jurisprudence makes it clear that **Art 6(3)(d)** applies only to accusatory witness statements made to the investigative authorities. Hearsay under English law can

Case	Facts	Principle and comment
		embrace all pre-trial statements satisfying the definition in **CJA 2003**. Lord Phillips stated (para 105) that the sole or decisive test if applied will in some cases result in acquittal of, or failure to prosecute, defendants where there is cogent evidence of their guilt. In *Al-Khawaja and Tahery v UK* (2011) the Grand Chamber failed to uphold the 'sole and decisive' rule, while stressing the need for strong safeguards.
R v Sellick [2005] 1 WLR 3257	Hearsay statements had been admitted under **CJA 1988**. In two cases the witnesses did not give evidence through fear. The appellants alleged this infringed **Art 6(3)(d)**. The court held that the evidence was properly admitted since the defendant had put the witness in fear. There had to be clear directions to the jury but in such a situation the defendant cannot claim that his rights have been infringed even if the hearsay evidence is the sole or decisive evidence against him.	The court took a robust approach to the admissibility of hearsay, particularly bearing in mind that the defendant was alleged to have caused the witnesses to be in fear. Controversially, it accepted that the conviction could stand even where the hearsay evidence was the main evidence.
R v Singh [2006] 1 WLR 1564	S's appeal turned on whether the prosecution should have been allowed to adduce evidence of entries in the memories of mobile phones. The inference from these was that S had taken part in a conspiracy. The court held that this evidence was an implied assertion and not hearsay as defined in the **CJA 2003**. In any case there were two other routes to admissibility, namely **s118(7)** as common enterprise or by the inclusionary discretion in **s114(1)(d)**.	This case makes it clear that the common law definition of hearsay (which included implied assertions) no longer prevails. *R v Kearley* (1992) is thus overruled.
R v Xhabri [2006] 1 All ER 776	A woman who claimed she had been imprisoned, raped, and forced to work as a prostitute had made statements to others about her plight. The prosecution statements were held to have been properly admitted, either under **s120(7)** or **s114(d)**, in a trial of her abductor. Appeal dismissed.	(i) Evidence may be admitted under **s114(1)(d)** even where the conditions for admissibility under s120 are not met. (ii) **Section 114** was compatible with **Art 6** since the court had the power to exclude hearsay evidence under **s126** and was under a duty to do so under **HRA 1998** where its admissibility would infringe **Art 6**.

Case	Facts	Principle and comment
		(iii) Since the hearsay provisions in **CJA 2003** applied to prosecution and defence, there was **equality of arms**.
Sparks v R [1964] AC 964	At S's trial for assaulting a young girl the victim was too young to testify. The defence was not allowed to tender a statement she had made to her mother shortly after the offence. She had said, 'It was a coloured boy.' S was white. The PC upheld the judge's ruling that the statement was inadmissible hearsay.	The rule against hearsay applies equally to defence and prosecution, and under the common law it was applied strictly. There was no judicial discretion to admit even arguably good quality evidence. The rule, if it applied, was inflexible.
Subramanian v DPP [1956] 1 WLR 965	S was convicted in British-held Malaya of having ammunition without lawful authority. He argued duress in his defence in that he had been threatened by terrorists. The appeal to the Privy Council turned on whether the alleged statements made by the terrorists to him should have been admitted or whether they were, as the trial court held, inadmissible hearsay. The PC held that they were not hearsay since the purpose of tendering them was not to suggest they were true or not but whether they were made. Appeal allowed.	This case illustrates the importance of the second aspect of the definition of hearsay. Even if made out of court a statement is only hearsay if it is tendered to suggest it is true or, as **s114 CJA 2003** now puts it, is 'admissible as evidence of any matter stated'. Here the purpose of putting evidence of the threats was simply to suggest that they had been made. The truth of their content was not in issue.

⑨⑨ Key debates

Topic	A review of the Grand Chamber judgment in *Al-Khawaja and Tahery* (2011) and the European Court of Human Rights judgment in *Ellis, Simms and Martin* (2012)
Author	B deWilde
Viewpoint	The abandonment of the absolute application of the 'sole and decisive rule' in relation to the admissibility of hearsay evidence and the opening up of the possibility of basing a conviction on anonymous witness statements has diminished the right to examine witnesses. Although the ECtHR has stressed the need for counterbalancing factors, the nature of these is not clear. The author argues that the right to a fair trial implies the right to question decisive witnesses, and if this is not possible or desirable the defendant should be acquitted.
Source	'A Fundamental Review of the ECHR Right to Examine Witnesses in Criminal Cases' (2013) 17/2 *E&P* 157

Exam questions
✳✳✳✳✳✳✳✳✳

Topic	The principles underpinning reform of the hearsay rule
Authors	P Roberts and A Zuckerman
Viewpoint	The hearsay sections in the CJA 2003 have flaws, including poor drafting, but overall they are progressive, and entrust the judges with discretion to operate the statute within the dictates of common sense and justice. Clear judicial directions to the jury are vital and, in particular, in the cases where hearsay is adduced by the prosecution, compliance with Art 6 and the common law require the judge to draw attention to problems associated with hearsay evidence.
Source	*Criminal Evidence* (OUP, 2010) pp432–441

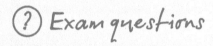 Exam questions

Essay question

'The first respect in which the hearsay rule deviates from common sense concerns its exclusion of evidence of innocence' (A Zuckerman, *The Principles of Criminal Evidence*, Clarendon Law Series, 1989).

Critically evaluate Zuckerman's observation in the light of the current law on the use of hearsay evidence in criminal proceedings.

 Online Resource Centre

To see an outline answer to this question visit www.oup.com/lawrevision/

Problem question

Anna and Fred are charged with stabbing John who has an allotment next to theirs. John had been found with a metal spike through his leg bleeding heavily. He died a few hours later. The prosecution case is that Anna, Fred, and John had a row over some missing garden tools and that Anna and Fred stabbed John with a metal tent spike. Harry, another allotment holder, had heard Anna, Fred, and John quarrelling before the stabbing. He told the Secretary of the Allotment Committee, Gloria, what he had heard. She made a report to the council official. Anna and Fred plead not guilty.

Discuss the admissibility of the following pieces of evidence:

(i) Evidence from Tom, who called the ambulance when he saw John injured on the allotment. John said to Tom, 'It was that monster Anna who did it.'

(ii) A text message from Sally, Anna's daughter, to her friend Harriet. In this she texted that Anna had told her that she had had nothing to do with the killing of John. Sally died in a motor accident before the trial.

(iii) The council official's record of what Gloria said Harry told her. Harry is unwilling to give evidence.

See the Outline Answers section in the end matter for help with this question.

Concentrate Q&As

For more questions and answers on evidence, see the *Concentrate Q&A: Evidence* by Maureen Spencer and John Spencer.

Go to the end of this book to view sample pages.

#7

Competence and compellability, special measures

Key facts

- The presumption in both criminal and civil trials is that all witnesses are competent and compellable, so a reason in statute or case precedent has to be found to apply an exception.

- The main criminal law exceptions in relation to competence are defendants testifying for the prosecution, or witnesses who are unable to give intelligible testimony.

- The main criminal law exceptions in relation to universal compellability are defendants themselves and spouses (or civil partners) and co-defendants testifying for the prosecution.

- The general expectation is that witnesses will give evidence on oath (**sworn evidence**).

- In criminal cases witnesses under the age of 14 years cannot give sworn evidence.

- In civil cases a child (a person under the age of 18 years) who understands the nature of the oath must give sworn testimony, while others may give unsworn evidence under certain conditions.

- Special measures for vulnerable witnesses in criminal trials are directed primarily at non-defendants but there are some limited protections for some defendants.

Chapter overview

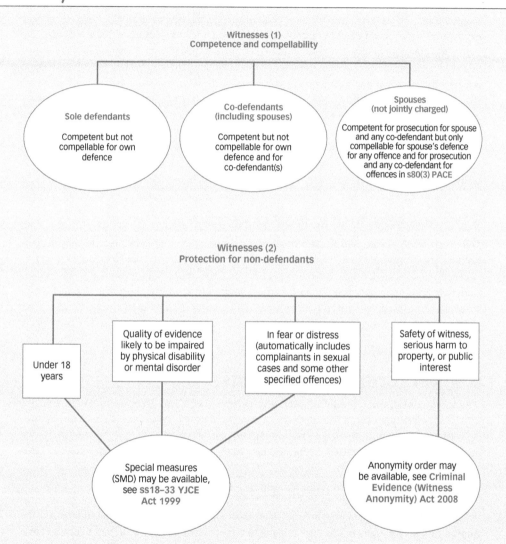

Related areas

These relate primarily to criminal trials. Chapter 8 covers some procedures regulating the examination and cross examination of witnesses in criminal trials and includes a summary of protections afforded certain classes of witness such as complainants in rape trials. The evidential consequences to the defendant of electing not to testify are covered in this chapter and the provisions here are closely related to the drawing of inferences from pre-trial silence covered in Chapter 3 and to the privilege against self-incrimination covered in Chapter 11. Another related area is that of hearsay, covered in Chapter 6, since increasingly witnesses are able to give evidence through written submissions rather than appearing in court. The close relationship between hearsay and compellability is illustrated in *R v L* (2009). The prosecution were permitted to admit a pre-trial statement by a non-compellable spouse at a trial where her husband was the defendant. The statement was admissible under s114(1)(d) Criminal Justice Act (CJA) 2003.

The assessment: key points

Questions in this area will mostly be on the exceptions to the general rule that all witnesses are competent and compellable. The limited special measures introduced to protect vulnerable defendants are recent and so may well form part of an assessment question. The controversial area of witness anonymity, where the government hastily introduced a statute to overrule a powerful decision by the House of Lords, raises many principled issues concerning fair trial rights which could form the basis of an essay question.

Key features and principles

The key statutes in this area are Criminal Evidence Act (CEA) 1898, Criminal Justice Act 2003, Criminal Justice and Public Order Act (CJPOA) 1994, Police and Criminal Evidence Act (PACE) 1984, Youth Justice and Criminal Evidence Act 1999 (YJCEA), Police and Justice Act 2006, amending the YJCEA to create a new s33A, and the Coroners and Justice Act 2009.

Criminal trials: the general rule on competence

A historically central principle in English trials is that oral evidence given under oath is the superior form of evidence. The reasoning is that this evidence can be subject to cross examination by the opposing side. Given the importance of this principle, known as the **principle of orality** in English trials, the rules regulating the attendance of witnesses assume special significance. This chapter covers the rules and practices which govern when and how witnesses are eligible to give evidence (ie are competent) and those which govern when they are required, under exercise of penalty for default, to appear (ie are compellable).

This is an area which is now largely covered by statute. The starting point is that all witnesses are competent. Section 53(1) YJCEA reads: 'At every stage in criminal proceedings all persons are (whatever their age) competent to give evidence.' There are exceptions, however, in relation to the defendant, who only became competent to testify in his defence in the CEA 1898 in a provision now enshrined in s53(1) YJCEA. Previously, the prevailing belief was that a defendant might give perjured evidence. He or she remains incompetent to testify for the prosecution under s53(4) YJCEA. This section also makes incompetent spouses who are jointly charged. Understandably, under s53(3): 'A person is not competent to give evidence in criminal proceedings if it appears to the court that he is not a person who is able to (a) understand questions put to him as a witness and (b) give answers to them which can be understood.' The former complicated and restrictive rules about child witnesses were liberalised by this provision. Guidance on the application of the provision is given in *R v Sed* (2004). The witness was a rape victim, 81 years old, who suffered from Alzheimer's disease. Her video-recorded evidence was admitted. Auld LJ stated (at para 46) it was 'for the judge to determine the question of competence almost as a matter of feel'. In effect the section does not require total comprehension by the witness.

Revision tip

You should be clear on the significance of the term 'compellable'. In *R v Yusuf* (2003), a witness to a murder failed to respond to a summons to testify. He was brought to court and cross examined as a hostile witness. He was found to be in contempt. Not all competent witnesses on the other hand are compellable. Although the general rule is that a witness who is competent is also compellable there are a number of exceptions to this based on public policy considerations as this chapter goes on to explain.

Criminal trials: exceptions to presumption of compellability

The starting point is the presumption of compellability of all witnesses, the three main groups of exceptions applying first to defendants, second to co-defendants, and third to spouses and civil partners.

Defendants and inferences from failure to testify

Defendants cannot be compelled to testify in their defence under s1(1) CEA 1898 since this would breach the privilege against self-incrimination. There is, however, indirect pressure to do so under s35 CJPOA 1994. This allows the court or jury, in determining whether the accused is guilty of the offence charged, to draw such inferences as appear proper from the failure of the accused to give evidence or his refusal, without good cause, to answer any question. The procedure which the court must follow is set out in the section. The leading case on its application is *R v Cowan* (1996).

Key features and principles

✳✳✳✳✳✳✳✳✳✳

The Court of Appeal, in that case, held that the judge must direct that

- the burden of proof remains on the prosecution;
- the defendant is entitled to remain silent;
- an inference from failure to testify alone cannot prove guilt;
- the jury must be satisfied that the prosecution have established a case to answer before drawing inferences from silence; and
- if the jury conclude that the silence can only sensibly be attributed to the defendant's having no real answer, or one that would stand up to cross examination, they may then draw an adverse inference.

In *R v Becouarn* (2005) the House of Lords held that a *Cowan* direction should be given where the defendant had refused to testify for tactical reasons. In *R v Dixon* (2013) the jury was entitled to draw an adverse inference from the defendant's failure to testify despite s35(1)(b). The defendant had a low IQ and learning difficulties which might have made it difficult for him to testify but that did not make it undesirable that he should do so.

In *O'Donnell v UK* (2015) the applicant, who had an IQ of 62, submitted that the trial judge erred in allowing the jury to draw an adverse inference under Art 4 Criminal Evidence (Northern Ireland) Order 1988, the equivalent to s35 CJPOA 1994. Expert psychiatric witnesses for the prosecution and the defence differed over whether he was able to testify. The judge accepted the prosecution evidence on this point. The court held that the judge had set out the expert evidence presented at trial regarding the applicant's intellectual disability, his limited capacity to understand English, as well as his limited capacity to provide a coherent account of his actions. The judge also explained that, regardless of whether or not the accused chose to testify, the prosecution retained the burden of proof beyond a reasonable doubt. Furthermore, the judge instructed the jury that they could only draw adverse inferences from the applicant's silence if they were satisfied beyond a reasonable doubt that the evidence relied upon by the applicant to justify his silence presented no adequate explanation for his absence from the witness box. There was no violation of Art 6.

The difference between judicial directions under s34 and s35 are addressed in *R v Doldur* (2000), where the Court of Appeal held that in deciding whether to draw adverse inferences under s35 the jury should be directed to consider the prosecution case only, whereas in relation to s34 it should additionally consider the defence evidence since the issue here turns on the contrast between what the defendant says pre-trial and in testifying.

Co-defendants

The law might appear complicated but bear in mind that under certain conditions, particularly if there is a 'cut-throat' defence put forward, the evidence of a co-defendant may assume the adversarial status of that of the prosecution. See Table 7.1.

Table 7.1 Competence and compellability (1)

Type of trial: two defendants: D1 pleading not guilty D2 pleading not guilty	
Are D1 and D2 competent for the prosecution?	No, see **s53(4) YJCEA**. *Note*: it follows that since D1 and D2 are not competent they are not compellable.
Are D1 and D2 competent for their own defence?	Yes, see **s53(1) YJCEA**. *Note*: same rules would apply if there was only one defendant.
Are D1 and D2 compellable for their own defence?	No, see **s1(1) CEA 1898**. *Note*: see earlier for evidential consequences to D1 and/or D2 of not testifying.
Is D1 competent for D2's defence (and vice versa)?	Yes, see **s53(1) YJCEA**.
Is D1 compellable for D2's defence and vice versa?	No, see **s1(1) CEA 1898**.

Revision tip

The rules change where the co-defendant becomes an 'ex-co-defendant'. This could happen where the co-defendant pleads guilty and is acquitted or a *nolle prosequi* is entered, see *R v Boal* (1965). In such a situation the ex-co-defendant is indistinguishable from other witnesses. In *R v McEwan* (2011) an appeal against the admissibility of evidence from a former accomplice who had pleaded guilty failed. The Court of Appeal held that **s53(5) YJCEA** made it clear that a person who pleaded guilty to an indictment was no longer incompetent to give evidence for the prosecution against others charged on that indictment. The judge had discretion whether to admit the evidence or exclude it under **s78 PACE** on the grounds that it was unreliable.

Witnesses, spouses, and civil partners

You will need to familiarise yourself with the various technical permutations of compellability which are summarised in Tables 7.2, 7.3, and 7.4. You will also need to prepare for the possibility of an essay question which will ask you to comment on the theoretical coherence, or lack of it, of the law. The general rule is that witnesses can be compelled to testify for the prosecution. The common law created an exception to this general rule, so that the defendant's spouse could not be compelled to testify. Cohabitees who are not married (and ex-spouses (see *R v Cruttenden* (1991))) are compellable under the common law rule, as are persons whose marriage is not recognised in English law (see *R v Khan* (1987)).

The spousal exception was said to protect the sanctity of marriage. Because of concern about domestic violence, the rules were changed in PACE 1984. Where the defendant is charged with assaulting, injuring, or threatening to injure his or her spouse or a person under 16, the spouse may be now compelled to testify at trial. Similarly, the spouse may

Key features and principles

✳✳✳✳✳✳✳✳✳✳✳

Table 7.2 Competence and compellability (2)

Type of trial: D is on trial for sexually assaulting his 19-year-old daughter. He is legally married to S.	
Is S competent and compellable for D's defence?	S is competent under the general rule in **s53(1) YJCEA**. She is compellable under **s80(2) and (4) PACE** since she is not charged herself.
Is S competent and compellable for the prosecution?	S is competent to give evidence for the prosecution under **s53(1) YJCEA** but she is not compellable under **s80(2A)(b) and (3) PACE** since the offence does not involve an assault on or injury etc to a wife, husband, or person under 16, nor is it a sexual offence against a person under 16.

Table 7.3 Competence and compellability (3)

Type of trial: husband (H) and wife (W) jointly charged and are both pleading not guilty, whether or not the same offence and whatever the offence.	
Are H and W competent for the prosecution?	No, see **s53(4) YJCEA**. *Note*: it follows that since H and W are not competent they are not compellable. See **s80(4) PACE**.
Are H and W competent for their own defence?	Yes, see **s53(1) YJCEA**.
Are H and W compellable for their own defence?	No, see **s1(1) CEA 1898** and **s80(4) PACE**.
Is H competent for W's defence (and vice versa)?	Yes, see **s53(1) YJCEA**.
Is H compellable for W's defence (and vice versa)?	No, see two overlapping provisions, **s1(1) CEA 1898** and **s80(4) PACE**.

Table 7.4 Competence and compellability (4)

Type of trial: two accused D1 and D2, both pleading not guilty, where the spouses/civil partners are called as witnesses, S1 and S2, and the charge is not covered by s80(3)(a). The general rules on competency apply to S1 and S2 as non-defendants, s53 YJCEA.	
Are S1 and S2 compellable to give evidence for the prosecution against D1 and D2 respectively?	No, **s80(2A)(b) PACE**.
Are S1 and S2 compellable to give evidence in defence of D1 and D2 respectively?	Yes, **s80(2) PACE**.
Is S1 compellable to give evidence for the defence of D2?	No, **s80(2A)(a)**. *Note*: the same rule applies to S2 giving evidence for the defence of D1. Note also S1's evidence for D2 could incriminate D1.

be compelled to testify about an allegation of a sexual offence against a person under 16. Roberts and Zuckerman (2010, pp312–317) point out some illogicalities in the law, including the limited range of offences covered (on this see *R v BA* (2012)), and the lack of protection for other potentially vulnerable persons, such as elderly or disabled people, whether members of the household or not. Nowadays, civil partners are in the same position as spouses. The term spouse or civil partner does not cover cohabiting partners even in the light of **Art 8 European Convention on Human Rights (ECHR)**. In *R v Pearce* (2002) a long-term unmarried partner was compellable for the prosecution.

 **Looking for extra marks?**

You will show a good grasp of the law in this area if you point out that there is a ban on the prosecution commenting on the failure of the defendant to call a spouse to give evidence. Section 80A PACE states that 'the failure of the spouse or civil partner of a person charged in any proceedings to give evidence in the proceedings shall not be made the subject of any comment by the prosecution.' This wording is a wide one and thus prevents comment even if it is based on a logical inference: see *R v Davey* (2006).

Table 7.5 Competence and compellability (5)

Type of trial: two accused, D1 and D2, both pleading not guilty, where the spouses/civil partners are called as witnesses, S1 and S2, and the charge is a physical attack on S1, spouse of D1.
The general rules on competency apply to S1 and S2 as non-defendants, s53(1) YJCEA. The offence is covered by s80(3)(a) PACE in that 'In relation to the spouse or civil partner of a person charged . . . it involves an assault on, or injury or threat of injury to, the spouse or civil partner'.

Is S1 compellable to give evidence in defence of D1?	Yes, **s80(2A)(a) PACE**.
Is S1 compellable to give evidence for the prosecution against D1 and D2?	(S)he is compellable against both as the spousal victim, **s80(2A)(b) PACE**.
Is S1 compellable to give evidence in defence of D2?	Yes, **s80(2A)(a) PACE**.
Is S2 compellable to give evidence for the defence of D1?	No, **s80(2A)(a) PACE**.
Is S2 compellable to give evidence for the prosecution of D1 and D2?	(S)he is not compellable for either prosecution case since (s)he is not the spousal victim, **s80(2A)(b) PACE**.
Is S2 compellable to give evidence for the defence of D2?	Yes, **s80(2) PACE**—general rules of spousal compellability apply.

Revision tip

Be careful in answering questions about spousal compellability that you are alert to the type of offence which is specified. In the example in Table 7.5, S2 would have been compellable to have given evidence for the prosecution against both D1 and D2 if the offence had involved a sexual or physical attack on a person, not necessarily in the household of D1 or D2, who at the material time was under 16 years.

Criminal trials: sworn evidence

A witness under 14 years cannot give sworn evidence, s55(2)(a) YJCEA. A witness who has attained the age of 14 can be sworn if he has 'sufficient appreciation of the solemnity of the occasion and of the particular responsibility to tell the truth which is involved in taking the oath' (s55(2)(b)). This non-religious test is the same as that set out in *R v Hayes* (1977). Witnesses are assumed, if they are able to give intelligible testimony, to have sufficient appreciation of this if no evidence tending to show the contrary is adduced. Otherwise, the witness may give unsworn evidence (s56). False unsworn evidence may still give rise to a perjury charge (s57).

Criminal trials: protective measures for vulnerable witnesses

In line with its policy of rebalancing the criminal justice system to give more protection to victims and witnesses other than the defendant the government introduced a number of measures protecting witnesses in the YJCEA 1999, as amended by the Coroners and Justice Act 2009.

What are the measures?

Note that live links are also available under s51 CJA 2003 (but not to defendants) if the court considers it is in the interests of the efficient or effective administration of justice and where relevant factors include the availability of a witness and the need for the witness to attend in person (see Table 7.6). Sections 34–36 prohibit the defendant from cross examining in person certain vulnerable witnesses, including children.

Who is eligible for special measures?

The measures apply to the following groups of witnesses:

- those under 18 years old (s16(1)(a));
- those where the quality of the evidence is likely to be diminished by reason of mental disorder, significant impairment of intelligence and social functioning, or physical disability or disorder (s16(1)(b) and (2)(a) and (b)). 'Quality' is defined in terms of the completeness, coherence, and accuracy of the evidence; and

Table 7.6 Outline Special Measures Directions (SMD) in criminal cases*

Statute	Protection	Circumstances
s51–56 CJA 2003	Live link	Court must consider if it is in the interests of the efficient or effective administration of justice; relevant factors include availability of witness and need for witness to attend in person. Applies to all witnesses.
ss137, 138 CJA 2003	Testimony video-recording	Applies to all witnesses in serious cases if events fresh in memory, not yet in force.
ss16–27; ss29–33 YJCEA 1999	• Screens • Live links • Evidence given in private • No wigs or gowns • Video-recorded evidence in chief • Use of intermediaries • Aids to communication	Apply to specific categories of witness: • Apply presumptively to all under 18 years (primary rule, note that the same provisions now apply to all child witnesses whatever the offence); or • Quality of evidence likely to be impaired by physical disability or mental disorder; or • Witness in fear or distress (automatically includes complainants in sexual cases and witnesses of assaults involving knives or firearms). Video-recorded cross examinations and re-examinations (s28) not yet in force.
ss32–39 YJCEA 1999	Judicial warning so that direction does not prejudice the accused	May be given during the trial or in the summing-up.

*These do not apply to defendants.
Source: Maureen and John Spencer, *Q&A Revision Guide. Evidence: 2013 and 2014* (OUP, 8th edn, 2013) pp30–31.

- those where the quality of the evidence is likely to be diminished by reason of the witness's fear or distress about testifying (s17). This section automatically includes adult complainants in sexual cases and other witnesses, including those to assaults.

What other conditions apply?

- The 'primary rule' (s21(3)) of the application of special measures applies presumptively to witnesses under 18 years (s16(1)(a)). Under the rule the court must provide for any relevant recording to be admitted if the child's evidence in chief has been video-recorded and must also provide for any additional evidence given by the witness in chief or cross examination to be given by means of a live link (s21(3)). The primary rule does not apply if the child so requests and the court is satisfied the quality of the evidence would not be diminished (s21(4)(b)) or if the court is satisfied that compliance with it would not be likely to maximise the quality of the witness's evidence so far as is practicable (s21(4)(c)). In the case of witnesses under s16(1)(b) the court must consider the witness's views.

Key features and principles

✳✳✳✳✳✳✳✳✳✳

- Adult complainants in sexual cases and some other offences (see earlier) are presumptively eligible for special measures unless the witness has told the court he or she does not wish to be so eligible (s17(4)) and in relation to other witnesses under s17(5)–(7) the court, in deciding whether to award special measures, should consider the nature and circumstances of the offence, the age of the witness, factors such as the social and cultural background and ethnic origins of the witness, and any religious beliefs or political opinions of the witness (s17(2)(a)–(c)). Other factors the court should bear in mind include the behaviour towards the witness on the part of the accused, his family, and associates, (s17(2)(d)) and also the views expressed by the witness (s17(3)).

How are the special measures applied?

- All the measures are available to witnesses eligible under s16, namely on grounds of age or incapacity (s18).
- Witnesses eligible for assistance on grounds of fear or distress about testifying are eligible for all measures apart from examination through an intermediary and aids to communication (s18).

What safeguards are there?

A judge must give the jury a warning to ensure that the fact a special measures direction was given in relation to a witness does not prejudice the accused (s32 YJCEA).

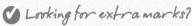 Looking for extra marks?

It is important you keep up to date with recent changes to the law as you prepare for the assessment. Be vigilant about the date of implementation of the controversial s28 YJCEA, which would allow cross examination by video recordings for vulnerable witnesses. This has at the time of writing remained unimplemented for 14 years but there are currently moves to bring it into force. Some commentators have expressed concerns that it will make for more unfairness for defendants, particularly in sexual cases.

Special measures for defendants

The Strasbourg court found breaches of Art 6 in the UK's treatment of child defendants, see *T v UK* (2000). However, the non-availability of special measures to the defendant has been held not to be a breach of Art 6 by several English judgments on the grounds that there are other safeguards for vulnerable defendants, in particular those derived from the courts' inherent powers. In *R (S) v Waltham Forest Youth Court* (2004) there was no breach where a special measures direction was not available for a 13-year-old defendant and in *R (D) v Camberwell Green Court* (2005) the House of Lords held that the ECHR does not guarantee a right to face-to-face confrontation with child accusers. The common law powers covering situations when it might be appropriate to allow a vulnerable defendant to be absent from the trial and also other technical means such as a video link to ensure participation are illustrated in *R v Ukpabio* (2008).

Some limited changes were introduced for vulnerable defendants in the Police and Justice Act 2006 and the Coroners and Justice Act 2009 creating ss33A, 33BA, and 33BB YJCEA. The accused may give oral evidence through a live link or intermediary if the court is satisfied that it is in the interests of justice and one of the following applies:

- the accused is under 18 years and his ability to participate effectively in the proceedings as a witness giving oral evidence is compromised by his level of intellectual ability, or

- social functioning and use of a live link or intermediary would enable him to participate more effectively in the proceedings, or

- the accused is over 18 years and suffers from a mental disorder (within the meaning of the Mental Health Act 1983) or otherwise has a significant impairment of intelligence and social function such that he is unable to participate effectively in the proceedings as a witness giving oral evidence in court and use of a live link or intermediary would enable him to participate more effectively in the proceedings.

Examining and cross examining young and vulnerable witnesses and defendants

The legal professions and the Ministry of Justice have devoted considerable attention to addressing the particular problems of examining and cross examining young and vulnerable witnesses. An important publication is the *Judicial College Bench Checklist: Young Witnesses Cases*, which aims at ensuring that such witnesses give their 'best evidence'. It gives guidance for case management and sets out questions and procedures to be employed in cross examination. The Advocacy Training Council (ATC) has also produced guidance, namely Para 3E.4 of the Criminal Practice Directions provides that all witnesses, both prosecution and defence, including the defendant, must be enabled to give the best evidence they can.

R v E (2011)

FACTS: E was charged with cruelty to a 5-year-old child, C. E denied the offence. There was conflicting evidence of the cause of C's injuries. The defence case was not put to her in cross examination. The defendant was convicted and appealed on the grounds that the trial was one-sided.

HELD: Appeal rejected. There was strong supporting evidence, the jury had been asked to make allowances for the defence difficulties, and the right to a fair trial had not been compromised.

Witness anonymity

✳✳✳✳✳✳✳✳✳✳✳

This case was one of the earliest examples of how, in the case of non-adult vulnerable witnesses, the advocate can move away from the normal practice of 'putting the case'. In *R v Lubemba* (2014) the court gave further guidance on the questioning of vulnerable witnesses. In this case the judge had managed the case appropriately. The court observed (at para 45):

> It is now generally accepted that if justice is to be done to the vulnerable witness and also to the accused, a radical departure from the traditional style of advocacy will be necessary. Advocates must adapt to the witness, not the other way round. They cannot insist upon any supposed right 'to put one's case' or previous inconsistent statements to a vulnerable witness.

Witness anonymity

The Criminal Evidence (Witness Anonymity) Act 2008 became law in July 2008. It had a **sunset clause** and its temporary provisions, which abolished the common law principles, are now incorporated in ss86–96 Coroners and Justice Act 2009. The 2008 Act was Parliament's extremely speedy reversal of *R v Davis* (2008), a powerful House of Lords judgment delivered on 18 June 2008. There the Lords had held that a murder trial was unfair and a violation of Art 6(3)(d) ECHR, where an order preserved the anonymity of a civilian witness. That evidence was in Lord Mance's words (at para 96) 'the sole or decisive basis on which alone the defendant could have been convicted'. The court held that the particular combination of protective measures violated Art 6 and observed, in addition, that it departed from common law principles. On the facts the measures adopted to protect witnesses, which included full anonymity, screens, voice distortion, and the use of pseudonyms, rendered the trial unfair. The cumulative effect of these measures meant that the defendant could not test the witness's credibility.

The 2009 Act allows various measures to be taken to protect the identity of a witness on the application by either the prosecution or defence. The measures include the use of a pseudonym and screening and voice modulation (s86). Different procedures apply to defence and prosecution (s87). The prosecution are only required to reveal to the court the identity of the person for whom a 'witness anonymity order' is sought, whereas the defence must inform the court and the prosecution but not any other co-accused. For an order to be granted the following three conditions must be satisfied (s88):

* Condition A: the measures must be necessary to protect the safety of the witness or another person or prevent serious damage to property or prevent real harm to the public interest (s88(3)(a)) having regard to reasonable fear on his part if he were identified or to protect the carrying on of activities in the public interest.

* Condition B: the taking of the measures would be consistent with the defendant receiving a fair trial (s88(4)).

* Condition C: the interests of justice require the order, since it appears to the court that it is important the witness should testify and the witness would not testify if the order were not made (s88(5); see *R v Powar* (2009)).

R v Willett (2011)

FACTS: W appealed against conviction for manslaughter on the grounds that the judge should not have granted an anonymity order to a prosecution witness (B) who gave evidence of an incriminating statement by W.

HELD: If the identity of the witness is known to the accused an anonymity order cannot serve to protect the witness. Condition A cannot therefore be met. The court considered, however, that even if the judge had erred in making an anonymity order in relation to witness B, it was satisfied that this did not have any adverse effect on the fairness of the trial or the safety of the conviction. The judge's directions about special measures were entirely apt to prevent the jury from holding witness B's anonymity against the appellant and to get them to concentrate on the evidence actually given by the witness, and there was nothing harmful to the defence in the directions given. Those directions ensured that no prejudice arose out of the fact that witness B remained anonymous.

Section 89(3) of the Act sets out relevant matters the court must consider, which include the general right of a defendant to know the identity of a witness, whether evidence given by the witness might be the sole or decisive evidence implicating the defendant, and whether the anonymous witness's evidence could be properly tested. Section 90(2) provides that: 'The judge must give the jury such a warning as the judge considers appropriate to ensure that the fact that [the witness anonymity] order was made in relation to the witness does not prejudice the defendant.'

The statutory regime applies to undercover police as well as other witnesses whereas critics have pointed out the superiority of the New Zealand scheme, which provides for separate regimes for civilians and police.

The 2008 Act was applied in a series of conjoined cases: *R v Mayers; R v Glasgow; R v Costelloe; R v Bahmanzadeh; R v P* (2008). The Court of Appeal allowed the appeal in *Mayers* because the court could not be confident that everything relating to the witness's credibility, motivation, and integrity had been revealed. The convictions in *Costelloe* and *Bahmanzadeh* were safe since knowledge of the true identities of undercover police officers was rarely of importance to the defendant. The conviction in *Glasgow* stood since the evidence of the anonymous witnesses could be tested. *R v P* involved the application of s116 CJA 2003, which required disclosure of the witness's name to the defence, and the prosecution's challenge to the trial judge's ruling on this was dismissed. The s114 inclusionary discretion could not be applied since that would involve rewriting the 2008 Act. It was not permissible to submit a hearsay statement anonymously.

Civil cases

All witnesses are presumed to be competent and compellable. The major exception is that of child witnesses. Section 96 Children Act 1989 provides that where a child under 18 years does not, in the opinion of the court, understand the nature of an oath, he or she may give unsworn evidence in civil proceedings provided he or she understands the duty to speak the truth and he or she has sufficient understanding to justify the evidence being heard. Thus,

Conclusion
✳✳✳✳✳✳✳✳✳

the test for competency for unsworn evidence, in referring to the duty to speak the truth, is stricter than under criminal law. Note, however, that a child's evidence may be more readily admissible by hearsay in civil cases.

① Conclusion

Traditionally, questions on competence and compellability form part of larger questions containing a number of other issues. However, the overlap of this area with the much broader question of policy towards victims as witnesses means it is subject to topical debate and therefore assumes larger importance. Compellability, and the consequential finding of contempt for failure to appear as a witness, is a reduced deterrent now that there are increased opportunities to appear as an anonymous witness or give evidence through special measures or by exceptions to the rule against hearsay. In spite of all these apparent concessions to the understandable reluctance of some witnesses to appear in court, you should not lose sight of the importance attached to the public duty of giving evidence in open court. As Rose LJ stated (at para 16) in *R v Yusuf* (2003): 'The role of the courts, in seeking to provide the public with protection against criminal conduct, can only properly be performed if members of the public cooperate with the courts. That co-operation includes participation in the trial process.'

The statutory provisions relating to special measures are very detailed and the earlier account is only an outline summary. A number of commentators are uneasy about the impact on the defendant. Munday (2015, p192) writes: 'Thanks to less restrictive tests of witness competence, together with special measures directions, cases are now coming to trial that formerly would have been unthinkable.' He cites *R v Watts* (2010), where four 'profoundly disabled' witnesses gave evidence of sexual assault by a home care worker.

✳ Key cases

Case	Facts	Principle and comment
R v Boal [1965] QB 402	B, one of the 'Great Train Robbers', sought in his appeal against conviction to adduce the evidence of an ex-co-defendant, C, who had pleaded guilty. B was not allowed to adduce this new evidence but the court held that C would have been a competent and compellable witness.	The general presumption of competence and compellability applies to a former co-defendant subsequently pleading guilty.

Case	Facts	Principle and comment
R v Cowan [1996] QB 373	The appellants, who had not testified at trial, appealed on the grounds that the trial judge had not given a proper direction on the application of **s35 CJPOA 1994**. They argued that the discretion to draw adverse inferences should only apply in exceptional cases.	The Court of Appeal rejected the arguments put. It specified, however, that the jury should be carefully directed on the uses to be made of the defendant's failure to testify.
R v Cruttenden [1991] 2 QB 66	The former wife of a council planning officer testified at his trial that he had corruptly received free petrol in return for favours. At the time of the alleged offences the two were married and she would have been incompetent as a witness against him. The law had been changed in 1986 so as to make a former spouse competent as a witness against his or her ex-spouse. The court held that the provision should not have been applied retrospectively.	Once a marriage is legally terminated a former spouse or civil partner is competent to testify about matters which occurred while the marriage existed.
R v Khan (1987) 84 Cr App R 44	The appeal turned on whether the second wife of a Moslem defendant whose first wife was alive at the time of marriage was both competent and compellable as a witness against him.	The position of a woman who had gone through a valid form of marriage which was of no effect in English law was no different from that of a woman who had not been through a ceremony at all or whose marriage was void because it was bigamous.
R v Pearce [2002] 1 WLR 1553	The defendant's long-term unmarried partner made statements which were prejudicial to him. At trial she gave answers which were inconsistent with her statements and was cross examined by the prosecutor as a hostile witness. His appeal on the grounds that the **ECHR** required his partner be treated as if she were his wife was dismissed.	The rules on the compellability of spouses do not apply to a cohabitee with whom the accused had not formed a marriage or civil partnership.
R v Pitt [1983] QB 25	Wife gave evidence as a prosecution witness at husband's trial without sufficiently appreciating her right to refuse to testify against him.	Once a spouse elects to give evidence, provided he or she has had the right of refusal clearly explained by the trial judge, he or she is to be treated as any other witness. Here the conviction was overturned. Note that in *R v L* (2009) Lord Phillips stated that neither law nor policy required that police inform a spouse of a right not to make a statement or give evidence against the defendant before taking a statement from the spouse.

Key debates

✷✷✷✷✷✷✷✷✷

 **Key debates**

Topic	Development of victims' rights as part of criminal justice
Author	K Starmer
Viewpoint	The author demonstrates how, over the past two decades, criminal law and evidence law have developed the concept of victims' rights as an integral part of positive human rights protection. This presents a challenge to the basic common law criminal justice model which has been in place in common law countries for centuries. *Doorson v Netherlands* (1996) is acknowledged as a landmark case in this sphere but much remains still to be done.
Source	'Human Rights, Victims and the Prosecution of Crime in the 21st Century' [2014] *Crim LR* 777

Topic	The law on competence and compellability for spouses and civil partners
Author	J Brabyn
Viewpoint	The author argues that it is important that the law in this area should continue to be based on helping to preserve marriages and that the case of *R v L* (2009) demonstrates the difficulties which arise in trying to achieve this objective.
Source	'A Criminal Defendant's Spouse as a Prosecution Witness' [2011] *Crim LR* 613

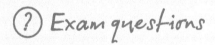 **Exam questions**

Essay question

Have the special measures provisions now available to witnesses undermined the protection of the defendant?

 **Online Resource Centre**

To see an outline answer to this question visit www.oup.com/lawrevision/

Problem question

Janet and John, who are married, are jointly charged with an assault on their child, Tim, who at the time of the alleged offence was 12. The alleged incident took place in the back garden of their home and was witnessed through the back window of the neighbouring house by Agnes, who is in her 90s and is suffering from the early stages of dementia. Janet is considering pleading guilty but John wishes to plead not guilty. John is also charged in the same indictment with cruelty to the family pet, a Labrador called Ron. The prosecution case is that John threw a garden spade at Ron as the dog tried to protect Tim.

Advise on the evidence, competence, and compellability of the witnesses.

See the Outline Answers section in the end matter for help with this question.

Concentrate Q&As

For more questions and answers on evidence, see the *Concentrate Q&A: Evidence* by Maureen Spencer and John Spencer.

Go to the end of this book to view **sample pages**.

#8

Issues in the course of trial

Key facts

Suspect evidence

- The general rule is that one piece of evidence is sufficient to convict but there are statutory exceptions to this where there is a need for **corroboration**, eg **s13 Perjury Act 1911**.

- The common law obligatory requirement for corroboration warnings in the case of certain categories of witnesses such as children was repealed in the **Criminal Justice and Public Order Act (CJPOA) 1994**. The emphasis now in looking for supportive evidence is more on the strength or otherwise of the evidence rather than the intrinsic nature of the witness.

- There is a requirement for the judge to give a direction (a *Turnbull* direction) of the need for care in cases of disputed identification.

- In cases where lies (in or out of court) told by the accused are presented as suggestive of guilt, the judge should give a 'care warning' (a *Lucas* direction).

- The judge has discretion to issue a care warning if there is reason to believe the witness might be unreliable.

- The **Police and Criminal Evidence Act 1984 (PACE) Code D** sets out the procedures for identification procedures and for video identification.

Examination in chief

- The witness is allowed to refresh his memory from documents under **ss120 and 139 Criminal Justice Act (CJA) 2003**.

- Previous consistent statements are inadmissible unless there is a statutory or common law exception.

- Parties are not allowed to cross examine their own witnesses except with leave of the judge under **s3 Criminal Procedure Act 1865** in cases where the witness changes their evidence from statements made pre-trial.

Cross examination

- There are statutory limits on the questions that may be asked of complainants in cases involving sexual offences, see **ss41–43 Youth Justice and Criminal Evidence Act (YJCEA) 1999**.

- Previous inconsistent statements of the witness may be admissible under **ss4 and 5 Criminal Procedure Act 1865**.

- A witness's answers to a collateral question should be treated as final. This rule of finality on collateral questions has a number of exceptions.

Chapter overview

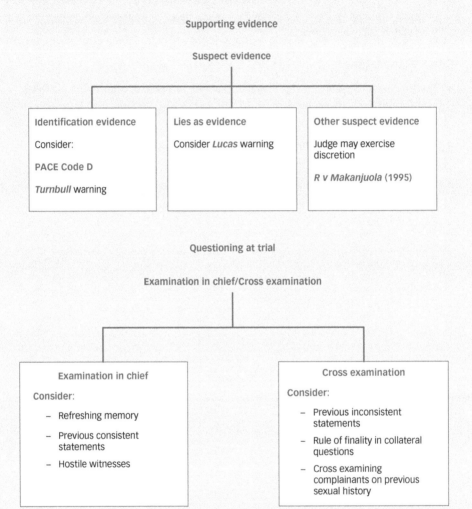

Supporting evidence

Suspect evidence

Identification evidence

Consider:

PACE Code D

Turnbull warning

Lies as evidence

Consider *Lucas* warning

Other suspect evidence

Judge may exercise discretion

R v Makanjuola (1995)

Questioning at trial

Examination in chief/Cross examination

Examination in chief

Consider:

- Refreshing memory
- Previous consistent statements
- Hostile witnesses

Cross examination

Consider:

- Previous inconsistent statements
- Rule of finality in collateral questions
- Cross examining complainants on previous sexual history

Related areas

This area is closely related to hearsay since much of it touches on the admissibility of out of court statements. Cross examination on previous sexual behaviour of complainants overlaps with character evidence and also with Chapter 7, which includes a discussion on vulnerable witnesses. Indirectly, the discussion on corroboration concerns inferences from silence since that is one area where a single piece of evidence, the inference of guilt, is not enough to found a conviction (see Chapter 3).

The assessment: key points

Since this area contains a disparate range of predominantly procedural issues it is more likely to form the basis of a problem question along with some other issues. You may have to discuss alternative ways of considering admitting evidence. Thus, for example, evidence of previous discreditable behaviour of a complainant in a sexual case may raise issues about bad character (see Chapter 5) as well as cross examination under s41 CJA 2003. The controversial question of the relative rights of defendants and witnesses is also covered in Chapter 7 on special measures and might well form the subject of an essay question particularly concerning the vexed question of the treatment of complainants in sexual cases.

You need to be clear about the difference between evidence of consistency and evidence of truth. Under the common law non-hearsay out of court statements admitted at trial could be evidence that the witness was telling the same account at trial. Under the CJA 2003 such statements are largely, but not entirely, evidence of the truth of their contents, thus creating an exception to the rule against hearsay.

This area forms a somewhat eclectic mix of evidential and procedural issues, highlighted by the fact that it is to be found in a disparate set of statutes and case law precedents. The key statutory sections are:

- Sections 4 and 5 Criminal Procedure Act 1865 on the admissibility of previous inconsistent statements,

- Section 3 Criminal Procedure Act 1865 on a party's questioning of their own witness whose evidence at trial differs from that at pre-trial,

- PACE 1984 Code D on the procedure for identification procedures,

- Sections 41–43 YJCEA 1999 on cross examination of victims in sexual cases,

- Sections 120 and 139 CJA 2003 on a witness's use of memory-refreshing documents at trial,

- Section 120(4) and (5) CJA 2003 on the admissibility and evidential status of identification evidence, and

- Sections 119 and 120 CJA 2003 on the evidential status of some previous consistent statements (others are covered by the common law).

Key features and principles

Suspect evidence

In English law a verdict can be based on evidence of a single witness or a confession. A small number of statutes provide that a conviction must be supported, or corroborated, by more than one piece of evidence.

Statutory erosion led to the removal of the need for corroboration warnings under the common law in s32 CJPOA 1994. Subsequently, the case of *R v Makanjuola* (1995) held that any warnings on the dangers of convicting on certain pieces of evidence should be decided on a case-by-case basis. See Table 8.1.

Revision tip

This is an area where technological change is putting strain on the law and you might have to answer a problem question on issues where the law is under review. An illuminating example is *R v Alexander and McGill* (2013) (see p160). The victim of a robbery identified his assailants by Facebook before he reported the incident. Before trial, defendants' requests for other Facebook pages to help them challenge the identification were ignored. It was held that the convictions were safe and a *Turnbull* warning had been given but (obiter) it was incumbent on investigators to provide as much information as possible to allow the reliability of the identification to be challenged.

Table 8.1 Situations where corroboration/warning may be required

Nature of corroboration/ care warning	Provision/comment
Judge must give a mandatory warning where identification evidence is disputed.	*R v Turnbull* (1976): Failure to give the warning will lead to an appeal. Elements of the warning are specified in the case.
Judge may exercise discretion to issue a care warning.	*R v Makanjuola* (1995): The judge has discretion whether to issue a warning and the nature of the warning. There are no categories of witness where a warning is necessarily required.
Corroboration required by statute.	Examples are s1 Treason Act 1795, s13 Perjury Act 1911, and s89(2) Road Traffic Regulation Act 1984. Under the latter a defendant cannot be convicted of speeding 'on the evidence of one witness to the effect that, in the opinion of the witness the person prosecuted was driving the vehicle at a speed exceeding a specified limit'.
Lies told by the defendant as evidence of guilt or as supportive of other evidence.	A judicial direction should be given to the jury when the prosecution proposes to rely on the defendant's lie or lies. The content of the direction is set out in *R v Lucas* (1981) and the occasions when the direction is necessary are set out in *R v Burge* (1996).

Identification evidence

In the 1970s, a spate of miscarriages of justice led to the setting up of the Devlin Committee to review procedures for identification evidence. It made some radical proposals for legislation in its 1976 Report but before these could be implemented the Court of Appeal decided the landmark case, *R v Turnbull* (1977). The current safeguards cover two areas. First, Code D issued under PACE 1984 specifies how police identification procedures should be organised. The Code is regularly revised. Second, the leading case, *R v Turnbull*, sets out mandatory directions which should be given to juries in cases of disputed identification.

Pre-trial procedures

Code D (see Annex A) provides that the suspect will normally be offered a video **identification parade** electronic recording (VIPER). The discretionary exclusion under s78 PACE applies to exclude prosecution evidence where the correct procedures have not been followed. The Code sets out procedures for three situations:

- when the suspect's identity is not known,
- when the suspect is known and available, and
- when the suspect is known but not available.

Revision tip

You may need to comment on other possible forms of identification which the police or prosecution may set up. Dock identifications, for obvious reasons, are not desirable. In *Tido v R* (2011) the Privy Council stated that although dock identifications were permissible, the trial judge should consider the possible threat to a fair trial and direct the jury carefully.

Code D does allow for group identifications and, as last resort, confrontations, particularly where the suspect will not attend a parade.

Further provisions in relation to identification evidence are summarised in Table 8.2.

In *R v Forbes* (2001) the House of Lords held that identification parades should always be held where the identification is disputed. As a result of this decision Code D was amended to allow more discretion on the holding of a parade. Thus, failure to hold a parade or video procedure will not now be necessarily fatal to the prosecution case. The result of this change has been to leave some uncertainty.

Procedures at trial

The lengthy *Turnbull* guidelines, which must be given by the judge in all cases of disputed identification, include the following provisions:

- the judge must warn the jury of the special need for caution if the case depends wholly or partly on one or more identification and should remind them that honest witnesses may be mistaken,

Key features and principles

✳✳✳✳✳✳✳✳✳✳✳

Table 8.2 Identification evidence: pre-trial provisions under PACE 1984 Code D

Situation	Provision
When should the police show a witness photographs?	When there is no suspect available to attend an identification. If there is to be a video identification or parade, the witness should not see photographs.
Can witnesses communicate before an identification?	No, there should be no risk of collusion. **Code D Annex A para 10** and **Annex B para 14**.
Can the officer involved in the investigation take part in the procedures for the identification under **Code D**?	No—**Code D para 3.11**.
What is the role of the defence lawyer in video identifications or parades?	She has a right to view the film and be present at the showing to witnesses and at a parade. If the accused does not have a representative present the parade should be videoed or a colour photograph taken.
When might **Code D** not apply?	It did not apply where the evidence was of a 'descriptive nature which was of elimination and not identification' (*R v Byron* (1999)).

- the jury must look closely at the circumstances of the identification, such as the light or any impediment to the witness's view,
- if the identification is of good quality it can be left to the jury, and
- the judge may withdraw the case if the witness had only a fleeting glance or longer observation in difficult circumstances and there is no other evidence.

It was decided in *Daley v R* (1994) that such a case could be withdrawn even if it did not meet the high standards of no case to answer set out in *R v Galbraith* (1981). In determining whether there is a case to answer the judge should have regard not only to the circumstances of the original identification but also subsequent factors such as breaches of Code D. The authorities suggest that recognition cases are less likely to fall in this category than identification of strangers (see *R v Ryan* (1990)).

In *R v Nash* (2004) the Court of Appeal stated that the judge should include in the *Turnbull* direction reference to miscarriages of justice arising out of mistaken identification. The judge may invite the jury to look for supporting evidence, and this might be the identification evidence from two different witnesses. In *R v Weeder* (1980), the court held that the judge must warn the jury in such cases that several honest witnesses may be mistaken.

Specific cases where Turnbull *warning is required*

If it is a 'recognition case':

In *R v Bentley* (1994) the defendant and victim knew one another. After a dispute the victim was wounded by having glass driven into his face. He identified the defendant who was convicted. His appeal was allowed since the judge had not given the *Turnbull* warning and it was possible the victim made a mistake even though recognition identifications were more reliable than those of strangers. See also *Shand v R* (1966) and *R v Oakwell* (1978).

If the accused admits his presence at the scene but denies participation and the scene is crowded:

In *R v Thornton* (1995) a man was attacked by a group at a wedding reception. T admitted being there but denied participation. Two witnesses identified him and he was convicted. The appeal was allowed since the judge should have given a *Turnbull* warning; particularly because several others at the wedding had been dressed like the accused.

If the witness is a police officer a *Turnbull* direction may still be required:

In *R v Moore* (2004) a police officer gave evidence of recognition of the offenders at a fight at a football match. The judge had failed to give a *Turnbull* warning about the difficulties of the sighting, such as the risk that the officer was distracted by his other duties.

Specific cases where a Turnbull *warning is not required*

Where accused claims witness is trying to 'frame' him:

In *R v Cape* (1996) the testimony of a publican who had witnessed a fracas was the main evidence. The defendants, who were known to him, claimed he was motivated by a grudge against them. Since the sole issue was truthfulness there was no need for a *Turnbull* direction.

Where the accused who admits his presence at the scene of the crime has unusual features:

In *R v Slater* (1995) a victim of a night-club assault identified his attacker, an unusually heavily built man who admitted being present but denied participation. No identification parade was held and no *Turnbull* guidelines given. The appeal against conviction failed since there was no evidence to suggest anyone like him was also present. In *R v Oakwell* (1978) the Court of Appeal stated that *Turnbull* was 'intended primarily to deal with the ghastly risk run in cases of fleeting encounters'. No warning was required in this case where the defendant agreed he was at scene of crime but denied he was the assailant.

Where the identification concerns a vehicle:

In *R v Browning* (1991) the Court of Appeal observed that there were important differences between cars and people and a *Turnbull* direction was not needed when the contested identification related to a car.

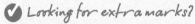

Looking for extra marks?

Increasingly, police surveillance may produce evidence of voice recordings as identification. In *R v Hersey* (1998) the Court of Appeal held that *Turnbull* guidance should be given if the evidence is presented at trial. In *R v Roberts* (2000) the Court of Appeal referred to the need for a modified *Turnbull* warning in the case of 'ear-witnesses'. Ormerod (2001) deplores the lack of statutory control in an area which may lead to miscarriages of justice.

See also *R v Flynn and St John* (2008) (p185) for the court's approach to expert evidence in such cases.

The overlap between this area and hearsay is shown by the variety of ways in which identification evidence may be admissible at trial as an exception to the hearsay rule as Table 8.3 illustrates.

The role of social media in identification was at issue in *R v Alexander and McGill* (2013).

R v Alexander and McGill (2013)

FACTS: A victim of a robbery identified his assailants from Facebook. A VIPER parade was held. The appellants appealed against convictions for robbery and attempted robbery having been initially identified by the victim informally through Facebook.

HELD: Identification by Facebook was valid. There had been serious failings of police procedure. Although it would have been highly desirable, had the judge used the terminology that had been used consistently for many years since *Turnbull*, the omission of the warning in the terms in which it should have been given, in the light of what the learned judge actually said, was not such that there was a material irregularity or material misdirection in the summing-up. If, as is to be anticipated, identifications occur in the way in which this identification occurred, namely by looking through Facebook, it is incumbent upon the police and the prosecutor to take steps to obtain, in as much detail as possible, evidence in relation to the initial identification. For example, it would be prudent to obtain the available images that were looked at and a statement in relation to what happened. The court recommended that the Director of Public Prosecutions and the Association of Chief Police Officers (now the National Police Chiefs Council) could, in conjunction with the relevant Ministry, give consideration so that *short* and *simple* guidance can be given in short order, so what happened in this case does not reoccur.

Defendant's lies as evidence

R v Lucas (1981), a case decided under the common law corroboration rules, set out the conditions under which lies by a defendant could amount to supporting evidence. The case is still good law in those situations where the prosecution seeks to rely on the defendant's lie or lies, either at interview or at trial, as evidence of guilt in the instant case. Such lies must be distinguished from other situations where untruthfulness is indirect evidence of lack of credibility (see Chapter 5). The *Lucas* direction must tell the jury to consider that the lie must be proved to be so beyond reasonable doubt and that a lie in itself is not evidence of

Table 8.3 Admissibility of out of court identifications

Admissibility	Authority
Declarant's performance of a relevant act	*R v MacCay* (1990). In this case a witness who had identified the suspect at a parade could not remember the number she had stated. The police officer was permitted to state the number. The court held that the evidence was correctly admitted either as the common law hearsay exception based on a statement accompanying an act or as a statutory exception for identification evidence under **PACE**.
As exception to the inadmissibility of previous consistent statements	Identification evidence was routinely admissible before the **CJA 2003** as an exception to this common law rule. The courts took a creative approach since this was likely to be cogent evidence.
As statutory exception	**Section 120 CJA 2003** specifically renders statements of identification admissible as evidence of their truth.

guilt since people may lie for other reasons such as wanting to hide embarrassment. In short, to be evidence of guilt the lie must

- be deliberate,
- relate to a material issue, and
- be prompted by a realisation of guilt and fear of the truth as opposed to an innocent reason.

R v Burge (1996) sets out the occasions on which a *Lucas* direction should be given. See Fig 8.1.

There is no need to give a *Lucas* direction if the lies told by the defendant relate to a central issue in the case. In *R v Middleton* (2001) the accused had an elaborate set of alibis to explain his non-involvement in a robbery. The prosecution alleged he was lying. It would confuse the jury to give a *Lucas* warning since there was no distinction between the issue of guilt and that of the lie. If they disbelieved him it followed that they must find him guilty.

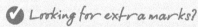 **Looking for extra marks?**

You will have to take care that you distinguish the elements of hearsay from that of lies. Note the case of *Mawaz Khan v R* (1966), where a statement concerning an alibi was admissible as non-hearsay since the purpose of adducing it was to show its falsity, not its truth.

Figure 8.1 Lies (non-hearsay) by defendant—see *R v Burge* (1996)

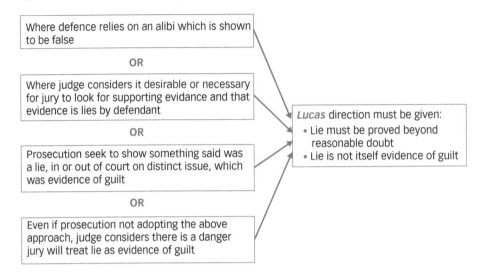

Where defence relies on an alibi which is shown to be false

OR

Where judge considers it desirable or necessary for jury to look for supporting evidence and that evidence is lies by defendant

OR

Prosecution seek to show something said was a lie, in or out of court on distinct issue, which was evidence of guilt

OR

Even if prosecution not adopting the above approach, judge considers there is a danger jury will treat lie as evidence of guilt

Lucas direction must be given:
- Lie must be proved beyond reasonable doubt
- Lie is not itself evidence of guilt

Examination in chief

Refreshing memory

Under s139 CJA 2003 a witness may refresh his memory from documents while giving evidence if

- he states in his oral evidence that the document records his recollection of the matter at that earlier time, *and*
- his recollection of the matter is likely to have been better at that time than it is at the time of his oral evidence.

Under s120(3) such a statement may be received in evidence and is evidence of the truth of its contents, thus creating a new statutory exception to the rule against hearsay. In *R v Chinn* (2012) the Court of Appeal addressed the construction of this section.

Previous consistent statements

The general rule is that a previous out of court statement cannot be admitted to support a statement made from the witness box. There are a number of exceptions to this common law rule. Three are now contained in s120 CJA 2003 and two governed by the common law:

CJA 2003

Such statements are admissible if the witness admits that to the best of his belief, first, that he made the statement and, second, that it is true and, third, that *any* of the following three conditions apply, namely identification or description, memory refreshing, and prior complaints:

1. the statement identifies or describes a person, object, or place (s120(5));

2. the statement was made when the matters stated were fresh in his memory and he cannot reasonably be expected to remember them well enough to give oral evidence (s120(6)); or

3. the statement is a complaint made by the witness who claims to be the person against whom an offence was committed, the offence is the subject matter of the proceedings, the complaint was not made as a result of a threat or a promise (but may be made as a result of a leading question, s120(8)) and before the statement is adduced the witness gives oral evidence in connection with its subject matter (s120(7)).

Revision tip

Bear in mind that examiners often draw on reported cases to set examination questions. The case *R v O* (2006) provides a number of pointers to the interpretation of the statute. Here, a complainant made an allegation to a friend about abuse by her stepfather, and four months later, she made the same complaint to her brother. It was held that the lapse of time was not a bar to admission and that the court could hear two complaints.

The complaint exception to the inadmissibility of previous consistent statements is a major development from the common law, which limited admissibility to complainants in sexual cases and then only as evidence of consistency and only if made as soon as reasonably practicable.

All three of the earlier categories of statements are admissible as evidence of any matter, thus creating another exception to the rule against hearsay (s120(4)). See *R v Chinn* (2012), where the Court of Appeal gave detailed guidance on this section.

Common law

Previous out of court exculpatory statements giving the accused's reaction to an accusation may be admissible under common law but only as evidence of consistency and thus to support the witness's creditworthiness. See *R v Storey* (1968), where the accused explained to police when they found illegal drugs on her premises that she had been forced against her will to keep them. The statement was admissible as relevant to the consistency of the accused's explanation. The statement does not have to be made immediately on first accusation but the length of time which has elapsed is a factor in admissibility, see *R v Pearce* (1979). Admissibility depends on the weight of the evidence and *R v Tooke* (1990) establishes that a statement will not be admitted if the evidence of the reaction on accusation is given adequately in alternative evidence.

Previous statements made to rebut an allegation of fabrication are also admissible under the common law, see *R v Oyesiku* (1971). If admitted these may now be taken as evidence of the truth of their contents under s120(2) CJA 2003.

Revision tip

An example of the overlap of hearsay and previous consistent statements is provided in the case of *R v Xhabri* (2005). The complainant alleged she had been raped and forced to work as a prostitute. She had made a number of telephone calls to her parents and others about her situation and the admissibility of these messages was at issue.

The trial judge allowed them in under s120(5) (previous identification) and s120(6) (a statement the witness could not be expected to recall) and s120(7) (a recent complaint). It was held that s120(7) was rightly applied but not the others. Alternatively, s114(1)(d) was appropriate (inclusionary discretion of hearsay). This was in compliance with **Art 6 ECHR**.

Unfavourable and hostile witnesses

If a party's witness does not '**come up to proof**', meaning that his answers to questions in examination in chief contradict his pre-trial statements, the following approaches are possible. The witness can be declared either 'unfavourable' or 'hostile', which are **terms of art**.

Unfavourable witnesses act in good faith and the effect of their unhelpful testimony can be nullified to some extent through other evidence. Such a witness cannot be cross examined, unlike a hostile witness. A hostile witness is one who shows no inclination to tell the truth. The party has to seek leave of court to declare the witness hostile and if that is granted the witness can be contradicted through other evidence or cross examined on a previous inconsistent statement. The procedure is governed by s3 Criminal Procedure Act 1865. An important change is that if a previous inconsistent statement is admitted in that way, then under s119 CJA 2003 it 'is admissible as evidence of any matter stated in it of which oral evidence by the person would be admissible'.

Cross examination

Previous inconsistent statements

If a witness makes statements which are inconsistent with his out of court statement he can be cross examined on them under ss4 and 5 Criminal Procedure Act 1865. Section 119 CJA 2003 makes such statements also an exception to the rule against hearsay. Under s124(2)(c), an out of court statement that is inconsistent with a hearsay statement that is admitted in evidence may be used to discredit the hearsay statement and is evidence of its contents.

The rule of finality on collateral questions

The general common law rule is that collateral questions may be asked of a witness but the answer must be treated as final. A collateral question is one which is relevant but does not relate directly to a fact in issue, but is specific to the witness, such as a question on credibility. There are three exceptions to this rule:

(i) If a witness is asked if they have any criminal convictions and they deny it, the conviction can be proved under s6 Criminal Procedure Act 1865.

(ii) If a witness is accused of bias they may be further questioned on their response. In *R v Mendy* (1976) a man was spotted taking notes in the public gallery while a prosecution witness was giving evidence and then describing the evidence to the accused's husband. When the husband denied this in cross examination the prosecution was allowed to call evidence in rebuttal. The scope of the concept of bias is illustrated in *R v Busby* (1981), which concerned the evidence of police officers who it was alleged had threatened a potential witness. The police denied this and the Court of Appeal held that the witness should have been allowed to give evidence of the threat by analogy with *Mendy*. It went on, however, to state that the issue of alleged impropriety was a fact in issue in the trial, not simply a collateral one.

(iii) A witness can be further questioned about any medical evidence of a disability which might have affected their evidence. In *Toohey v MPC* (1965) medical evidence of the liability of the witness to hysteria was called.

Cross examining complainants in sexual cases on previous sexual history

The difficulty of successfully prosecuting rape is well documented. It has been argued that complainants may not come forward because they fear hostile questions from defence counsel. Special measures protection is afforded to such witnesses (see Chapter 7) and in addition there are restrictions on cross examination. The key section is s41 YJCEA 1999, which repealed the controversial s2 Sexual Offences Amendment Act 1976. The complex s41 will be summarised and then the relevant case law examined.

(1) The section relates to trials where a person is charged with a sexual offence, defined as any offence under Part 1 Sexual Offences Act 2003. The Secretary of State has power to add or subtract from this listing.

(2) Except with the leave of the court no evidence may be given or no question asked in cross examination by or on behalf of the accused at the trial about the sexual behaviour of the complainant. Sexual behaviour means any behaviour or other sexual experience, whether or not involving any accused or other person but excluding (except as specified in point (3)) anything alleged to have taken place as part of the event which is the subject matter of the current charge.

Cross examination

(3) The court may give the defence leave if one of the following four situations applies (note that the section does not apply to prosecution applications):

(a) The question or evidence relates to a relevant issue which is *not an issue of consent* (s41(3)(a)). This applies to situations where the defence is either the offence did not take place or that the defendant reasonably believed the victim had consented. This is so since 'issue of consent' is defined in s42(b) as

any issue whether the complainant in fact consented to the conduct constituting the offence with which the accused is charged (and accordingly does not include any issue as to the *belief* of the accused that the complainant so consented)

OR

(b) The question or evidence relates to a relevant issue which is an issue of consent and the complainant's sexual behaviour is alleged to have taken place *at or about the same time* as the subject matter of the charge (s41(3)(b))

OR

(c) The question or evidence relates to a relevant issue which is an issue of consent. The complainant's sexual behaviour is alleged to have been *so similar* to the alleged sexual behaviour of the complainant *during* the event, which is the subject matter of the charge or to any other sexual behaviour that took place *at or about the same time as* that event, that the similarity cannot reasonably be explained as coincidence (s41(3)(c)(i) and (ii))

OR

(d) The question or evidence relates to any question adduced by the prosecution about any sexual behaviour of the complainant and in the opinion of the court would go no further than is necessary to enable the evidence to be rebutted or explained by or on behalf of the accused (s41(5)).

The general effect is that the complainant can only be questioned about other sexual behaviour with anybody, including that with the alleged offender, if one or more of the following apply:

- it is not an issue of consent,
- it is an issue of consent and the relevant sexual behaviour took place at or about the same time as the alleged offence,
- it is an issue of consent and the sexual behaviour was so similar to behaviour which took place during the offence *or* at or about the same time as the alleged offence that the similarity cannot be a coincidence, or
- it is necessary to rebut the prosecution evidence.

In addition, even if one of the above situations applies, before the court can give leave for cross examining the complainant it has to consider the following:

- Leave can only be granted if a refusal 'might have the result of rendering unsafe a conclusion of the jury or (as the case may be) the court on any relevant issue in the case' (s41(2)(b)). This in effect means danger of a miscarriage of justice.

- Leave for questioning should not be granted even if the above conditions apply 'if it appears to the court to be reasonable to assume that the purpose (or main purpose) for which it would be adduced or asked is to establish or elicit material for impugning the credibility of the complainant as a witness' (s41(4)).

- The evidence or question must relate to a specific instance or instances of the complainant's sexual behaviour.

Figure 8.2 illustrates this section's summary of s41 YJCEA.

Figure 8.2 Cross examination of complainant on previous sexual history (s41 YJCEA 1999).

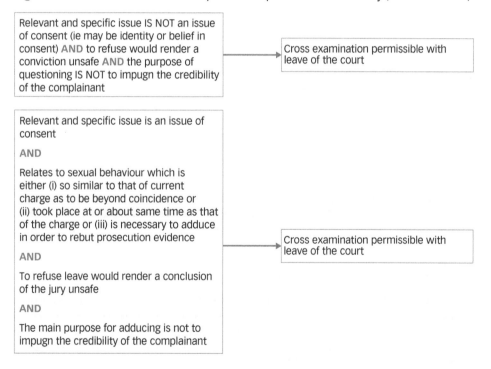

Protection of witnesses from cross examination by accused in person

Sections 34 to 39 YJCEA 1999 set out restrictions against the accused cross examining certain categories of witnesses in person. Section 34 covers complainants in sexual offences. Section 35 covers complainants and child witnesses who may not be complainants for specified offences. Section 36 gives the court a discretion to extend such protection to other witnesses who may not be covered by these two sections but does not cover a witness who is a co-defendant. Section 38 allows for defence representation for the purposes of cross examination in the situations covered by these sections and s39 specifies that if a defendant in a trial on indictment is prevented from cross examining a witness in person under s34, 35, or 36 the judge must give such a warning to the jury as he or she 'considers necessary to ensure that the accused is not prejudiced' by any inferences that might be drawn from the fact that the cross examination is not permitted or that it has been carried out by a legal representative.

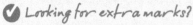 **Looking for extra marks?**

In answering essay questions on s41 you need to be familiar with the fertile academic debate in this area. Birch and Temkin have taken, respectively, a critical and a supportive stance on s41 and you should familiarise yourself with their debate in the pages of the *Criminal Law Review* in 2002–3, see references in the selected bibliography.

The following questions have arisen in the application of s41 YJCEA 1999:

Does s41 breach a defendant's right to a fair trial?

In *R v A* (2001) the House of Lords considered whether s41 could be operated in compliance with the Human Rights Act 1998 and in particular Art 6. The appellant had been convicted of rape. His defence was consent or, in the alternative, belief in consent and he claimed that he had an earlier continuing and consensual relationship with the complainant. Questioning of the complainant on this was excluded at trial. Before the Court of Appeal, the prosecution accepted that evidence of the earlier relationship was admissible under s41(3)(a) in relation to the issue of belief in consent but the Court of Appeal held that it was inadmissible in relation to the issue of consent. It stated that directing the jury that the evidence was solely relevant to belief in consent might result in an unfair trial since the sexual relationship might be relevant to consent as well. The House held that it was possible to read s41, particularly s41(3)(c), as implying that evidence would not be inadmissible if it was needed to comply with Art 6. Thus, logically relevant evidence could be admitted. The case was referred back to the trial judge to determine admissibility on that basis.

In relation to this important case, Emson (2010, p507) comments:

> Section 41(3)(c) has therefore been judicially rewritten to represent the general common law position that the accused may adduce or elicit any evidence which is relevant to his defence of consent unless its probative value is insufficiently high when weighed against competing considerations, the most important of which in this context are the importance of protecting the complainant from vexation and preventing the accused from misleading the jury.

Revision tip

You will gain marks in the assessments if you familiarise yourself with the individual speeches in the landmark judgment *R v A*. You should research cases where the ruling has been considered. To give two examples: *R v S* (2010) concerned a rape allegation against an estranged husband. ➜

➡ *R v A* was considered but the court held in this case that, 'There is no logical connection between the last act of consensual intercourse between husband and wife and the event of the alleged rape.' By contrast, *R v A* was followed in *R v Andrade* (2015). The defence, which was based on consent, was denied an opportunity to cross examine the complainant on her previous sexual history with the defendant. The court referred to the 1998 Human Rights Act and considered that '*R v A* provided that the important question arising in cases where the previous sexual history was suggested to have been with the defendant himself was that, under s 41(3)(c) of the 1999 Act, construed where necessary by applying the interpretive obligation under s 3 of the 1998 Act, and due regard always being paid to the importance of seeking to protect the complainant from indignity and from humiliating questions, the test of admissibility was whether the evidence, and questioning in relation to it, was nevertheless so relevant to the issue of consent that to exclude it would endanger the fairness of the trial under art 6 of the Convention. If that test was satisfied, the evidence should not be excluded.' The appeal against conviction was allowed.

How have the courts defined 'sexual behaviour'?

As evidence students, you are well aware that each case is fact specific. A precise definition of 'sexual behaviour' is not to be found in the cases but you should study the judgments carefully. An illuminating discussion is to be found in *R v Mukadi* (2003). The Court of Appeal held that evidence that the complainant had, some hours before the alleged rape, climbed into the car of an older male driver and exchanged telephone numbers with him should have been admitted. In that case the court stated (para 14), 'It would not be possible to try to define sexual behaviour further. It probably would be foolish to do so. It is really a matter of impression and common sense.' Such behaviour could include solitary activity such as viewing pornography. In *R v Ben-Rejab* (2011) the Court of Appeal (at para 35) cited s41 and stated, 'It will be noted that "sexual behaviour or experience" need not involve any other person. The expression is plainly wide enough, in our view, to embrace an activity of viewing pornography or engaging in sexually-charged messaging over a live internet connection. That being the case, the question for the court is whether an indulgence by answering questions in a sexually explicit quiz is "any sexual behaviour" within the meaning of the section. In our judgment it is.'

Is the allegation of making a false complaint in the past 'sexual behaviour' for the purposes of cross examination under s41(1)?

In *R v Davarifar* (2009) the Court of Appeal stated that making a false allegation is not 'sexual behaviour' under s41(1) and so was not excluded. There has to be a reasonable basis of fact for the falsity of the allegation. However, s41 may apply if the evidence relates to actual sexual behaviour as well as the content of the false allegation. In *R v S* (2003), a defence allegation that the claimant had lied about her previous sexual behaviour by lying about her virginity at the time of the rape which was the subject of the charge was held to be about sexual behaviour.

Cross examination

✳✳✳✳✳✳✳✳✳✳

Revision tip

Problem questions about offences of sexual activity with children require you to be aware of the difficulties of applying s41. This section cannot apply to such offences since there can be no issue of consent with under 16-year-olds. *R v P* (2013) is a good illustration of this point. The case involved P's alleged sexual assault on his stepdaughter when she was a child. He was refused leave to question her about helping her obtain an abortion when she was 17 years old in order to suggest that they had a good relationship. The judge said such questions were caught by s41. The Court of Appeal held they were not about sexual behaviour but relevant to the complainant's allegation about her view of his actions. Similarly, s100 was not engaged since an abortion was not 'reprehensible behaviour'.

Is the allegation of making a false complaint 'impugning the credibility of the complainant' under s41(4)?

Credibility may be in issue if a fair defence is threatened. In *R v Martin* (2004) the defendant was entitled to adduce evidence that the complainant had made a false allegation of sexual assault since this was necessary for a fair presentation of his defence.

In two conjoined appeals, *R v T; R v H* (2001) the complainants had allegedly made false allegations of sexual assaults in the past but this evidence was ruled inadmissible at trial since the purpose was to impugn the witness's credibility. The appeals were allowed since the questions in both were relevant in the normal non-statutory sense. They were not automatically excluded under s41 even if they went principally to credibility. There must, however, be a proper evidential basis for asserting that the complainant made the statement and that it was untrue.

See *R v M* (2009) for an example of how difficult the judges find it to apply this test. There the conviction was overturned since the judge had erred in holding that the proposed cross examination on an earlier allegedly false allegation by the complainant was about sexual behaviour so s41 applied.

Note also the requirements of s100 CJA 2003, the bad character provisions which apply to non-defendant witnesses. It may be necessary for the defence to seek leave under s100(4) CJA 2003. See *R v V* (2006).

✔ *Looking for extra marks?*

Consider whether the case of *R v Edwards* (1991) would be decided in the same way today. The case involved the complex question of the cross examination of police officers by defence counsel and the application of the principle of the rule of finality to collateral questions. It illustrates the close connection of this with character evidence. In this case, evidence could not be called in rebuttal of a denial by officers of the West Midlands Crime Squad, who were giving evidence, that they were involved in an earlier case where perjury had been alleged, and which had resulted in an acquittal. This was an issue of credit only and was collateral.

It is arguable there will be greater scope for such cross examination under s100(1)(b) CJA 2003, as important explanatory evidence. Emson (2010, p167) calls this reasoning 'reverse similar facts'.

Key cases

Case	Facts	Principle and comment
R v A [2001] UKHL 25	The appellant had been charged with rape. His defence was consent or, in the alternative, belief in consent and claimed that he had an earlier continuing and consensual relationship with the complainant. Questioning of the complainant on this was excluded at trial. Before the Court of Appeal the prosecution accepted that evidence of the earlier relationship was admissible under **s41(3)(a)** in relation to the issue of belief in consent but the Court of Appeal held that it was inadmissible in relation to the issue of consent. The House of Lords held that it was admissible. The case was referred back to the trial judge to determine admissibility on that basis.	The House of Lords considered whether **s41** could be operated in compliance with the **Human Rights Act 1998** and in particular **Art 6**. The House held that it was possible to read **s41**, particularly **s41(3)(c)**, as implying that evidence would not be inadmissible if it was needed to comply with **Art 6 ECHR**. Thus, logically relevant evidence could be admitted.
R v Burge (1996) 1 Cr App R 163	Two defendants lied about the circumstances of their murder of an elderly man in the course of a robbery. They claimed he had been alive when they left the scene and that the neighbour who was known to them had killed him. The judge gave the jury a warning about the lies told to the police. The defence appealed on the grounds that the warning also ought to have been given in relation to lies told in court. Appeal dismissed since the directions had been adequate.	The Court of Appeal held that a *Lucas* direction should be given if accused relies on evidence of alibi, *or* where the judge directs the jury that the lies may be supporting evidence, *or* where the prosecution rely on a lie as evidence of guilt, *or* there is a real danger the jury may treat the lie as evidence of guilt.
R v Flynn and St John [2008] 2 Cr App R 266	The defendants were convicted of conspiracy to rob. The evidence against them included covert recordings from a probe placed in the van used in the robbery. Police officers claimed the voices on the recording matched those of the defendants which they had heard following arrest. The defendants successfully appealed to the Court of Appeal.	Although it was highly desirable, it was not mandatory that voice recognition be carried out by experts. Minimum standards had not been observed in this case. Where voice recognition was properly admitted the jury should be permitted to compare the recorded voices with the voices of the defendants if they heard them giving evidence.

Key cases

****

Case	Facts	Principle and comment
R v Forbes [2001] 1 AC 473	The victim of an attempted robbery made a street identification of the defendant. A request for an identification parade was refused. The defendant was convicted. The House of Lords rejected his appeal. There should have been an identification parade but in this case the conviction was safe.	A procedure under **Code D** is mandatory unless the suspect is well known to the witness or there are exceptional circumstances. Note that the wording of **Code D (para 3.12(ii))** now contains the words 'an identification procedure shall be held unless it is not practicable or would serve no useful purpose in proving or disproving whether the suspect was involved in committing the offence. For example, when it is not disputed that the suspect is already well known to the witness who claims to have seen them commit the crime.'
R v Makanjuola [1995] 1 WLR 1348	The appellant had been convicted of an indecent assault. He had denied the charge at the pre-trial interview and did not testify. His counsel cross examined the complainant to the effect that she had a grudge against the defendant. There was no judicial direction on her testimony. The appeal failed since there was no basis for regarding the complainant as unreliable.	The court stated that where a witness was demonstrably unreliable the judge might consider whether or not to give a warning. Whether a warning should be issued and in what form was a matter for judicial discretion. Such discretionary warnings decided on a case-by-case basis replace the mandatory warnings removed by statute.
R v Slater [1995] 1 Cr App 584	The defendant had been arrested after his alleged victim had described his unusual build to police. He admitted being present at the scene of the attack but denied participation. There was no identification parade and no *Turnbull* warning. He appealed and his appeal was dismissed.	There is not necessarily a need for a *Turnbull* warning when the defendant admits being present at the scene but denies the offence. Rose LJ stated that whether a *Turnbull* direction is required or not depends on the circumstances of the case. Here one factor was the unusual build of the defendant.
R v Turnbull [1977] QB 224	Police, as a result of information, had kept watch at the site of a planned robbery. A man was recognised by police as Turnbull. He appealed on conviction. The appeal was dismissed.	Other evidence supported the identification and, although the officer had only caught a fleeting glimpse of the defendant, the conviction was safe. Guidelines were set out for judicial directions in cases which depended wholly or substantially on disputed identification evidence.

Case	Facts	Principle and comment
R v Weeder (1980) 71 Cr App R 228	The victim of an assault had caught sight of his attacker and identified him at a parade. An onlooker also identified two assailants whom she recognised. The judge directed that the jury could take into account each witness's evidence as mutually supportive. The defendant was convicted and appealed. His appeal was dismissed.	One identification can support another as long as the judge warns that even honest witnesses may be mistaken.

⑨⑨ Key debates

Topic	Sexual history of complainant in rape trials
Authors	L Kelly, J Temkin, and S Griffiths
Viewpoint	Defence lawyers use a number of methods to circumvent s41(4) YJCEA 1999. Report recommends (at p76) 'A new exception to the rule of exclusion should be inserted into section 41, allowing for evidence of previous or subsequent sexual behaviour with the accused. This exception could have a time limitation'.
Source	*Section 41: An Evaluation of New Legislation Limiting Sexual History Evidence in Rape Trials*, Home Office Online Report 20/06, London, available at http://217.35.77.12/research/england/justice/rdsolr2006.pdf

Topic	Identification and miscarriages of justice
Author	A Roberts
Viewpoint	Draws on recent psychological research to highlight the continuing dangers of mistakes in identification.
Source	'The Problem of Mistaken Identification: Some Observations on Process' (2004) 8/2 *E&P* 100

⑦ Exam questions

Essay question

'It is well known that identification evidence, like confession evidence, has contributed to a significant number of miscarriages of justice' (A Choo, *Evidence* (OUP, 2015) p153).

Exam questions

✳✳✳✳✳✳✳✳✳

Examine whether the current rules and procedures governing the use of identification evidence in criminal trials ensures fairness.

Online Resource Centre

To see an outline answer to this question visit www.oup.com/lawrevision/

Problem question

Rory is charged with the attempted rape of Gloria. She reported the incident, which she says took place at a pop festival, to the police several days after it allegedly occurred and there is no forensic evidence. Rory denies the offence. Gloria went home the day after the festival and her mother asked her why she was looking so depressed and whether 'anything had happened at the festival?' She then told her mother that she had been assaulted. When first arrested Rory denied the offence. The defence wish to call evidence that Gloria had made false allegations of rape before.

Advise Rory on evidence.

See the Outline Answers section in the end matter for help with this question.

Concentrate Q&As

For more questions and answers on evidence, see the *Concentrate Q&A: Evidence* by Maureen Spencer and John Spencer.

Go to the end of this book to view **sample pages**.

#9

Opinion evidence

Key facts

Criminal and civil cases

- The general rule is that courts can hear evidence of fact not opinion but there are a number of exceptions.
- Under the common law expert opinion is admissible where the matter is outside the experience of judge or jury.
- The judge decides on admissibility in relation to whether the court should be assisted and whether expert has the required expertise.
- Expertise is decided on a case-by-case basis.
- The expert gives opinion on basis of facts which must be proved by admissible evidence.

Criminal cases only

- The common law principle is that an expert cannot give an opinion on the very fact the tribunal has to decide (the ultimate issue rule) but in practice this is often ignored.
- The **Criminal Procedure Rules 2015 Part 19** applies where a party wants to introduce expert opinion evidence.

Civil cases only

- The **Civil Procedure Rules (CPR)** set out details of how expert evidence is to be presented including the use of court appointed experts.
- The ultimate issue rule has been abolished by **s33(1) Civil Evidence Act 1972**.

Chapter overview

Reception of expert evidence in criminal trials

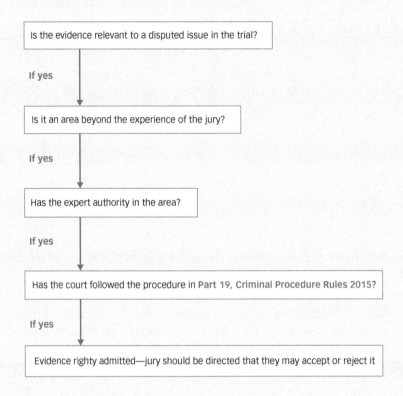

Is the evidence relevant to a disputed issue in the trial?

If yes

Is it an area beyond the experience of the jury?

If yes

Has the expert authority in the area?

If yes

Has the court followed the procedure in **Part 19, Criminal Procedure Rules 2015**?

If yes

Evidence righty admitted—jury should be directed that they may accept or reject it

Related areas

There is some overlap with the rule against hearsay since it is usually the case that the experts have to base their opinions on material generated out of court which is produced to establish the truth of its contents. In civil cases the rule against hearsay itself has been abolished by the Civil Evidence Act 1995. In criminal cases also the rule has been affected by statute. Under s127 Criminal Justice Act (CJA) 2003 the expert may rely at trial on statements prepared by other persons at the judge's discretion. Under s30 CJA 1988 expert reports are admissible with leave if the witness is not attending court. Note also the link with confessions as far as evidence from psychiatrists is concerned.

The assessment: key points

The rule on opinion evidence is historically one of the major exclusionary rules in evidence but it has been much eroded. Expert opinion evidence is the major exception and expert scientific evidence particularly is of significant topical interest. Questions may centre on how misuse of medical evidence in particular has led to miscarriages of justice. It is particularly important here to approach problem questions logically and examine to what extent the opinion evidence is based on general scientific knowledge and to what extent it is eyewitness testimony or hearsay testimony based on what a bystander has said. Even experts may also be acting as ordinary witnesses. You should bear in mind that expert opinion is only that and may be rejected by the jury or the trier of fact in a civil court. This is an area where there is considerable mixture of case law and statute, which you should draw on for your authorities. As a result English law has been accused of taking an overly piecemeal and incoherent approach. This controversy is covered in an outline answer to an essay question at the end of the chapter.

Key features and principles

The Supreme Court addressed the considerations which govern the admissibility of skilled evidence in *Kennedy v Cordia Services Ltd UK* (2016), a Scottish case which involved a breach of health and safety provisions. The court identified four:

(i)   whether the proposed skilled evidence will assist the court in its task,

(ii) whether the witness has the necessary knowledge and experience,

(iii) whether the witness is impartial in his or her presentation and assessment of the evidence, and

(iv) whether there is a reliable body of knowledge or experience to underpin the expert's evidence.

Key features and principles

✳✳✳✳✳✳✳✳✳

It is important to stress that expert witnesses owe their duty to the court rather than the party for whom they are a witness. See *Myers v The Queen* (2015) (p185).

The increasing role of science in criminal and civil investigation has transformed the trial process and the admission of expert evidence is now commonplace. DNA in particular plays a key part in criminal appeals, sometimes exonerating those convicted of crimes many years before. This area of evidence law is very topical since flawed evidence by experts is one of the major causes of miscarriages of justice. In other words what happens when experts make mistakes is very serious. It is an area where you need to keep clear in your mind the difference between civil and criminal procedures. It is still dominated by case law and English law has been criticised as being based on pragmatism as a result and being to some extent incoherent by comparison with arguably the more fully reasoned United States' approach.

Revision tip

Your answers will also be improved in this area perhaps more than any other by an intelligent reading of serious newspapers as well as academic journals. For example, official or parliamentary reports, such as that by the House of Commons Science and Technology Committee, may well be reviewed in *The Times* or *The Guardian* before they reach the scholarly press and your answers to an essay question will benefit by knowledge of their findings. In an essay question in this area you should show in particular that you are familiar with the recommendations of the Report of the Law Commission, *Expert Evidence in Criminal Proceedings in England and Wales* (2011), which, drawing in part on the United States case *Daubert v Merrell Dowe* (1993), proposes that the trial judge should take on more of a gatekeeper role in relation to admitting expert evidence.

Although the subject is taught in evidence courses as predominantly one concerning the exclusionary rule on opinion evidence and expert evidence as an exception, it is arguable that expert evidence forms a field in its own right. Roberts and Zuckerman (2010, p469) point out, 'It is more illuminating to see expert evidence as a topic organised around issues of forensic authority, the transparency of the inferential process, and the durability of trust in the legitimacy of criminal verdicts.' In other words, it is a matter of knowledge as much as opinion, although the fallibility of the expert knowledge may be an issue. This has led to several miscarriages of justice: see *R v Clark* (2003) and *R v Cannings* (2004). In *R v Henderson* (2010) the Court of Appeal gave guidance in situations where expert evidence is the only evidence of guilt. See also *R v Kai-Whitewind* (2005), where *Cannings* was distinguished and the conviction for causing the death of an infant upheld.

Many of the areas of expertise relevant to trials are in the scientific and medical fields and some understanding of statistics in particular would be useful. Finally, there are a number of areas of current controversy such as the survival of the ultimate issue rule in criminal cases and whether new areas of expertise such as **facial mapping** or **psychological profiling** are appropriate for expert testimony. These will be outlined in this chapter.

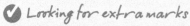 **Looking for extra marks**

Law courses differ in the extent to which they expect students to demonstrate numerical knowledge. It is advisable, however, that you do show some understanding of the specific problems of statistical probability in the area of DNA profiling. Note that in *R v Adams* (1996) the Court of Appeal held that it was not appropriate to use Bayes' Theorem in criminal trials since they were about common sense not mathematical or scientific reasoning. See Naughton and Tan (2011).

Criminal cases

Opinion evidence: the exclusionary rule and exceptions

The rule against the admissibility of opinion is simply stated and based in part on the ideal of appreciation of facts in a trial by a lay and impartial jury who should not be exposed to a witness who is possibly subjectively biased or afforded too high a status as a specialist. Thus, for example, witnesses should not be asked to give opinions on other witnesses' testimony. The two exceptions to the rule relate to the admissibility of the evidence of experts who will be unlikely to have perceived events at first hand and of lay opinion evidence for certain restricted areas from witnesses who are likely to have first-hand knowledge of the circumstances giving rise to the proceedings.

Who is an expert and what areas are appropriate for expert evidence?

Does an expert need formal qualifications?

R v Silverlock (1984): an expert does not need to have professional qualifications. Here, a solicitor was allowed to give expert evidence on handwriting, which was a hobby he had pursued for a number of years.

How competent does an expert have to be and does he, for example, have to have respect from his peers?

Judicial control of the assessment of whether an expert witness is eligible is apparent in this judgment:

R v Robb (1991)

FACTS: An expert on voice recognition, a lecturer in phonetics was allowed to give evidence relying on his own methodology, which was not generally approved of by other experts in the field since it did not include a procedure called acoustic analysis.

HELD: The Court of Appeal held that the expert's opinion was admissible although his methods did not have majority approval in the relevant scientific community. The court attached importance to judicial directions that the jury was entitled to reject the evidence.

This remains a controversial decision in particular since the jury was not made aware that the expert's methodology was not widely accepted.

What areas are appropriate for expert testimony?

The following cases give an indication of the sort of considerations which the court will address.

Experts are not needed for areas which come within the common experience of judge and jury:

R v Turner (1975)

FACTS: T was charged with murder of his girlfriend. He claimed the killing was a reaction to hearing the news that she had been unfaithful and that her child was not fathered by him. H wished to call expert evidence as to his mental state. The trial judge refused.

HELD: Expert evidence was rightly denied since the question of provocation came within ordinary human experience on which the judge/jury could pronounce without expert help. Contrast this case with that of *Stockwell*, see Table 9.1.

Table 9.1 *R v Stockwell* (1993)

Facts: S was convicted of robbery and attempted robbery. Security camera footage showed that in one incident the robber was clean-shaven and disguised with glasses and a wig, and in the other was clean-shaven. S had grown a beard before arrest. At trial N, a facial mapping expert, gave evidence as to whether the man in the photos and S were the same man.

S appealed.

Defence grounds of appeal	Court of Appeal held
1. The issue did not justify the reception of expert evidence.	1. **Rejected**. In the light of the admitted change of appearance an expert could provide information and insight. The issue was not straightforward.
2. N was not an expert in the area.	2. **Rejected**. N had no formal qualifications but had expertise as an artist in the field of science and medicine.
3. N's evidence violated the 'ultimate issue' rule.	3. **Rejected**. The ultimate issue rule was a matter of form not substance. Expert evidence can be given on the ultimate issue as long as the jury is warned they can reject it.
4. N's evidence should have been excluded under s78 PACE as it was more prejudicial than probative.	4. **Rejected**. That matter went to weight, not admissibility. **Conviction upheld.**

(See also *R v Atkins* (2009).)

Revision tip

A good performance in answering questions on opinion evidence requires that you adopt an interdisciplinary approach and familarise yourself with the principles of statistics. Keane and McKeown (2015, p593) refer to the 'relaxed' approach of the courts in cases such as *Robb* (1991) and *Luttrell* (2004). The courts are arguably not sufficiently aware of such dangers as the absences of a statistical database and of relying on subjective opinion.

Is expert evidence admissible as to the mental state of defendant or other witness?

The general rule is that expert evidence on mental state is not admissible since the jury is capable of coming to a decision. However, this is subject to two somewhat overlapping exceptions.

First exception: mental disability

Keane and McKeown (2016, p583) comment that 'many of the decisions reflect the view that expertise is only called for in the case of a person suffering from a mental illness, a view which, it is submitted, is unnecessarily inflexible.' The courts have been slow to accept expertise on other forms of mental instability. Thus, for example, in *R v Weightman* (1991) (at para 297) the court referred to the undesirability of admitting such evidence to help the jury decide on the reliability of a confession. The jury did not need to hear a 'psychiatrist talking about "emotional superficiality" and "impaired capacity to develop and sustain deep or enduring relationships"'. However, this overly narrow conception is now modified in relation to the reliability of confessions: see *R v Ward* later and Table 9.2.

Toohey v MPC (1965)

FACTS: T was allegedly the victim of an assault. He had been found by police in a hysterical state.

HELD: The House of Lords held that expert medical evidence as to his mental state was admissible and was relevant to his credibility and to the fact in issue: whether the assault had happened. The House stated, 'when a witness through physical (in which I include mental) disease or abnormality is not capable of giving a true or reliable account to the jury, it must surely be allowable for medical science to reveal this vital hidden fact to them'. There was an objective reason for the difficulty the witness had in telling the truth.

Second exception: who to believe

Exceptionally, psychiatric evidence may be admissible to help the jury decide which of two defendants is more likely to be telling the truth:

R v Lowery (1975)

FACTS: Two men were accused of murdering a girl. Each maintained that the other had done the killing. L's co-defendant called a psychiatrist to give evidence that L's personality made it more likely he was the killer.

Criminal cases

****

> **HELD:** The Privy Council held the evidence had been rightly admitted. The psychiatrist's evidence was relevant to show that the co-defendant's version of the facts was more likely than L's and to negative L's case. This formed an exception to the usual rule that expert evidence is not admissible on matters for which the jury requires no assistance.

Table 9.2 Expert evidence and mental state

Case	Offence	Mental condition	Expert evidence admissible? Y/N
R v Smith (1979)	Murder	Automatism	Yes. Medical condition was outside ordinary juror's experience.
R v Toner (1991)	Attempted murder	Minor hypoglycaemic state	Yes. Defence should have been permitted to cross examine doctor who gave evidence as to whether the condition could have negatived T's intent to kill.
R v Masih (1986)	Rape	No psychiatric illness but IQ of 72	No. Generally speaking expert evidence should be admitted only if accused has IQ of 69 or below.
R v Chard (1971)	Murder	No diagnosed mental disorder	No. Judge correct to exclude report of prison doctor that C had no intent to kill.
R v Jackson-Mason (2014)	Fraud by false representation	Learning disability, low IQ, vulnerability to exploitation	No. J's defence was she was not dishonest since she believed she was helping men who had approached her. Jury did not need expertise on her state of mind. Save in relation to confession evidence, expert evidence concerning defendants with an IQ greater than 69 was inadmissible (see also *R v Walker* (2003).
R v Ward (1993)	Murder	Abnormal personality disorder	In the case of confession evidence, expert evidence of a psychologist or psychiatrist may be admissible if the defendant has a significantly abnormal personality disorder which might make a confession unreliable and there is evidence that the condition pre-dated confession (see also *R v Walker* (1998) and *R v Blackburn* (2005). In *R v Blackburn* (2005) the court held that evidence of a forensic psychologist was admissible as relevant to the reliability of the confessions of a vulnerable teenager who did not have a mental disorder. See also *R v Everett* (1988) (p183).

You must be careful how you cite this Privy Council case since it is of limited authority. Note that the Court of Appeal in *Turner* (1975) (at p842) was of the view that this case had 'been decided on its special facts. We do not consider that it is an authority for the proposition that in all cases psychologists and psychiatrists can be called to prove the probability of the accused's veracity. If any such rule was applied in our courts, trial by psychiatrists would be likely to take the place of trial by jury and magistrates. We do not find that prospect attractive and the law does not at present provide for it.'

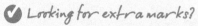 **Looking for extra marks?**

You will impress the examiners if you link your knowledge of confessions to that of expert evidence. The courts have shown greater willingness to admit expert evidence on intellectual impairment in assessing the reliability of confession evidence under s76(2)(b) PACE. Here the arbitrary line of whether the IQ was below 69 or 70, is less stringently observed. The key questions for admissibility of expertise are the extent of deviation from the norm and whether the abnormality has pre-dated the making of the confession.

This was held to be so in one of the most notorious miscarriages of justice in recent years, that involving Judith Ward, whose suggestible personality had led her to confess to IRA terrorist acts she had not committed (*R v Ward* (1993)). By contrast in *R v Everett* (1988) expert evidence was not admissible because there was no evidence of mental handicap or retardation so as to put the defendant outside the normal range of intelligence.

Can an expert give evidence on the very issue on which the jury/court must pronounce?

The ultimate issue rule at common law prevented all witnesses from testifying on matters that should properly belong to the trier of fact. In practice it is often applied flexibly as the case of *Stockwell* (see Table 9.1) illustrates. There the expert gave evidence on disputed identification. In *Pora v R* (2015), a New Zealand murder case, the Privy Council reviewed the law on the ultimate issue. It referred to the expert evidence of Professor Gudjonsson:

> The expert witness should be careful to recognise, however, the need to avoid supplanting the court's role as the ultimate decision-maker on matters that are central to the outcome of the case. Professor Gudjonsson trenchantly asserts that Pora's confessions *are* unreliable and he advances a theory as to why the appellant confessed. In the Board's view this goes beyond his role. It is for the court to decide if the confessions are reliable and to reach conclusions on any reasons for their possible falsity. It would be open to Professor Gudjonsson to give evidence of his opinion as to why, by reason of his psychological assessment of the appellant, Pora might be disposed to make an unreliable confession but, in the Board's view, it is not open to him to assert that the confession is in fact unreliable.

DPP v A&BC Chewing Gum Ltd (1968)

FACTS: The defendants were charged under the **Obscene Publications Act 1959** with publishing so-called battle cards. The magistrates refused to allow the prosecution to call experts in child psychology to show that the cards would have a tendency to deprave or corrupt children.

Criminal cases

✳✳✳✳✳✳✳✳✳

> **HELD:** The Court of Appeal held that the evidence was admissible. Lord Parker CJ observed (p164):
>
> with the advance of science more and more inroads have been made into the old common law principles. Those who practise in the criminal courts see every day cases of experts being called on the question of diminished responsibility, and although technically the final question, 'Do you think he was suffering from diminished responsibility?' is strictly inadmissible, it is allowed time and time again without any objection.

Note, however, the limitations of this decision since the court was of the view that if the case had only concerned adults, expert evidence should not have been admitted.

Revision tip

Opinion evidence seems initially quite a straightforward area of evidence law and problem questions do not usually present much difficulty for the well-prepared student. Increasingly, however, some examiners are setting essay questions which can only be answered well by reading widely. Commentaries on the Law Commission Report continue to appear in the pages of the academic journals. One recurrent theme is the extent to which legal practitioners need to be familiar with non-legal (exogenous) knowledge. Edmond (2012, p65) points out that common law legal systems have evolved in ways that discourage judges (and jurors) from undertaking their own inquiries and investigations. He observes, 'Legal institutions, and particularly judges, disregard exogenous knowledge, advice and authority as well as information about the effectiveness of legal procedures at considerable risk, not only to the innocent, but to their own social legitimacy.'

How does the court approach new areas of knowledge and expertise?

In essence the list of areas for which expert evidence is admissible is not closed. The test remains whether it is within the general experience of the trier of facts. There is, however, not surprisingly somewhat of a conservative view as to what are valid areas of new knowledge.

Consider the following contrasting examples to see how the courts approach this.

R v Luttrell (2004): The Court of Appeal was prepared to accept evidence from a lip-reading expert since the tests for admissibility had been satisfied. They were that

- the evidence was relevant and outside of the jury's experience,
- study or experience gave the opinion of the witness an authority that those not so qualified did not have,
- the witness was qualified to express an opinion,
- the judge gave the appropriate warnings, and
- it was not necessary that the results should be verifiable under cross examination.

By contrast, other areas are not appropriate for expert evidence. *R v Gilfoyle* (2001) is a controversial case. One issue which the Court of Appeal had earlier addressed was whether evidence of a 'psychological autopsy' was admissible. This would have been given in relation to the victim's mental state to help the court decide if she had taken her own life. The Court of Appeal agreed with the trial judge that this evidence should not be admitted. The court commented that 'unstructured and speculative conclusions are not the stuff of which admissible expert evidence is made'. There were no acceptable standards by which to assess the work. The question is, therefore, how reliable is the evidence? Here it was so unreliable as to have no probative value.

Revision tip

This is an area which is rapidly changing as formerly novel areas of expertise become mainstream. It is helpful to have an awareness of the way science progresses generally. One key question is that the expert must be able to demonstrate the reproducibility of the experimental results. *R v Dallagher* (2003) is a useful case where the Court of Appeal implicitly accepted that ear-printing was a possible field of expertise even though the method used was questionable. Another controversial area is that of voice recognition. In *R v Flynn and St John* (2008) the evidence against the defendants had included voice recordings made covertly by police. The Court of Appeal held that it was desirable but not mandatory for experts to carry out voice recognition procedures. See p171.

How is expert evidence given?

Criminal cases

Two statutory sections cover the presentation of expert evidence. Section 30(1) CJA 1988 essentially provides an exception to the rule against hearsay for expert reports. It defines an expert report as 'evidence of any fact or opinion of which the person making it could have given oral evidence'. It provides that an 'expert report shall be admissible as evidence in criminal proceedings, whether or not the person making it attends to give oral evidence in the proceedings'. If the person making the report is not giving oral evidence the written report is only admissible with the leave of the court. In giving leave the court has to have regard

- to the contents of the report,
- the reasons the person making the report is not giving oral evidence,
- any risk of unfairness to the accused caused by the admission or the exclusion of the report, and
- any other relevant circumstances.

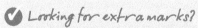 Looking for extra marks?

An area of increasing interest is that of the role of police officers in giving expert evidence. This was examined by the Privy Council in *Myers v The Queen* (2015). One Sergeant Rollins had given evidence on the nature of gang membership in Bermuda. Commenting on this, the court stated (para 60) that 'once he is tendered as an expert he is not simply a part of the prosecution team, but has a separate duty to the court to give independent evidence whichever side it may favour'. He should make full disclosure of the nature of his material. The judgment reviews the complex evidential issues at stake including hearsay evidence. Referring to *R v Tirnaveanu* (2007), the court pointed to the need for the expert police witness to distinguish bad character evidence under s98(a) CJA 2003 (see p87). The court expressed satisfaction that Rollins had discharged his duty as an expert witness.

Criminal cases

✳✳✳✳✳✳✳✳✳✳✳✳

The CJA 2003 includes sections relevant to expert evidence. Section 118(8) preserves the common law rules under which, in criminal proceedings, an expert witness may draw on the body of expertise relevant to his field. In *R v Abadom* (1983) the Court of Appeal held that expert opinion was admissible although the expert had relied on statistics supplied by the Home Office. The expert was entitled to rely on his research in forming his opinion and such evidence did not violate the rule against hearsay.

Section 127 CJA 2003 allows an expert to base an opinion on a statement prepared by another who had personal knowledge of the matters stated and which was prepared for the purposes of criminal proceedings. The accompanying Explanatory Note makes it clear that the provision is designed to address the problem which arises where information that the expert relies upon is outside his or her personal experience and cannot be proved by other admissible evidence. Thus, the rules about advance notice are amended so as to require advance notice of the name of any person who has prepared information on which the expert has relied. In summary, an expert's opinion may be based on statements he or she has not prepared if the following conditions are met:

- the statement was prepared for the purposes of criminal proceedings; and
- any person who prepared the statement had, or may reasonably be supposed to have had, personal knowledge of the matters stated.

You will see that the provisions are not dissimilar to those relating to the admissibility of business documents.

The Criminal Procedure Rules 2015 Part 19 now sets out the procedure for the conduct of expert witnesses. They draw on the 'active case management' principles already established in civil cases, see later in this chapter. The Law Commission Report, *Expert Evidence in Criminal Proceedings* (2011) had recommended a statutory admissibility test to be applied in appropriate cases. Under this, expert opinion would be admissible in criminal proceedings if it passed the 'reliability test'. The judges would be provided by statute with a single list of generic factors to apply. These proposals have not been accepted because of cost. Instead amendments have been made to the Criminal Procedure Rules. (See **Outline Answer to Essay Question**, Chapter 9 for academic commentary, including that of Redmayne, on these changes.)

> ### ✅ *Looking for extra marks?*
>
> Handwriting as a form of identification makes a not infrequent appearance in problem questions. Your answer will be improved if you are able to distinguish between three types of situation in relation to disputed handwriting: eyewitness testimony, opinion evidence, and comparison of handwriting.
>
> - It is relatively uncontroversial that, for example, a witness may testify that he saw someone sign a document.
> - A lay witness may testify to an opinion that a piece of writing is that of a specific person. He might do that on the basis of letters received, for example. In the words of a nineteenth century case, *Doe d Mudd v Suckermore* (1837), 'The servant who has habitually carried ➡

➡ letters addressed by me to others has an opportunity of obtaining knowledge of my writing though he never saw me write or received a letter from me.'

- The final question of comparison of handwriting is more complex. Under s8 Criminal Procedure Act 1865 (which applies to civil and criminal trials) where there is a dispute over authorship, a document proved to have been written by the person in question may be compared with the disputed piece. Although evidence on the comparison may be given by an expert or a lay person, case law has established that in criminal trials a judge should not invite the jury to make a comparison without expert guidance. See *R v Tilley* (1961). (For a full discussion on this, see Tapper (2010), pp676–677.)

Civil cases

This is covered extensively by statute. Key sections are as follows under the Civil Procedure Rules (CPR) 1998, the Civil Evidence Act (CEA) 1972, and the Civil Evidence Act (CEA) 1995. Significant changes were made to the CPR as a result of the Woolf Report which were aimed at reducing the numbers and consequential expense of expert reports. The test for admissibility is set out in rr35.1–35.6 CPR 1998 (see later). In essence the admissibility of evidence is more strictly controlled by the court than is the case in criminal proceedings. The presumption also is that evidence will be given by written report. See Table 9.3.

Lay opinion evidence

Civil proceedings

This area is dealt with under s392 CEA 1972. Where a person is called as a witness in any civil proceedings a statement or opinion by him on any relevant matter on which he is not qualified to give expert evidence, if made by way of conveying relevant facts personally perceived by him, is admissible as evidence of what he perceived.

This has replaced the common law, making it possible for non-expert opinion evidence to be given on any issue.

Criminal proceedings

In practice it is often impossible for a witness's testimony to avoid making inferences from facts which may take the form of opinions. The common-sense practice is therefore that witnesses can give opinions when this is the accepted way of relaying information on what had been observed. Such matters include most frequently identification evidence, and the speed of vehicles. The fine dividing line between fact and opinion is illustrated in the following case.

In *R v Davies* (1962), which involved driving while unfit through alcohol, the lay witness was allowed to give his opinion as to whether the defendant had been drinking. He could give an account of the primary facts which had formed the basis of the opinion.

Lay opinion evidence

Table 9.3 Civil proceedings: procedure for admission of expert evidence

Provision	Overview of the provisions relating to civil proceedings only
s2 CEA 1972	Rules of court may be made to regulate the admissibility and presentation of expert reports.
s3(2) CEA 1972	Where a person is called as a witness his opinion on any relevant matter on which he is not qualified to give expert evidence is admissible if that statement is made by way of conveying relevant facts. (Note that this provision in effect abolishes the 'ultimate issue rule' in civil proceedings.)
rr35.1–35.6 CPR 1998	Expert evidence is restricted to that which is reasonably required to resolve the proceedings and the court has power to restrict expert evidence and require that it be given in a written report. No party may call an expert as a witness without the court's permission. A party may put written questions to an expert instructed by another party. The expert has an overriding duty to the court, see *Stevens v Gullis* (2000). The party was debarred from calling an expert witness who had failed to fulfil the requirement to provide the court with a declaration that he understood his duty to the court.
rr35.7–35.14 CPR 1998	The court has power to direct that evidence is to be given by a single joint expert. If the parties cannot agree who should be the expert the court may appoint one. Each party may give instructions to the single joint expert. A party who fails to disclose an expert's report may not use the report at trial or call the expert to give evidence orally unless the court gives permission.
CPR 1998 Practice Direction 35	The expert has a paramount duty to the court.

He was *not* allowed to testify whether the defendant was unfit to drive for two reasons. First, because such an opinion could only be given by an expert and second, because this was the very issue the court was to determine (but see discussion earlier on the ultimate issue).

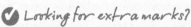 Looking for extra marks?

If you are asked to advise on evidence generally you will get credit for dealing not only with the question of admissibility in a problem question on opinion evidence but, if the question concerns a criminal trial, also for including, where appropriate, judicial directions to the jury. Thus, in relation to the use of statistics at trial when presenting DNA evidence you should show that you are aware that the use of Bayes' Theorem was criticised by the Court of Appeal in *R v Adams* (1996). The need to consider how to present DNA evidence to the jury was also at issue in *R v Doheny* (1977), where guidance was given on how to direct the jury bearing in mind that people find statistics difficult.

Key cases

Case	Facts	Principle and comment
DPP v A&BC Chewing Gum Ltd [1968] 1 QB 159	The defendants were charged under the **Obscene Publications Act 1959** with publishing so-called battle cards. The magistrates refused to allow the prosecution.	Lord Parker CJ observed at p165: '[W]ith the advance of science more and more inroads have been made into the old common law principles. Those who practise in the criminal courts see every day cases of experts being called on the question of diminished responsibility, and although technically the final question "Do you think he was suffering from diminished responsibility?" is strictly inadmissible, it is allowed time and time again without any objection.'
R v Cannings [2004] EWCA Crim 01	Another case, like *Clark*, involving multiple sudden infant deaths.	Where expert opinion was seriously divided about the causes of the multiple infant deaths and there was no evidence other than the fact of the deaths to suggest murder, the prosecution should not be brought.
R v Chard (1971) 56 Cr App R 268	At C's trial for murder, his counsel sought to adduce the report of a prison doctor to the effect that C had no mental disorder but had had no intention to kill. The judge's decision to exclude the doctor's report was upheld on appeal.	Where there was no evidence of any mental disorder and the defendant was entirely normal, there was no room for expert medical evidence on the defendant's intent. That was a matter for the jury to decide.
R v Clark [2003] EWCA Crim 1020	Both her children having suffered cot deaths, the defendant was convicted of murder. Evidence suggesting that the deaths were natural was not disclosed and a leading paediatrician testified that the odds of two such deaths by accident was greater than those of tipping the Grand National winner four years in a row. The Court of Appeal overturned the conviction.	Although the appeal turned on non-disclosure of prosecution medical evidence the Court of Appeal expressed concern about the use of statistical evidence. Before admitting statistical generalisations in evidence, the court should examine the evidence carefully to make sure the jury are not misled. See also *R v Cannings* (2004), another case involving multiple cot deaths.

Key cases

✱✱✱✱✱✱✱✱✱

Case	Facts	Principle and comment
R v Gilfoyle [2001] 2 Cr App R 57	G's wife was found hanging in the garage of the family home. He maintained she had committed suicide, but was convicted of her murder. On appeal he sought to adduce expert psychiatric evidence to cast light on the deceased's state of mind. The court refused to admit the evidence.	An expert's opinion was admissible to provide the court with scientific information that was likely to be outside the jury's experience. But the jury could form an opinion unaided on the proven facts. Expert evidence of how someone's mind operated at the time of an offence was inadmissible unless there was an issue of insanity or diminished responsibility.
R v Henderson [2010] 2 Cr App R 185	The appellants (H, B, and O) in joined cases involving shaken baby syndrome, appealed against their convictions for manslaughter, causing grievous bodily harm, and cruelty; and for murder. They sought to adduce new expert medical evidence. B's conviction was overturned on the basis of the new evidence but the other convictions were held to be safe.	The Court of Appeal gave detailed case management guidance for situations where expert evidence was the only evidence of guilt. The evidence should be properly organised before it is presented to them. The problem for the court was how to manage expert evidence so that a jury could be directed in a way which would, so far as possible, ensure that any verdict they reached was justified on a logical basis.
R v Hodges [2003] 2 Cr App R 15	At his trial for drug dealing, a police officer was allowed to give evidence that the amount of drugs found was more than would be required for H's own use—allowing the jury to infer that he was a dealer. The admission of the police officer's evidence was upheld on appeal.	An experienced police officer could act as an expert witness, particularly as he could be cross examined and evidence could be called to rebut his evidence.
R v Lowery [1974] AC 85	Two men were accused of murdering a girl. Each maintained that the other had done the killing. L's co-defendant called a psychiatrist to give evidence that L's personality made it more likely he was the killer. The Privy Council held the evidence had been rightly admitted.	The psychiatrist's evidence was relevant to show that the co-defendant's version of the facts was more likely than L's and to negative L's case. This is an exception to the usual rule that expert evidence is not admissible on matters for which the jury requires no assistance.

Case	Facts	Principle and comment
R v Turner [1975] QB 834	T admitted having killed his girlfriend, but claimed he had been provoked by her saying he was not the father of her expected child. He sought to call a psychiatrist to say that he was not violent by nature but that his personality was such that he could have been provoked in the circumstances and that he was likely to be telling the truth. The Court of Appeal upheld the exclusion of the psychiatric evidence.	The evidence was irrelevant because T's mental health was not in issue. There was no general rule that psychiatric evidence was admissible to prove that a defendant was likely to be telling the truth. His veracity and the likelihood of his being provoked were matters for the jury.

⟨99⟩ Key debates

Topic	How poor understanding of scientific evidence has caused wrong decisions in criminal proceedings
Author	G Edmond
Viewpoint	Argues that there is an idealised view of scientific evidence, particularly by the appeal court, which can be addressed by exploring the conceptual disparity between the assessment of scientific evidence used to acquit and that used to convict.
Source	'Constructing Miscarriages of Justice: Misunderstanding Scientific Evidence in High Profile Criminal Appeals' (2002) 22/1 *OJLS* 53

Topic	The Law Commission Report on Expert Evidence
Author	T Ward
Viewpoint	The author notes that, two years after the publication of the Law Commission's reform proposals, the prospect of legislation is remote given the fear about costs. He disagrees with critics of this delay in implementing a radical overhaul. He argues that the basic principles of the common law are sound, although in some cases they have not been adequately applied. He identifies these principles as a broad test of prima facie admissibility coupled with a power to exclude evidence whose potential prejudicial effect outweighs its probative value.
Source	'Expert Evidence and the Law Commission: Implementation without Legislation?' [2013] *Crim LR* 561

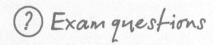

Exam questions

Essay question

'The principal weakness in the English law concerning the reception of expert evidence is that its development has been based on pragmatism rather than principle' (A Roberts, 'Drawing on Expertise: Legal Decision-making and the Reception of Expert Evidence' [2008] Crim LR 443, p443).

Assess the validity of this observation in relation to criminal trials.

Online Resource Centre

To see an outline answer to this question visit www.oup.com/lawrevision/

Problem question

Pat is suing the police for trespass to the person arising out of her treatment when she was arrested at a demonstration. She claims to have suffered serious injuries to her hip. She plans to produce expert medical evidence from Dr Sprog which suggests her injuries were inflicted by deliberate blows. The police plan to produce expert evidence from Mr Clifford that she most likely suffers from brittle bones. Clifford is basing his evidence on experiments conducted by professors at an American university. The police also want to produce evidence from a psychiatrist, Clementine Friend, that Pat is a habitual fantasist and is not likely to be telling the truth.

Advise the parties.

See the Outline Answers section in the end matter for help with this question.

Concentrate Q&As

For more questions and answers on evidence, see the *Concentrate Q&A: Evidence* by Maureen Spencer and John Spencer.

Go to the end of this book to view **sample pages**.

#10

Public interest immunity, closed material procedures, and disclosure

Key facts

Public interest immunity

- Public interest immunity (PII) is a common law doctrine whereby potentially relevant evidence may be excluded at trial.

- If PII is applied neither party may use the evidence, preserving equality of arms.

- Exclusion of evidence on grounds of PII is a recognition of the public interest in non-disclosure, which outweighs that of access to evidence of the parties to the proceedings.

- The principle mainly relates to non-disclosure of documents rather than oral testimony.

- A claim for non-disclosure may be made by the parties, by the court, or by third parties, including the state or a public body.

- Non-disclosure claims may be made for a specific document (contents claim) or a series of documents (a class claim).

- Areas of public interest which are covered by possible PII claims include national security, defence and foreign policy, the identity of police informers, protection of children, and confidential records held by public bodies.

- PII claims primarily occur in civil cases. The main area in criminal cases is the protection of informers.

- The Justice and Security Act 2013 (JSA) has replaced PII with closed material procedures in the ordinary civil courts where national security requires it.

Key facts

✳✳✳✳✳✳✳✳✳

Disclosure (brief outline only in this chapter)

- In criminal proceedings disclosure is governed by the **Criminal Procedure and Investigations Act (CPIA) 1996** (as amended by the **Criminal Justice Act 2003**) and the **Criminal Procedure Rules 2015**.

- In civil proceedings disclosure is governed by the **Civil Procedure Rules (CPR) 1998**.

Chapter overview

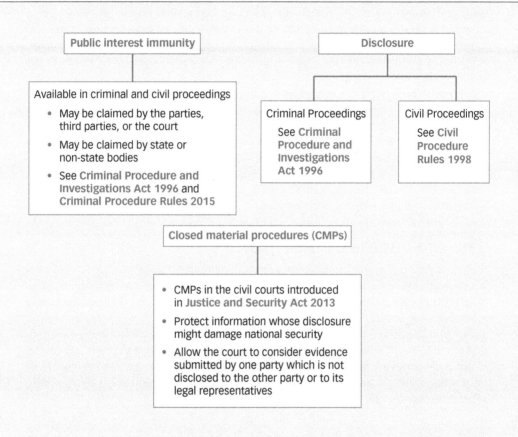

Public interest immunity

Available in criminal and civil proceedings

- May be claimed by the parties, third parties, or the court
- May be claimed by state or non-state bodies
- See **Criminal Procedure and Investigations Act 1996** and **Criminal Procedure Rules 2015**

Disclosure

Criminal Proceedings

See **Criminal Procedure and Investigations Act 1996**

Civil Proceedings

See **Civil Procedure Rules 1998**

Closed material procedures (CMPs)

- CMPs in the civil courts introduced in **Justice and Security Act 2013**
- Protect information whose disclosure might damage national security
- Allow the court to consider evidence submitted by one party which is not disclosed to the other party or to its legal representatives

Related areas

Since the outcome of a PII claim may be non-disclosure of a document it has affinities with legal professional privilege, under which principle, information may be withheld at trial in order to protect lawyer–client confidentiality. There are, however, major differences between the two: first, legal professional privilege belongs to the parties to the proceedings, it cannot be claimed by the court; and second, a claim for privilege may be waived by the individual to whom it belongs.

Public interest immunity forms a part of a wider area which is procedural as well as evidential in scope. That is, the question of disclosure, or pre-trial exchange of evidence by the parties. Most undergraduate evidence courses do not discuss this in depth since it is very detailed and to an extent is more appropriate for the law professional course. It will not be covered here except insofar as it relates to the specific issue of PII.

A final related area is that of allegedly improperly obtained evidence, since, in criminal cases, claims for non-disclosure are sometimes made in response to allegations that police undercover activities have led to entrapment.

The assessment: key points

Your public law course may have included a consideration of PII since it is as much an aspect of administrative law as of the law of evidence. Thus, although it is a fairly technical question of whether certain evidence should be presented at trial, it also raises fundamental human rights issues about freedom of information and access to justice. You may well then have an essay question on the constitutional issues raised by PII. These may be relevant to both civil and criminal matters. Archival research, for example, has shown that the national security claim in the landmark case of *Duncan v Cammell Laird* (1942) may have had as much to do with bureaucratic considerations of litigation management as protecting the nation in time of war (see Spencer (2004)).

Key features and principles

The common law doctrine of PII is an attempt to reconcile two interests or rights, namely the right to a fair trial and the public interest in protecting a public good such as the safety of the state or the protection of the identity of those who inform to the authorities about an individual's wrongdoing.

Public interest immunity used to be called **Crown privilege** and the new name indicates that it is open to any body or group to apply for non-disclosure. Until the landmark case of *Conway v Rimmer* (1968) the courts would not challenge a PII claim, which was normally made by a minister. In *Conway*, however, the court inspected the documents and denied the application. It is arguable, however, that the earlier approach as applied in *Duncan v Cammell Laird* (1942) still applies in cases of national security. The European Court of Human Rights (ECtHR) has examined a number of cases where a challenge has been made to an order for non-disclosure on the grounds that there is consequently a threat to the right to a fair trial enshrined in **Art 6 European Convention on Human Rights (ECHR)**.

Landmark cases

Most of the landmark cases are in civil law and the current approach in criminal law is very much regulated by statute rather than case law. The civil and criminal law positions, therefore, have very much diverged in recent years. Nonetheless, leading civil law cases may have an effect in criminal evidential law, particularly, for example, in defining the scope of a national security claim. Similarly, the grounds of claims are similar and therefore the categories set out in the civil case of *Duncan v Cammell Laird* (1942) apply also in criminal cases. In essence of course the two areas are very different since it would never be appropriate to deny a defendant in a criminal case information which might raise doubt as to their guilt. On the other hand the balancing act between the public and individual interest does not raise such momentous issues in civil cases. The following chronologies (in Tables 10.1 and 10.2) set out the landmarks in civil and criminal evidence separately.

Table 10.1 Civil law landmarks

Year	Event	Comment
1942	*Duncan v Cammell Laird*	Possible grounds of PII claims include 'material injurious to national defence, diplomatic relations, or where the practice of keeping a class of documents secret is necessary for the proper functioning of the public service'. The decision of the Minister on non-disclosure was binding on the courts.
1947	**Crown Proceedings Act 1947**	Act preserves the right for authorities to claim Crown privilege.
1968	*Conway v Rimmer*	Judges should inspect document(s) and make final decision on disclosure. *Duncan* was overruled on this point but it is arguable that it still applies in national security cases. The test was set out for decisions on disclosure, which is that the judge must weigh up the competing benefits and disadvantages to the public and the litigant.
1979	*D v NSPCC*	Sources that need to be protected include those involving authorised bodies as well as government departments.
1980	*Burmah Oil Co Ltd v Bank of England*	There was no class of documents that was totally immune from production.
1983	*Air Canada v Secretary of State for Trade and Industry*	The party seeking disclosure should not embark on a fishing expedition but should demonstrate the potential relevance of the evidence before judge inspects.

Key features and principles

2011	*Al Rawi v Security Service*	Supreme Court ruled that use of secret evidence in civil courts is against the common law.
2013	*Justice and Security Act*	Allows closed material procedures in common law civil courts where national security demands it.

Table 10.2 Criminal law landmarks

Year	Event	Comment
1890	*Marks v Beyfus*	A defendant could not normally require that a police informer's identity be revealed to him. However, if the identity is necessary to establish innocence it will be revealed. In **R v Agar (1989)** the Court of Appeal held that disclosure of an informer in a drugs case was necessary where the defendant claimed to have been set up by the informer and the police acting together.
1986	*R v Rankine*	PII may be claimed for police observation points.
1992	**Matrix Churchill trial**	The criminal prosecution of businessmen charged with sending arms to Iraq collapsed after the judge ordered disclosure of government documents for which PII had been claimed.
1993	*R v Ward*	PII applied in criminal cases and the court must make the final decision on the claim to withhold evidence. A failure to do so would jeopardise the right to a fair trial.
1994	*R v Keane*	The case set out the modern test for disclosure of identity of informers. If the material may prove that the accused is innocent the court should order disclosure.
1996	**Report of Scott Inquiry**	The Report criticised government ministers over the Matrix Churchill PII applications and doubted whether class claims could be made in criminal cases.
1996	**Criminal Procedure and Investigations Act 1996**	The Act set out procedure for PII claims.
2001	**Auld Review of Criminal Courts in England and Wales**	The Review recommended (Recommendation 206) use of special independent counsel in PII cases to protect defendants' interests.
2004	*R v H*	For details see Fig 10.1.

The following key features govern the law on PII:

- in both criminal and civil cases the courts are the final arbiters on disclosure,
- PII may be claimed by non-state bodies, and
- class claims should be rarely made in criminal cases but may be appropriate on occasion in civil suits.

Class claims are controversial and in *R v Lewes JJ, ex p Home Sec* (1973) the House of Lords noted that there would be a heavy burden of proof on any authority making such a claim. The government announced in 1996 that class claims would no longer be made in relation to government documents. Note, however, that class claims may still be made by non-government bodies such as the police: see *Taylor v Anderton* (1995). See also *Kelly v MPC* (1997). Choo (2015, p206) comments, 'What is required now is legislation which makes the approach of the Government of general application.' Tables 10.3 and 10.4 set out the statutory provisions which specify the procedure for making claims in criminal and civil cases.

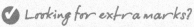

Looking for extra marks?

Many of the criminal cases are on informers and you should be clear that this relates not only to the police. Whistleblowers can be carrying out a civic duty and they can operate in many areas, not just that of the police. *D v NSPCC* (1978) concerned informers on child abuse and in *Rogers v Home Secretary* (1973) the Gaming Board was informed secretly on the suitability of applicants for gaming licences.

Table 10.3 Statutory procedure for claiming PII in criminal cases

Authority	Procedure
s23(1) CPIA 1996 and para 6.12 Code of Practice (2005)	Lists 13 categories of 'sensitive material' which might be appropriate for PII claims.
Criminal Procedure Rules 2015 Part 15 and s17 CPIA 1996	Prosecution make an application requiring • notification to the defence, • specification of the nature of the material subject to PII, and • both parties to make representations to the judge. *But* procedure must be *ex parte* in case of sensitive material and in some extreme cases the defence may not even know of the application.
s15(3) CPIA 1996	Judge must keep any decision for non-disclosure under review as trial proceeds.

Key features and principles

✳✳✳✳✳✳✳✳✳

Table 10.4 Statutory procedure for claiming PII in civil cases

Authority	Procedure
r31.3 CPR	Party to whom a document has been disclosed has a right to inspect it unless the disclosing party has a right or duty to withhold inspection.
r31.9 CPR	Party can make *ex parte* application to withhold existence of document on grounds of PII.

Article 6 and PII

Article 6 ECHR requires equality of arms before the parties and so potentially withholding information could jeopardise the defendant. However, since English law requires that a defendant cannot have a fair trial without prosecution disclosure of evidence it has usually been taken to be Convention compliant. The rights under Art 6 are not absolute.

A number of Strasbourg cases have examined English law:

Rowe and Davis v UK (2000)

FACTS: Three men had been convicted of a series of robberies on the basis of information supplied by police informers. On appeal the defendants sought disclosure of the identity of the informers. This was refused, but the Court of Appeal did see the documents and still upheld the convictions. An informer had been paid and all had been involved in the offences and granted immunity from prosecution.

HELD: The ECtHR found a violation of Art 6 in that the principle of equality of arms had been breached. The ECtHR accepted that it is possible in principle for non-disclosure by the prosecution not to jeopardise a fair trial. The decision on disclosure must be made by the judge.

The matter was referred back to the Court of Appeal, which quashed the convictions. Permitting non-disclosure may not violate Art 6. The decision, however, must be made by the judge, not the prosecution. Here, the procedures used when deciding on disclosure did violate Art 6.

Edwards v UK; Lewis v UK (2005)

FACTS: Both E and L, in separate proceedings, claimed they had been entrapped by the police; in E's case in connection with drug dealing and in L's case in connection with counterfeit money. The prosecution successfully made *ex parte* applications to prevent certain evidence from being disclosed.

HELD: The ECtHR held there had not been a fair trial. The judge was the tribunal of fact on the issue of entrapment and the *ex parte* procedure here violated Art 6. The accused were not able to present their case effectively. Undisclosed evidence may have been relevant to a question of fact to be determined by the trial judge.

Edwards led to a review of the law by the House of Lords in *R v H* (2004) (see Fig 10.1). In *Jasper v UK; Fitt v UK* (2000) the *ex parte* PII procedure was not a violation of Art 6 because the defence were able to make representations to the judge outlining the nature of the case. In addition, the judge, after the *ex parte* hearing on disclosure, monitored this during the trial. If circumstances changed he could order disclosure at that later stage. Contrast this situation with that in *Edwards*.

PII and informers in criminal cases

R v H; R v C (2004)

FACTS: The appellants, who had been convicted of conspiracy to supply heroin, demanded disclosure of details of police undercover surveillance relating to the charges. The judge had ruled in favour of the appointment of a special advocate.

HELD: The House of Lords dismissed the appeal. On the facts this was not a borderline case where a PII hearing should be held. The judge had not considered the nature of the material that was the subject matter of the PII claim and so the decision to seek the appointment of a special advocate was premature. Their Lordships, per Lord Bingham, set out the test for considering PII claims in criminal cases in the light of the Strasbourg court's decision in *Edwards*.

See Fig 10.1.

Revision tip

There has been much recent discussion about the future of class claims. You need to distinguish here the approach of the government and the approach of other bodies. You first of all need to examine the nature of the public interest which is at stake. If the claim is potential damage to national security a class claim may well prevail. As far as government documents are concerned the government ➡

Figure 10.1 Diagrammatic representation of test for public interest immunity claim set out in *R v H; R v C* (2004)

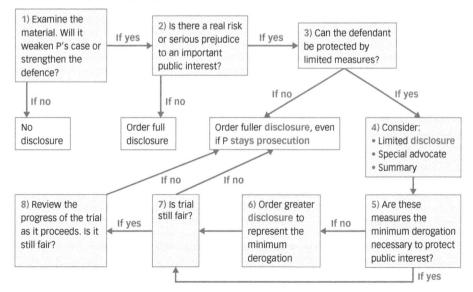

➡️ has stated it will rarely make class claims. Two cases, *R v Chief Constable of the West Midland Police, ex p Wiley* (1995) and *Taylor v Anderton* (1995) illustrate a more flexible approach in relation to non-central government bodies. Even police informer cases are treated on a case-by-case basis.

From PII to CMPs

The common law doctrine of public interest immunity preserves the principle of equality of arms in that, if the court accepts the claim, neither side to the proceedings may use the evidence. Increasing concern over national security has led to replacing PII with a statutory based procedure in civil courts, namely closed materials procedures (CMPs). The legislative change was prompted by the landmark majority judgment of the Supreme Court:

Al Rawi v Security Service (2011)

FACTS: The claimants alleged involvement of the security services in their detention and torture in foreign locations, including Guantanamo Bay. The defendants wished the court to consider material which should not be disclosed to the claimants on security grounds. The trial judge allowed the defendants' claim as a conventional *ex parte* PII hearing but the Court of Appeal refused.

HELD: The Supreme Court upheld the Court of Appeal decision. There was no power at common law under PII procedure to order closed material procedures in the common law civil courts. A closed procedure is the very antithesis of a PII procedure. Such a change to equality of arms could only be achieved by legislation.

Closed material procedures had been introduced in statutory tribunals by legislation in 1997 and the use of special advocates had been accepted by the civil courts as part of the PII applications where any disclosed material is available to both parties as well as the court. The courts have thus acknowledged the need to accommodate national security interests while balancing this with fair trial rights. In *R (Mohammed) v Secretary of State for Defence* (2012) the Administrative Court held that there was no objection to a 'confidentiality ring' in considering a PII application whereby material would be available to lawyers not their clients. This would operate with the consent of the lawyers of both parties.

The Justice and Security Act was passed in 2013. Part II enables the civil courts to order a closed material procedure for material which would, in the court's view, damage the interests of national security. It applies to civil proceedings before the High Court, Court of Appeal, and Supreme Court. The judge exercises discretion to impose such an order but the Act does not include a balancing test, which is the basis of PII applications. *CF v the Security Service* (2013) was the first case in which the statutory proceedings were considered. See Table 10.5.

Disclosure

Disclosure more properly belongs to the area of civil and criminal procedure rather than evidence and is not usually covered in any detail in Evidence undergraduate courses. It refers to the responsibility of the parties to exchange, before the trial, the evidence they plan to use. The

Table 10.5 Difference between PII and CMPs

	Under PII	Under CMP
1. **Would the excluded material be available only to Y or to both or to neither?**	To neither X or Y	Y only
2. **Would excluded material be available to X or Y's lawyers?**	No	Y only
3. **Can the special advocate consult with X and Y before the closed proceedings begin?**	N/A	Yes
4. **Can X instruct the special advocate?**	N/A	No
5. **Can the special advocate consult with X after seeing the closed material?**	N/A	No
6. **Can X ask to have the services of an expert witness?**	N/A	Only one who is security vetted

Note: *X is suing Y (a government body). The court may impose a CMP procedure under the JSA and impose a special advocate. The alternative would be to accept a PII claim by the government body. Table 10.5 shows the possible effects of these alternatives. Note that special advocates may be used in sensitive PII applications.*

defendant thus knows the prosecution or the claimant's case and justice is served. Rule 31 in the Civil Procedure Rules sets out what should be done in civil cases. In criminal cases the rules relating to the prosecution are to be found in the Criminal Procedure and Investigations Act 1996, accompanied by the current Criminal Procedure Rules. The main sections are ss3–8 and 11. A controversial rule is that the defendant is required to indicate in advance what he disputes about the case against him. Section 11 covers 'Faults in disclosure by accused'. The court, or any other party, may make comment on the defence's failure to comply with the Rules and the jury may draw 'inferences as appear proper' in deciding guilt. The prosecutor has a duty to disclose to the accused any unused material 'which might reasonably be considered capable of undermining the case for the prosecution against the accused or of assisting the case for the accused'.

✅ Looking for extra marks?

In cases involving police informers the examiner may require you to demonstrate your knowledge of waiver in this area. Authority for the proposition that even if a police informer is willing to have his identity revealed the final decision is still a matter for the court is found in the case of *Savage v Chief Constable of Hampshire* (1977). There might still be wider interest at stake. A good answer would also note the refinement of this approach in the case of class-based claims. The court accepted here that, if the claim was in respect of a particular body of people such as the occupants of premises, the willingness of an individual to be identified should be considered in pronouncements on disclosure since the primary aim of the class claim no longer applied.

Key cases

Case	Facts	Principle and comment
	Public interest immunity	
	CIVIL CASES	
Air Canada v Secretary of State for Trade (No 2) [1983] 2 AC 394	The airline claimed disclosure of ministerial documents relating to increases in charges which it was alleged were *ultra vires*. The House of Lords held that the party seeking disclosure must present a convincing case for it. This had not been made here. The fact that the documents were Cabinet minutes did not mean they were immune from disclosure.	The effect of this case is to put more obstacles in the way of the litigant who wants to secure disclosure.
Burmah Oil v Bank of England [1980] AC 1090	In challenging a transfer of shares to the Bank after a rescue operation, the oil company's request for disclosure of documents was opposed by the government. The House of Lords held that the documents, which concerned high level policy, were not relevant to the case. The House, however, firmly rejected the argument based on candour as a reason for non-disclosure.	This decision makes it clear that even high level policy documents might not be immune from disclosure.
Conway v Rimmer [1968] AC 910	C, a probationer police officer, sued a police superintendent for malicious prosecution. Crown privilege was claimed against a demand for the production of probation reports. The House of Lords allowed their production, there being nothing in the documents which was detrimental to the proper functioning of the police force or to the public interest.	Following this case a claim for PII is not conclusive of the issue. The court will inspect the documents and attempt to balance the public interest against disclosure with that of the interests of justice in disclosure. See Spencer and Spencer (2010).
D v NSPCC [1978] AC 171	A mother requested the identity of the person who had made a complaint to the NSPCC about her cruelty to her child. The allegation turned out to be baseless. The House of Lords stated that the public interest in the need for a flow of informers meant the disclosure should not be granted.	This case is an important illustration of the principle that authorised bodies as well as central government departments may claim PII.

Case	Facts	Principle and comment
Duncan v Cammell Laird [1942] AC 624	A Royal Navy submarine sank on her maiden voyage in Liverpool Bay with the loss of 99 lives. The vessel had been commissioned by the Admiralty. Dependants of the civilian victims requested disclosure of official documents to assist their suit for damages against the ship owners. The government refused and the House of Lords held that the courts could not look behind a properly constituted claim for Crown privilege.	Although *Conway v Rimmer* overruled part of this judgment it is arguable that the courts will still not look behind claims made on the specific grounds of national security. Note, however, *R (Mohamed) v Secretary of State for Foreign and Commonwealth Affairs* (2010), where the Court of Appeal upheld the decision to disclose documents and refused the Foreign Secretary's appeal.
R v Chief Constable of West Midlands Police, ex p Wiley [1995] 1 AC 274	The question arose in relation to potential proceedings against two Chief Constables whether their documents created for the purpose of an investigation into the police under **Part IX PACE** were covered by class immunity. The House held there was here no compelling reason to create such a class immunity. There could, however, be a contents claim.	In *Taylor v Anderton* (1995) in another claim against the police the Court of Appeal accepted that there may be a class claim for a subset of documents dealing with the actual police reports on professional colleagues or members of the public.
CRIMINAL CASES		
Marks v Beyfus (1890) 25 QBD 494	M sued for malicious prosecution and sought discovery from the DPP of the identity of the person who had informed against him. The DPP's refusal to disclose was upheld.	Most of the criminal cases involving PII concern police informers. The court recognised, however, that if disclosure was necessary to ensure a fair trial it should prevail.
R v Keane [1994] 1 WLR 746	K was charged with counterfeiting notes. He argued he had been tricked. The Court of Appeal upheld the decision to refuse to disclose the identity of the informant. The court set out the procedure for deciding on disclosure. It must examine the material and balance the public interest for and against disclosure. If the material may establish innocence it must order disclosure.	In the subsequent case of *R v Turner* (1995) the Court of Appeal discussed the potential problem of defences being fabricated in order to obtain disclosure. Thus, the judge is required to hear details of the defence in any application.

Key debates

✳✳✳✳✳✳✳✳✳✳

Case	Facts	Principle and comment
R v Rankine (1986) 83 Cr App R 18	An alleged drug dealer was watched from an observation point by police. At his trial he requested details of the post. The Court of Appeal refused.	The reasoning is analogous to that dealing with police informers and the same test for disclosure applied.
R v Ward [1993] 1 WLR 619	A mentally disturbed woman who fantasised about associating with the IRA had confessed to bombings she did not commit. Government scientists had withheld material on the basis that it might damage the prosecution case. The Court of Appeal held that this was an improper ground of PII.	This notorious miscarriage of justice case led to a change in the procedures for claiming PII in criminal cases. In *R v Davis* (1993) the Court of Appeal set out procedures for PII applications. The current rules are in the **Criminal Procedure Rules 2015**.

⑨ Key debates

Topic	Reform of public interest immunity
Author	I Leigh
Viewpoint	The article is a detailed account of the Matrix Churchill trial and the implications of the Scott Inquiry. It is an important contribution to understanding the evolution of public interest immunity and helps explain the context of the subsequent changes to the law in this area.
Source	'Reforming Public Interest Immunity' [1995] 2 *Web JCLI* 89

Topic	Secret evidence
Author	J Jackson
Viewpoint	Reviews the implications of the introduction of closed materials procedures in civil hearings and considers the extent of the threat to open justice. In the light of these changes, impelled by the threat to national security, the author sets out the minimum standards of procedural fairness needed to comply with the ECHR.
Source	'Justice, Security and the Right to a Fair Trial: Is the Use of Secret Evidence Ever Fair?' [2013] *PL* 720

Exam questions

Problem question

James is charged with unlawful possession of controlled drugs. They were found in his front garden after a lawfully conducted raid on his house. He had never been convicted of drugs offences before. His defence is that someone had deliberately placed them in his garden without his knowledge. He wants to know who informed on him so that the police carried out the raid. He suspects that his neighbour Joan, who is a known drug user, told the police. She had borne him a grudge since he had refused to buy heroin from her.

Advise him on whether he is likely to succeed in an application to have the informer identified.

See the Outline Answers section in the end matter for help with this question.

Concentrate Q&As

For more questions and answers on evidence, see the *Concentrate Q&A: Evidence* by Maureen Spencer and John Spencer.

Go to the end of this book to view sample pages.

#11
Privilege

Key facts

- Both legal professional privilege and the privilege against self-incrimination are doctrines whereby potentially relevant evidence may be excluded at trial. The rules relating to both differ.

Legal professional privilege

- Legal professional privilege is the only privilege which applies by rule to communications between a professional adviser and his client, its purpose being to ensure the parties to legal action proceedings are not constrained in preparing their action. It applies in civil and criminal proceedings.

- Legal professional privilege is a common law principle, which is acknowledged in **s10 Police and Criminal Evidence Act (PACE) 1984**.

- Legal professional privilege is implicitly but not explicitly contained within **Art 6 of the European Convention on Human Rights (ECHR)**.

- This privilege covers: (1) **advice privilege**: communications conveying legal advice between a lawyer and his client; there does not have to be litigation in mind; (2) **litigation privilege**: communications between lawyer, client, and third parties (eg other professionals) for the purpose of pending or contemplated litigation.

- The privilege does not protect communications covering fraud.

- The privilege remains even if the party to whom it attached could gain no further benefit from it.

- The privilege prevents facts from being disclosed but does not prevent facts in the documents from being proved by other means.

- The privilege may be lost by waiver, deliberate or accidental.

The privilege against self-incrimination

- The principle is protected by common law, by statute, and Art 6.

- The privilege is based on the concept that an individual should not be expected to offer evidence to the state or answer questions which might lead to his conviction.

- The privilege is enshrined in s14(1) Civil Evidence Act 1968.

Chapter overview

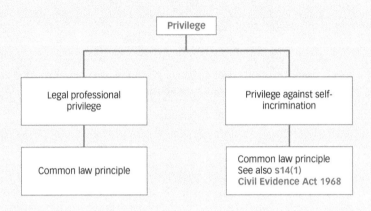

Related areas

Legal professional privilege

It is helpful also in revising this area to recall the work you have done on discretionary exclusion of evidence under s78 PACE or the procedure to stay a prosecution, see Chapter 4. If the prosecution improperly use material which is subject to legal professional privilege these procedures may be applied. The privilege is at issue in relation to the erosion of the right to silence under the Criminal Justice and Public Order Act (CJPOA) 1994. If a suspect claims legal advice as a reason for refusing to respond to police questions he may have to disclose details of communications with his solicitor. He cannot be asked, however, to waive the privilege. Finally, consider what you have learnt about competence and compellability and the application of the well-known maxim 'there is no property in a witness'. The fact that communications with a witness may be privileged does not preclude the opposing party's right to call the witness to testify.

Privilege against self-incrimination

Clearly, this area also overlaps with that of the right to silence covered in Chapter 3. The common law privilege is of course much wider and applies particularly in civil law. Another related area is that of witness compellability and the position of spouses and civil partners in criminal proceedings.

The assessment: key points

Legal professional privilege

You are most likely to be asked about legal professional privilege in a civil context although in the light of the controversial decision in *R v Derby Magistrates' Court, ex p B* (1996) you may be asked an essay question examining the justification for this absolutist approach to the privilege. Although you must keep clear the distinction between the civil and criminal case law the key principles are common to both and they will be treated together in this chapter.

Note that the privilege does not cover objects or documents which are pre-existing in that they did not come into existence for the purpose of obtaining legal advice. The test for objects or documents which are pre-existing is whether or not to make them available to the other side would have the effect of revealing the content of the legal advice that was subsequently given, in which case they would be privileged. Thus, if a problem question concerns a document that may have passed through several hands be careful to look at its origins. *R v King* (1983) is a useful case.

Privilege against self-incrimination

It is helpful in this area to have some knowledge of the history of evidence in order to appreciate how the law on the privilege against self-incrimination evolved. In an essay question on this area you should demonstrate how the law has gradually been eroded over the centuries, in part because it is arguable that the defendant in a criminal trial has sufficient protection from abuse of state power by the stricter controls that have been put on the police.

A key question here is distinguishing essay questions on the right to silence, which may simply require an analysis of the provisions in CJPOA 1994, from the larger question of the privilege against self-incrimination (see Chapter 3). You will need also to distinguish the principles in Art 6 from those derived from the common law, which are broader.

Key features and principles

Legal professional privilege

Protected by statute

The current definition is to be found in s10 PACE. The purpose of this section is to specify which items are protected from the entry, search, and seizure provisions of the Act.

Key features and principles
✳✳✳✳✳✳✳✳✳

Section 10 PACE gives the meaning of 'items subject to legal privilege':

(1) Subject to subsection (2) below, in this Act, 'items subject to legal privilege' means—

    (a) communications between a professional legal adviser and his client or any person representing his client made in connection with the giving of legal advice to the client;

    (b) communications between a professional legal adviser and his client or any person representing his client or between such an adviser or his client and any other person made in connection with or in contemplation of legal proceedings and for the purposes of such proceedings; and

    (c) items enclosed with or referred to in such communications and made—

        (i) in connection with the giving of legal advice; or

        (ii) in connection with or in contemplation of legal proceedings and for the purposes of such proceedings, when they are in the possession of a person who is entitled to possession of them.

(2) Items held with the intention of furthering a criminal purpose are not items subject to legal privilege.

Case law has amplified the definition here and *R v R* (1994) provides some useful guidelines. In that case the Court of Appeal held that the reference in s10(1)(c) to 'made' was wide enough to include a sample of blood obtained and held in a particular container.

The courts take an absolutist approach

The courts have a principled approach to the privilege.

R v Derby Magistrates' Court, ex p B (1996)

FACTS: B confessed to his solicitor to the murder of a 16-year-old girl. He retracted his confession before trial and blamed his stepfather. He was acquitted and his stepfather subsequently charged and convicted. He had failed to secure disclosure of B's confession.

HELD: The House of Lords held that the communication was protected by legal professional privilege.

Revision tip

In critiquing this area of law you should be aware of its intimate relationship with access to justice and the state's claim of the need to balance this with security concerns. In *Re McE* (2009), in a majority judgment, the House of Lords held that Part II of the Regulation of Investigatory Powers Act 2000 permits covert police surveillance of a suspect's confidential interview with a lawyer. The House did not pronounce on the admissibility of such evidence, but Lords Hope and Carswell expressed the view that legal professional privilege should preclude admissibility.

The European Court of Justice has set out a detailed test for disclosure of legally privileged material taking into account the public as well as client interest, see *Kingdom of Sweden v Council of the European Union* (2009).

The privilege only applies to legal professionals

R (Prudential plc) v Special Commissioners of Income Tax (2013)

FACTS: The appellant companies (P) refused to disclose documents containing legal advice from their accountants to the Revenue on the ground that they were covered by legal advice privilege. The Revenue had issued a notice under **s20 Taxes Management Act 1970** requiring disclosure of documents relating to a tax avoidance scheme.

HELD: The Supreme Court upheld the Court of Appeal decision that legal advice given by accountants in respect of tax matters was not covered by legal advice privilege.

Legal advice includes advice given in a relevant legal context

---

Three Rivers (No 6) (2004)

FACTS: The claimants sought disclosure of documents (which had not been the subject of the court order in an earlier case). The newly requested documents concerned communications with solicitors about the presentation of the Bank of England's evidence to the official inquiry.

HELD: The House of Lords held that these were covered by legal advice privilege.

The decision leaves some doubt as to whether a '**dominant purpose**' test has to be applied to legal advice privilege as to litigation privilege. Lord Scott framed the relevant test to be first to establish that the advice 'relates to the rights, liabilities, obligations, or remedies of the client either under private law or under public law'. Then the question to be asked (at para 84), is: 'Is the occasion on which the communication takes place and is the purpose for which it takes place such as to make it reasonable to expect the privilege to apply?'

Advice privilege only applies to two-way communications between client and legal adviser

Note that the main distinction between advice privilege and litigation privilege is that the former only covers direct communications. Note also that in *Three Rivers DC v Bank of England (No 5)* (2003) the Court of Appeal took a narrow view of who was a client. The effect of this decision for large corporations is that they must be careful to specify who among their employees constitutes the client in order to be covered by legal professional privilege. Those outside this group constitute third parties.

Key features and principles

✳✳✳✳✳✳✳✳✳✳

A 'legal adviser' is not necessarily a lawyer in private practice

The definition includes in-house lawyers and even non-legally qualified staff, such as legal executives who may attend suspects at police stations. Statutes have extended the privilege to communications with others, such as licensed conveyancers and trade mark agents.

Litigation privilege does not cover inquisitorial proceedings

In *Re L (A Minor) (Police Investigation)* (1997), during care proceedings concerning a child whose parents were drug addicts, an expert's report on the mother's explanation of certain events was passed to her solicitors. She appealed the disclosure of the report. The appeal was dismissed by the House of Lords since litigation privilege did not arise in relation to non-adversarial proceedings.

The privilege may be waived deliberately or accidentally

At a trial the claimant's counsel read out an account of an unprivileged conversation from a document which also contained privileged information. Counsel had not been aware that the additional material was privileged and had not intended to waive privilege. It was held that the whole memorandum was privileged and the waiver therefore applied to its entirety. See *Great Atlantic Insurance v Home Insurance* (1981). Note also that the privilege attaches only to the original document and that copies may be adduced. See *Calcraft v Guest* (1898).

The privilege will not be lost if fraud or deceit is involved in obtaining documents from the other party

> **Guinness Peat Properties Ltd v Fitzroy Robinson Partnership** (1987)
>
> **FACTS:** The solicitors of the claimant were sent privileged documents by mistake. The solicitor copied them before returning them. The owner sought an injunction to prevent the claimant using them.
>
> **HELD:** The injunction was granted. The privilege is not lost if disclosure is obtained by fraud or by means of making use of an obvious mistake.

In such instances the injunction to halt disclosure, a discretionary remedy, has to be made promptly. See also *Ashburton v Pape* (1913). **Rule 31.20 Civil Procedure Rules 1998 (CPR)** provides that a party who is allowed to inspect a privileged document by inadvertence may only make use of it with permission of the court.

Contrast *Guinness* with the criminal case of *R v Tompkins* (1977), where the privilege was lost. The prosecution was allowed to cross examine the defendant on the contents of a note which had been found on the floor of the court. The evidence had come into the prosecution's hands innocently. Munday (2013, p120) comments, 'Ethically speaking, this is a dubious decision'.

The privilege will not protect fraud or criminal activity

R v Central Criminal Court, ex p Francis and Francis (1989)

FACTS: In a police investigation into drug trafficking, a judge ordered disclosure of a document held by the solicitors of a member of the suspect's family, G. The solicitors applied for judicial review to have the order quashed citing **s10(2) PACE**, whereby 'items held with the intention of furthering a criminal purpose are not items subject to legal privilege'.

HELD: The House of Lords held that even if G was an unknowing benefactor of the proceeds of drugs, **s10(2)** applied. The statute reflected the common law principle that communications furthering crime or fraud are not covered.

See also *JSC BTA Bank v Ablyazov* (2014), which concerned alleged dishonesty in relation to disclosure of assets. Note that fraudulent activity does not necessarily have to be criminal. See also *R v Cox and Railton* (1884).

The 'dominant purpose' test must be applied in applications for litigation privilege

---

Waugh v BRB (1980)

FACTS: W was the widow of a man killed in a railway accident. She sued the BRB and sought disclosure of an internal accident report made two days after the accident by engineers and sent to the BRB solicitors.

HELD: The House of Lords ordered disclosure since in order to be covered by litigation privilege the dominant, if not the sole, purpose of the submission of the document had to be pending litigation. This was not the case here.

Note also the definition in s10(1)(b) PACE. Although other professionals and experts will often be the **third party** in questions involving litigation privilege this is not always the case. Other prospective witnesses, including lay ones, may be covered, including their identities.

Revision tip

Be very careful that you make it clear you are aware of the different procedures for remedying the situation where privileged documents are obtained by the opposing party in civil and in criminal proceedings. In civil procedures application would be for an injunction, a discretionary remedy. In a criminal case consideration should be given to stay of prosecution or discretionary exclusion of evidence by s78 PACE.

✅ Looking for extra marks?

R v Derby Magistrates' Court, ex p B (1996) is clearly a case where arguably a defendant was denied access to evidence which might have raised a reasonable doubt about his guilt. You will gain extra credit if you refer also to the absolutist nature of the privilege as demonstrated by the case of *R v Grant* (2005). The difference is that the defendant here benefited from the Court of Appeal's ➡

➡ decision. By secretly recording conversations between a suspect and his solicitor the police had violated the principle of legal professional privilege. In this instance no evidence had been obtained against G as a result of this impropriety. Nonetheless, the Court of Appeal quashed the conviction since the trial should have been abandoned as an abuse of process.

Privilege against self-incrimination

The privilege against self-incrimination has in various ways been observed in English law for several centuries. In the House of Lords' judgment in *R v Director of Serious Fraud Office, ex p Smith* (1993), Lord Mustill stated that the privilege was part of a disparate group of immunities, which differ in nature, origin, incidence, and importance, and as to the extent to which they have been encroached upon by statute. Note that the privilege does not apply to administrative proceedings. Figure 11.1 illustrates this.

Figure 11.1 *R v Director of Serious Fraud Office, ex p Smith* (1993)

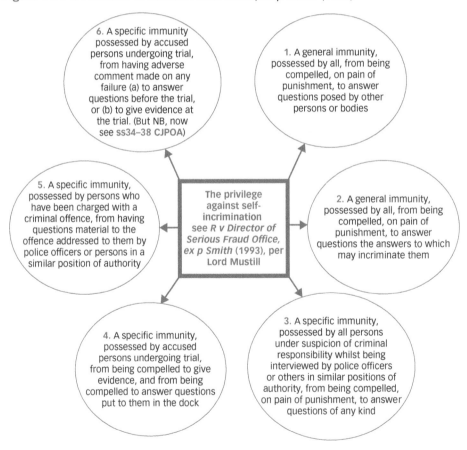

6. A specific immunity possessed by accused persons undergoing trial, from having adverse comment made on any failure (a) to answer questions before the trial, or (b) to give evidence at the trial. (But NB, now see ss34–38 CJPOA)

1. A general immunity, possessed by all, from being compelled, on pain of punishment, to answer questions posed by other persons or bodies

5. A specific immunity, possessed by persons who have been charged with a criminal offence, from having questions material to the offence addressed to them by police officers or persons in a similar position of authority

The privilege against self-incrimination see *R v Director of Serious Fraud Office, ex p Smith* (1993), per Lord Mustill

2. A general immunity, possessed by all, from being compelled, on pain of punishment, to answer questions the answers to which may incriminate them

4. A specific immunity, possessed by accused persons undergoing trial, from being compelled to give evidence, and from being compelled to answer questions put to them in the dock

3. A specific immunity, possessed by all persons under suspicion of criminal responsibility whilst being interviewed by police officers or others in similar positions of authority, from being compelled, on pain of punishment, to answer questions of any kind

In *R v Hertfordshire CC, ex p Green Environmental Industries Ltd* (2000) the privilege did not protect against the use of compelled questions in an administrative enquiry. It does not cover material having an existence independent of the will of the suspect. According to *Saunders v UK* (1997) this included 'documents acquired pursuant to a warrant, breath, blood and urine samples and bodily tissue for the purpose of DNA testing'. The principle was made clear also in *C plc v P* (2007). In this case the claimant did not succeed in preventing the submission of pornographic images on a computer to the prosecuting authorities. These had been discovered as a result of an official search on another matter, see also *R v S* (2009). Another limitation of the privilege is that it may be limited in its application if that limitation pursues a legitimate objective and is proportionate.

In *Brown v Stott* (2003) the Privy Council accepted such a limitation. Section 172(2)(a) Road Traffic Act 1988 required the occupants of a car that was speeding to identify who was driving. Criminal penalties could be imposed for non-responses. B responded and was convicted of speeding. The conviction was upheld.

In *Luckhof v Austria* (2008) the Strasbourg court found no violation of Art 6(1) ECHR on similar facts. There was a legitimate public interest in road safety.

Revision tip

Contrast the case of *Brown v Stott* (2003) with that of *Heaney v Ireland* (2001). There, the degree of compulsion to respond to questions effectively abolished the privilege against self-incrimination. The applicants faced charges under anti-terrorist legislation which made it an offence not to give an account. The Strasbourg court could not justify 'a provision which extinguishes the very essence of the applicant's rights to silence and against self-incrimination guaranteed by Article 6(1) of the Convention'.

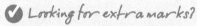 Looking for extra marks?

You need to be on the lookout for questions on compellability which may be inserted in questions on the privilege against self-incrimination. Examiners may, for example, refer to spouses in a problem in civil proceedings concerned with the privilege. Note that s80A PACE (introduced by the CJA 2003) provides that the failure of the spouse or civil partner of a person charged in any proceedings to give evidence in the proceedings shall not be made the subject of any comment by the prosecution. Section 14(1)(a) and (b) Civil Evidence Act 1968 uphold the privilege in civil proceedings to witnesses, spouses, and civil partners. Not surprisingly, under s1(2) Criminal Evidence Act 1898, a defendant cannot claim the privilege in relation to questions on the current charge.

 Conclusion

The connecting thread between public interest immunity (PII) and privilege is that they both deal with ways potentially relevant evidence may be excluded at trial for extrinsic policy rather than intrinsic fair trial procedural reasons. The doctrines have quite distinct rules and you should study

Conclusion

them separately. However, it is helpful to keep in mind the main differences, particularly between legal professional privilege and PII. They are set out in Table 11.1.

The privilege against self-incrimination is a more diffuse concept and it has been subject to continuing statutory encroachment, such as s31(1) Theft Act 1968.

The case of *Saunders v UK* (1997) shows that statutory encroachments have to be Convention compliant. In *Beghal v DPP* (2015) the Supreme Court considered the privilege in the light of the power to stop and search under the Terrorism Act 2000, which provided that a person questioned at a port for the purposes applying in the Act must answer or be prosecuted. In a majority judgment the court held that there was no violation of Art 6 since the purpose of the questioning and search was not the accumulation of an evidential case against the subject. The subject was not a person charged for the purpose of Art 6, which thus had no application to him. There was not a breach of the common law privilege against self-incrimination. Lord Kerr, dissenting, said,

> There is, currently, no guarantee that someone who gives a self-incriminating answer in the course of a Schedule 7 inquiry will not be confronted by those answers in a subsequent criminal trial. He may succeed in having evidence of those answers excluded but he cannot ensure that he will not be prosecuted on foot of them. I consider therefore that the requirement in Schedule 7 that a person questioned under its provisions must answer on pain of prosecution for failing to do so is in breach of that person's common law privilege against self-incrimination. On that account it is incompatible with article 6 of ECHR.

Table 11.1 Differences between PII and legal professional privilege

PII	Legal professional privilege
Non-disclosure is a duty.	Non-disclosure is a right.
PII may be claimed by the court or by a third party.	Privilege can only be claimed by parties to the proceedings.
Cannot be waived by the party claiming it (possible exception for an informer on non-disclosure of identity).	Can be purposefully or accidentally waived by party claiming it.
In civil proceedings, party may apply to court ex parte that even the existence of the document should not be disclosed to the other side (r31.19(1) CPR). (In very exceptional cases such ex parte applications may be made in criminal proceedings.)	Existence of disputed document must be revealed to other side during 'discovery'.
Secondary evidence of the relevant document cannot be adduced.	The privilege attaches to the original document and secondary evidence may be adduced.
Disclosure or stay of prosecution may be ordered if establishing innocence is threatened by non-disclosure.	Disclosure will not necessarily be ordered even if necessary to establish innocence.

The privilege in its current form in civil proceedings has been held to be archaic. Lord Templeman, in *AT&T Istel Ltd v Tully* (1993), stated: 'I regard the privilege against self-incrimination exercisable in civil proceedings as an archaic and unjustifiable survival from the past when the court directs the production of relevant documents and requires the defendant to specify his dealings with the plaintiff's property or money.'

 **Key cases**

Case	Facts	Principle and comment
	Legal professional privilege	
Great Atlantic Insurance v Home Insurance [1981] 1 WLR 529	At a trial the claimant's counsel read out an account of an unprivileged conversation from a document which also contained privileged information. The counsel had not been aware that the additional material was privileged and had not intended to waive privilege. It was held that the whole memorandum was privileged and the waiver therefore applied to its entirety.	Here counsel was acting as the client's agent and thus waived privilege on his behalf.
Guinness Peat Properties Ltd v Fitzroy Robinson Partnership [1987] 1 WLR 1027	The solicitors of the claimant were sent privileged documents by mistake. The solicitor copied them before returning them. The owner sought an injunction to prevent the claimant using them. The injunction was granted. The privilege is not lost if disclosure is obtained by fraud or by means of making use of an obvious mistake.	In such instances the injunction to halt disclosure, a discretionary remedy, to be made promptly. **Rule 31.20 CPR** provides that a party who is allowed to inspect a privileged document by inadvertence may only make use of it with permission of the court.
R v Central Criminal Court, ex p Francis and Francis [1989] AC 346	In a police investigation into drug trafficking a judge ordered disclosure of a document held by the solicitor of a member of the suspect's family, G. The solicitor applied for judicial review to have the order quashed citing **s10(2) PACE**, whereby 'Items held with the intention of furthering a criminal purpose are not items subject to legal privilege.' The House of Lords held that even if G was an unknowing benefactor of the proceeds of drugs **s10(2)** applied.	The principle here is the common law one that communications furthering crime or fraud are not covered, see *R v Cox and Railton* (1884). The fraudulent activity does not have to be necessarily criminal.

Key cases

✳✳✳✳✳✳✳✳✳

Case	Facts	Principle and comment
R v Derby Magistrates' Court, ex p B [1996] 1 AC 487	B confessed to his solicitor to the murder of a 16-year-old girl. He retracted his confession before trial and blamed his stepfather. He was acquitted and his stepfather subsequently charged and convicted. He had failed to secure disclosure of B's confession. The House of Lords held, overruling earlier authorities, that the communication was protected by legal professional privilege.	Lord Taylor CJ said (at p507) 'a man must be able to consult his lawyer in confidence, since otherwise he might hold back half the truth. The client must be sure that what he tells his lawyer in confidence will never be revealed without his consent. Legal professional privilege is thus much more than an ordinary rule of evidence . . . It is a fundamental condition on which the administration of justice as a whole rests.'
Re L (A Minor) (Police Investigation) [1997] AC 16	During care proceedings concerning a child whose parents were drug addicts an expert's report on the mother's explanation of certain events, was passed to her solicitors. She appealed the disclosure of the report. The appeal was dismissed by the House of Lords since litigation privilege did not arise in relation to non-adversarial proceedings.	Note, however, that the *Three Rivers* series of cases establishes that legal advice privilege may be available in non-adversarial proceedings.
Three Rivers DC v Bank of England (No 5) [2003] QB 1556	Facing an action for misfeasance in public office the Bank of England claimed legal advice privilege in relation to documentary evidence produced for an official inquiry into the collapse of the BCCI. The documents had been generated some time before the current action. The court held that the advice privilege only attached to a small group of individuals in the Bank.	The controversial decision in this case had the effect of narrowing the group of people who could be called 'clients'. In effect, corporate bodies must now take care who they nominate as the 'client' if they wish to protect confidential documents. Employees who are outside this nominated group will be third parties.
Three Rivers (No 6) [2004] 3 WLR 1274	The claimants sought disclosure of further documents (which had not been the subject of the court order in the case above). The newly requested documents concerned communications with solicitors about the presentation of the Bank's evidence to the official inquiry. The House of Lords, reversing the Court of Appeal, held that these were covered by legal advice privilege.	The House extended the scope of legal advice privilege to cover documents generated in a relevant legal context even if they were not specifically directed to legal matters. The case also confirmed that legal advice privilege, whether or not there is impending or potential litigation, applied.

Case	Facts	Principle and comment
Waugh v BRB [1980] AC 521	W was the widow of a man killed in a railway accident. She sought disclosure of an internal accident report made two days after the accident by engineers and sent to the BRB solicitors. The House of Lords ordered disclosure since in order to be covered by litigation privilege the dominant, if not the sole, purpose of the submission of the document had to be pending litigation. This was not the case here.	The public interest in disclosure here prevailed over an extension of litigation privilege.

Privilege against self-incrimination

Case	Facts	Principle and comment
Blunt v Park Lane Ltd [1942] 2 KB 253	In an action for slander the claimant challenged the requirement to respond to interrogatories on her alleged promiscuity on the grounds that her responses might lead to penalty or censure by an ecclesiastical court for adultery. The court held that answering did not infringe her privilege against self-incrimination.	In this case the only likely penalty was to have the sacraments refused and this did not constitute a penalty within the scope of the rule.
R v Hertfordshire CC, ex p Green Environmental Industries Ltd [2000] AC 412	The **Environmental Protection Act** made it an offence for local authorities not to give information about their waste management. It was held that this did not breach **Art 6**.	The outcome shows how the courts will distinguish responses which might be used in criminal proceedings and those used for administrative inquiries.
Saunders v UK (1997) 23 EHRR 313	In a criminal trial for false accounting and theft, evidence was produced from S's responses to questions from DTI inspectors. They had powers under the **Companies Act** to compel responses.	**Article 6** was breached by the use in a criminal trial of answers which were obtained under compulsion.

 Key debates

Topic	The rationale behind the decision to exclude legal professional privilege from inquisitorial proceedings
Author	A Zuckerman
Viewpoint	Discusses the relationship between the decision in *Re L* and that in *ex p B* and suggests that an alternative and fairer approach would have been to declare *ex p B* wrongly decided.

Exam questions

✳✳✳✳✳✳✳✳✳

Source	'Legal Professional Privilege: The Cost of Absolutism' (1996) 112 *LQR* 535
Topic	The reasons for protecting the privilege against self-incrimination
Author	M Redmayne
Viewpoint	Discusses the reasons for protecting the privilege and maintains one is the need for distance from a powerful state.
Source	'Rethinking the Privilege against Self-Incrimination' (2007) 27/2 *OJLS* 209

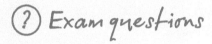 (?) Exam questions

Essay question

Does the current law on legal professional privilege undermine or ensure the right to a fair trial? Answer, giving reasons, in relation to legal professional privilege in civil and criminal proceedings.

 Online Resource Centre

To see an outline answer to this question visit www.oup.com/lawrevision/

Problem question

Freda is suing the Pets Holiday Camp (PHC) for negligently causing the death of her pet dog by leaving it in a van without water on a hot summer day. She had paid to have the dog in the kennels for a week. Martin is a member of a charity organisation called Keep Pets Safe. He works as a clerk with Fixit, the lawyers acting for PHC. He sends to Freda anonymously a copy of an email PHC's insurers have sent to Fixit which refers to poor staffing levels in PHC.

Advise Freda whether she can adduce the text of this email at trial.

See the Outline Answers section in the end matter for help with this question.

 Concentrate Q&As

For more questions and answers on evidence, see the *Concentrate Q&A: Evidence* by Maureen Spencer and John Spencer.

Go to the end of this book to view sample pages.

Exam essentials

One important skill to develop in answering evidence examination questions is to recognise what the question is about. Most problem questions set out an imaginary scenario and then ask you to advise on the evidential issues. Thus, they may not necessarily directly indicate the areas of law involved. You must make a list of the potential witnesses and put a brief note beside them setting out the aspect of evidence law which you will need to address. The first matter to determine of course is whether the question involves civil or criminal evidence. Many an evidence student has been swept onto the rocks by ignoring this crucial preliminary matter. It is also a good idea to write an introductory line or two indicating how you are going to shape your answer, whether by taking each witness in turn or by taking a chronological stance. The following brief overview of the areas discussed in this *Concentrate* will help you recognise how questions are shaped. See also the flow chart on pA4.

Burden and standard of proof

This is implicit in all questions and you may be expected to state the general rule and how the judge should direct the jury. You should be alert to more complex issues if the following are referred to in the question. First, there may be an extract from a statute, real or imaginary, which shifts the burden of proof and you will need to consider whether this is the evidential or the legal burden. Second, the defendant may claim a common law defence such as non-insane automatism and you will then refer to the evidential burden. Finally, in civil cases the controversial issue is the standard of proof where there is a quasi-criminal allegation.

Confessions and the defendant's silence

This is an enormous area and you can be sure that it will appear in any evidence examination. You should work carefully through the provisions of ss76 and 78 PACE to determine if the exclusionary rules or the exercise of discretion should apply. Section 82 PACE may be called into play if the judge decides that evidence has been wrongly admitted. Be sure to recognise the particular provisions referring to co-defendants, namely s76A. In relation to silence as well as revising the voluminous case law on judicial directions under ss34–38 CJPOA you should not ignore the common law, which may apply if the parties are on even terms. This area has close connections with that on character. Thus, for example, if there is an allegation that the police are lying about the circumstances of a confession being admitted be aware that s100 CJA 2003 may apply in relation to the admissibility of the character of a non-defendant witness.

Improperly obtained evidence other than confessions

Clues to questions involving this are references to undercover police who may be engaged in entrapment and real evidence obtained as a result of a breach by those in authority of a law or an administrative provision. It is an area you should not attempt unless you are familiar with the Strasbourg case law and the significance of Art 8 as well as Art 6. Remember that the possible remedies are stay of prosecution or exclusion of evidence.

Character

This is one of the most notoriously difficult areas of evidence and may well dominate even a question mixed with other areas. It is vital that you separate the law relating to good and bad character and that for defendants and non-defendants. Arguably, the law has become more straightforward after the sweeping changes in the 2003 Act. There is a growing number of Court of Appeal decisions but you have to avoid applying them mechanically. Consider the implications of the specific facts you are given.

Hearsay

This exclusionary rule is now regulated almost entirely by statute and you must be aware how the changes have been part of the move to protect victims so that there may be ways their evidence can be given without the requirement for them to appear in court. A major change under the CJA 2003 is that implied assertions are not hearsay. This approach has generated quite a significant amount of case law, many on drugs-related cases on the relevance and status of text messages on mobile phones and social media material. The complex question of implied assertions still causes difficulty.

Competence and compellability, special measures

You will be alerted that these issues may come up by references to reluctant witnesses such as spouses called to testify for the prosecution and by vulnerable witnesses such as children or rape victims.

Issues in the course of trial

Your evidence course will probably have concentrated on specific areas of this broad and somewhat procedural set of issues. One topical issue is the problem of previous allegedly false allegations by the complainant. They may not be covered by the exclusion under s41 YJCEA 1999 but the case law shows the difficulty of determining this.

Opinion

This area has been subject to an important Law Commission Report and although it is not as yet enshrined in law the content of the report will help illuminate the issues for you.

Public interest immunity

This will largely come up in civil cases, apart from the question of police informers in criminal cases.

Privilege

Legal professional privilege is closely protected but you should be aware of the inroads made by ss34–38 CJPOA 1994. The privilege against self-incrimination is important in both civil and criminal cases but most of the questions on the latter would also be embraced by the application of the law on the defendant's silence.

And finally

Be up to date and address the question

As part of your examination preparation do make sure that you are up to date on the recent cases and journal articles because your examiners will often draw on them as inspiration for questions. It is very important you direct your answer to the question set. Most problem questions on evidence involve advising on admissibility, commenting on how the judge should address the jury, or advising if there are grounds of appeal because of judicial misdirections which may be listed in the question. You have to apply the law as it is. Essay questions will expect you to be more critical of the law as it is and also to be familiar with proposals for reform. You may also be expected to show your knowledge of academic debates in scholarly journals.

Exam essentials

✳✳✳✳✳✳✳✳✳✳

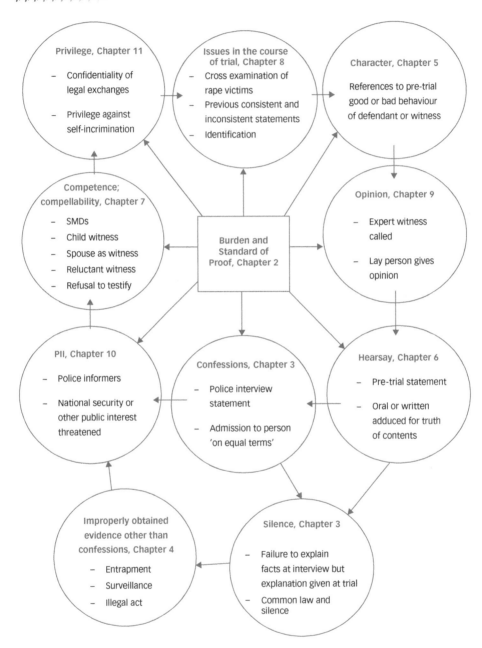

Selected bibliography

Ashworth, A, 'Criminal Proceedings after the Human Rights Act: The First Year' [2001] Crim LR 855

Birch, D, 'Rethinking Sexual History Evidence: Proposals for Fairer Trials' [2002] Crim LR 531

Birch, D, 'Untangling Sexual History Evidence: A Rejoinder to Professor Temkin' [2003] Crim LR 370

Burton, M, Evans, R, and Sanders, A, 'Vulnerable and Intimidated Witnesses and the Adversarial Process in England and Wales' (2007) 11/1 E&P 1

Choo, A L-T, *Evidence* (OUP, 2015)

Crinion, C, 'Adducing the Character of the Prosecution Witnesses' [2010] Crim LR 570

Dennis, IH, 'Reverse Onuses and the Presumption of Innocence' [2005] Crim LR 901

Dennis, IH, 'Case Comment. Human Rights: *Al Khawaja and Tahery v UK*' [2012] Crim LR 375

Dennis, IH, *The Law of Evidence* (Sweet and Maxwell, 5th edn, 2013)

Doak, J, and McGourlay, C, *Criminal Evidence in Context* (Law Matters, 4th edn, 2015)

Edmond, G, 'Constructing Miscarriages of Justice: Misunderstanding Scientific Evidence in High Profile Criminal Appeals' (2002) 22/1 OJLS 53

Edmond, G, 'Is Reliability Sufficient? The Law Commission and Expert Evidence in International and Interdisciplinary Perspective, Part 1' (2012) 16/1 E&P 30

Emson, R, *Evidence* (Palgrave Macmillan, 5th edn, 2010)

Glover, R, *Murphy on Evidence* (OUP, 14th edn, 2015)

Hoyano, L, 'Variations on a Theme by Pigot: Special Measures Directions for Child Witnesses' [2000] Crim LR 250

Hoyano, L, 'Special Measures Directions Take Two: Entrenching Unequal Access to Justice?' [2010] Crim LR 345

Hyland, K, and Walker, C, 'Undercover Policing and Underwhelming Laws' [2014] Crim LR 555

Jackson, J, 'Justice, Security and the Right to a Fair Trial: Is the Use of Secret Evidence Ever Fair?' [2013] PL 720

Keane, A, and McKeown, P, *The Modern Law of Evidence I* (OUP, 2016)

Laudan, L, *Truth, Error and Criminal Law: An Essay in Legal Epistemology* (CUP, 2008)

Law Commission, *Expert Evidence in Criminal Proceedings in England and Wales* (Law Com No 325, 2011)

Law Commission, *Criminal Liability: Insanity and Automatism. A Discussion Paper* (Law Com, 2013)

Leigh, I, 'Reforming Public Interest Immunity' [1995] 2 Web JCLI 89

Lloyd Bostock, S, 'The Effect on Juries of Hearing about the Defendant's Previous Criminal Record: A Simulation Study' [1973] Crim LR 734

Lloyd Bostock, S, 'The Effect on Lay Magistrates of Hearing that the Defendant is of "Good Character", Being Left to Speculate, or Hearing that He Has a Previous Conviction' [2006] Crim LR 189

Mirfield, P, 'The Argument from Consistency for Overruling *Selvey*' [1991] CLJ 490

Munday, C, *Core Text: Evidence* (OUP, 8th edn, 2015)

Naughton, M, and Tan, G, 'The Need for Caution in the Use of DNA Evidence to Avoid Convicting the Innocent' (2011) 15 E&P 245

O'Brian, W, 'Confrontation: The Defiance of the English Courts' (2011) 15/2 E&P 93

O'Floinn, M, and Ormerod, D, 'Social Networking Sites, RIPA and Criminal Investigations' [2011] Crim LR 766

Selected bibliography

O'Floinn, M, and Ormerod, D, 'Social Networking Material as Criminal Evidence' [2012] Crim LR 486

Ormerod, D, 'Sounds Familiar? Voice Identification Evidence' [2001] Crim LR 595

Ormerod, D, 'Case Comment: *R v Bains*' [2010] Crim LR 937

Ormerod, D, 'Case Comment: *R v Thakrar*' [2011] Crim LR 399

Pattenden, P, 'Should Confessions be Corroborated?' (1991) 107 LQR 317

Redmayne, M, 'Expert Evidence and Criminal Justice' (OUP, 2001)

Redmayne, M, 'Rethinking the Privilege against Self-Incrimination' (2007) 27/2 OJLS 209

Redmayne, M, 'Recognising Propensity' [2011] Crim LR 177

Redmayne, M, 'Hearsay and Human Rights: Al-Khawaja in the Grand Chamber' (2012) 75 MLR 865

Redmayne, M, *Character in the Criminal Trial* (OUP, 2016)

Roberts, A, 'Drawing on Expertise: Legal Decision-making and the Reception of Expert Evidence' [2008] Crim LR 443

Roberts, A, 'Case Comment' [2011] Crim LR 642

Roberts, P, and Doak, J (eds), 'Mastering Evidence and Proof: A Tribute to Mike Redmayne' (2016) 20/2 E&P 89(a special issue of the journal)

Roberts, P, and Zuckerman, A, *Criminal Evidence* (OUP, 2010)

Spencer, M, 'Bureaucracy, National Security and Access to Justice: New Light on *Duncan v Cammell Laird*' (2004) 55/3 Northern Ireland Legal Quarterly 277

Spencer, M, and Spencer, J, 'Coping with *Conway v. Rimmer* [1968] AC 910: How Civil Servants Control Access to Justice' (2010) 37/3 JLS 387

Spencer, M, and Spencer, J, *Questions and Answers on Evidence* (OUP, 2016)

Tandy, R, 'The Admissibility of a Defendant's Previous Criminal Record: A Critical Analysis of the Criminal Justice Act 2003' (2009) Statute Law Review 201

Tapper, C, 'Privilege, Policy and Principle' (2005) 121 LQR 181

Tapper, C, 'The Law of Evidence and the Rule of Law' [2009] CLJ 67

Tapper, C, *Cross and Tapper on Evidence* (OUP, 12th edn, 2010)

Temkin, J, 'Sexual History Evidence—Beware the Backlash' [2003] Crim LR 217

Tribe, L, 'Triangulating Hearsay' (1974) 87 Harv LR 957

Twining, W, *Rethinking Evidence: Exploratory Essays* (Blackwell, 1990)

Ward, T, 'Expert Evidence and the Law Commission: Implementation without Legislation?' [2013] Crim LR 561

Witting, C, 'Res Ipsa Loquitur: Some Last Words' (2001) 117 LQR 392

Worthen, T, 'The Hearsay Provisions of the Criminal Justice Act 2003: So Far Not So Good?' [2008] Crim LR 431

Zuckerman, A, *Principles of Criminal Evidence* (Clarendon Press, OUP, 1989)

Zuckerman, A, 'Legal Professional Privilege: The Cost of Absolutism' (1996) 112 LQR 535

Outline answers

Chapter 2

Problem answer plan (a)

First list the elements of the offence and any statutory defences. The offence consists of setting traps to kill rats. It is assumed this is an offence requiring *mens rea*.

The elements of the offence/statutory defences are:

- knowingly setting traps to kill rats,
- where there is a risk that humans will be harmed.

You should then state the general rule, which is that the burden of proof lies on the prosecution subject to any statutory or common law exceptions, see *Woolmington v DPP* (1935) and Art 6 ECHR. There is little doubt that the task of proving *mens rea* in relation to the setting of the traps lies on the prosecution.

The court will address the question of who has the legal burden of establishing that humans were unlikely to be harmed. On the basis of the statutory construction it is not clear if the question of the likely harm to humans is an element of the offence or a defence which takes the form of an 'exception, etc, following s101 Magistrates Courts Act'. According to *Edwards* (1975), confirmed in *Hunt* (1987), the burden could impliedly shift to the defence. This applied whether the offence was tried summarily or on indictment.

If on its construction the burden is shifted to the defence the question is whether this is a proportionate response in the light of the HRA 1998. Applying *Lambert* (2002) and *Sheldrake* (2004) factors to consider include:

- the moral blameworthiness of the offence,
- the size of the penalty, and
- the ease of production of the proof.

Here the offence appears to be a regulatory one. It has some similarities with *Johnstone* (2003) in that it is imprisonable. It could be argued that this is the sort of situation Dennis (2005) refers to as 'a voluntary assumption of risk'. It is likely that the legal burden will be on the defendant Harold. It is arguable in particular that he would find it easier to prove the actual situation in his yard. The standard of proof is the civil one (*Edwards* (1975)).

Problem answer plan (b)

This question requires you to show familiarity with the difference between the evidential and the legal burden of proof. The general rule is that the legal and the evidential burden is on the prosecution. However, it is not the case that the prosecution has to anticipate every defence the defendant might put forward. The judge has a role in deciding if there is enough evidence for any specific defence that is not an essential part of the prosecution case, and (outside of the *Woolmington* exceptions) to be put to the jury. On these issues the defence has the evidential burden. The placing of the evidential burden on the defence on a specific issue may be derived from statute or from the common law. Self-defence is a common law defence and there is authority to explain that on this the evidential burden is on the defence while the legal burden remains on the prosecution. The case you should cite is *R v Lobell* (1957), where the accused pleaded self-defence to a charge of wounding with intent. The Court of Appeal overturned the conviction because the trial judge had stressed that the burden of proof lay on the accused. The only 'burden' on the accused was the evidential burden. The judge should consider, in deciding whether to put the defence, whether there was sufficient evidence to raise a reasonable doubt in the minds of the jury.

You might refer also to the case of *R v O'Brien* (2004), where the judge had wrongly failed to direct the jury that it was for the prosecution to prove that the defendant was not acting in self-defence. In this question it is likely that Jane has very strong grounds of appeal.

Outline answers

✳✳✳✳✳✳✳✳✳✳

Chapter 3

Problem answer

Points to cover:

- Is Dorrit's silence when accused by David admissible?
- Are Nell's two confessions admissible?
- If they are not admissible for the prosecution can Dorrit adduce them as part of his defence?
- Can the jury be told of the existence of the poison?
- What is the effect of Tim's 'no comment' interview, failure to testify, and of his barrister's line of defence?
- Can an inference of guilt against Tim be drawn from his barrister's adoption of the defence that Pip may have committed suicide?

Taking each in turn:

David is not charged with investigating crimes so ss34–38 CJPOA do not apply. Dorrit is arguably on even terms with him so his silence might amount to a confession of guilt. See *Parkes* (1976) and *Osborne* (2005).

Nell should have been told that the legal advice was free so there appears to be a breach of PACE Code C para 6.1. She is also a vulnerable suspect. The denial of the solicitor plus her emotional state provides the 'something said or done' in the 'conditions existing at the time' to make for possible exclusion under s76(2)(b). See *Harvey* (1988). Her second interview appears to be properly conducted but her resolve may have been tainted by the first so both may be excluded under s76(2)(b) if the prosecution cannot prove beyond reasonable doubt that s76(2)(b) was not breached. See *McGovern* (1990).

Dorrit may adduce Nell's confession exonerating him if it is held to be relevant and he can prove, on the balance of probabilities, that it should not be excluded under s76A(2)(b).

The prosecution may inform the court that they have found the poison but not how they came to knowledge of its whereabouts, see s76(4) PACE.

Tim's barrister may have engaged s34 CJPOA against Tim. He has arguably adopted an explanation, ie the possible suicide of Pip, which Tim might have given earlier. This applies even where the defendant does not testify, see *R v Webber* (2004). Tim runs the risk of s34 CJPOA 1994 being engaged since his barrister is offering an explanation at trial which Tim might reasonably be expected to have given at interview (see *R v Webber* (2004) and *R v Argent* (1997)). The judge may invite the jury to draw an adverse inference from this and the failure to testify, see s35 CJPOA. Tim should be advised that the judge must give the prescribed judicial directions on both issues, see *R v Cowan* (1996).

Chapter 4

Problem answer

The question is asking you to apply the law on entrapment evidence to this scenario. You should review the case law and in particular consider whether there should be a stay of proceedings or exclusion of evidence.

- State the common law position and the extent of the discretion under s78 PACE.
- Entrapment is not a defence but there may be exclusion of evidence if there would be unfairness to the proceedings, which means considering defence and prosecution, ie public good in diminution of crime.
- Test for exclusion set out in *Smurthwaite* (1994), see also *Texeira v Portugal* (1998).
- Did Tamara do more than offer Janet an unexceptional opportunity?
- Is it significant that there had been concern about theft on the estate so the police were not simply engaging in a fishing exhibition?
- How active or passive was Tamara?
- How serious is the offence?
- See *Looseley* (2001) and *Warren v A-G for Jersey* (2011): would the criminal justice system be brought into disrepute if the evidence is admitted?
- Correct response may be to stay proceedings if there is no other evidence than that obtained by entrapment and Tamara is considered to have incited the offence.

Chapter 5

Problem answer

The question raises the issue of what is known as joinder. The bad character of the defendant may be revealed not only by prior convictions but by combining several charges on one indictment. In order to answer the question fully you need to have knowledge of the Court of Appeal decision *R v Freeman* (2008), which clearly sets out the extent to which the character provisions of the CJA 2003 have replaced the common law rules. You need to address two issues, first, can the evidence on one charge be supportive evidence for the other charges and second, if the answer is yes to this question, how should the judge direct the jury in relation to the evidence. A related issue is whether there is any risk of collusion between the complainants, Jane and Alice.

The prosecution is likely to succeed in having the three counts against Swann heard concurrently. The preliminary test is that of relevance. This principle of admissibility was well established at common law. It is arguable in this case that the evidence on each charge is more probative of guilt on the others than it is prejudicial to the defendant although the defence may argue there are marked differences in the offences. The ages of the complainants are different. On the other hand they are all offences of a sexual nature. One issue will be the specific defence which Swann presents and whether it is the same on all counts, whether mistaken identity or innocent association.

The prosecution will rely on the decision in *Freeman* (2008), where the appellant was convicted of three counts of indecent assault and two counts of sexual assault of a child. He appealed on the grounds that the judge was wrong to refuse to sever the indictment, that the directions given to the jury were insufficient, and that the judge erred in referring to bad character at all in his summing-up. The appeal was dismissed.

The Court of Appeal held that evidence in relation to one count in an indictment was capable of being admitted as bad character evidence in relation to any other count in the indictment if it met any of the criteria in s101(1) of the 2003 Act. Here, the three charges clearly fall into the definition of bad character in s98 CJA 2003, as amplified by s112, as 'other reprehensible behaviour'. The 'gateway' to admissibility is likely to be s101(1)(d) as it was in *Freeman*.

In relation to directions to the jury the court in *Freeman* stressed that it might not always be helpful to concentrate on the concept of propensity when the nature of the evidence was such that in itself it was capable of being probative in relation to another count. In other words the evidence on each count made it more likely either that the offence had been committed or that the defendant had committed it. Whilst a jury had to be reminded that it had to reach a verdict on each count separately, it was entitled in determining guilt in respect of any count to have regard to the evidence in regard to any other count, or to any other admissible bad character evidence, and was not required to determine first whether it was satisfied on the evidence in relation to one of the counts of the defendant's guilt before it could use the evidence in relation to that count in dealing with any other count on the indictment.

The court cited *R v Chopra* (2007), where a dentist was charged with indecent assault on three teenage patients on three separate occasions. Common law rules in relation to treatment of the evidence no longer applied. The court in *Freeman* stated that 'whether or not the incidents were capable of establishing a propensity each was admissible itself as evidence to support the truth of the other allegations'. The court distinguished *Hanson* (2005), where the impression may have been given that the jury in its decision-making process in cross admissibility cases should first determine whether it is satisfied on the evidence in relation to one of the counts of the defendant's guilt before it can move on in using that evidence in relation to the other count in the indictment. That was 'too restrictive an approach' (para 20). The prosecution thus may invite the jury to consider the cumulative effect of the evidence of each of the counts as to whether Swann's defence is innocent association or mistaken identity. In *R v Mitchell* (2016) the Supreme Court considered the application of s10(1)(d). It stated (para 54) that the proper question to be posed is whether the jury is satisfied that a propensity has been established. That assessment depends on an overall consideration of the evidence available, not upon a segregated examination of each item of evidence in order to decide whether it has been proved beyond reasonable doubt.

One final question is that Swann may raise the possibility of collusion between Jane and Alice. This question is one for the judge to decide in the test set out in s107(1)(b)(ii) CJA 2003. The section requires the judge to stop the case where the evidence is 'contaminated', including that resulting from collusion between the witnesses and others.

Chapter 6

Problem answer

(i) John's statement to Tom fulfils the definition of hearsay to be found in ss114, 115, and 121 CJA 2003. It is being tendered to suggest that it is true, namely that Anna killed John. It may be admissible under s116 as oral first-hand hearsay where the reason for not calling John is that he is dead. Alternatively, it may be admitted under the common law exception *res gestae*: see *Andrews* (1987).

(ii) The defence may want to produce the text Harriet received from Sally since it is exculpatory evidence. It is clearly hearsay in that it is being adduced to suggest she did not carry out the killing. It is a document not covered by s117, see *Taylor* (2006), since it is multiple hearsay and is not received in the course of trade etc. It is, therefore, only admissible by exercise of the discretion under s121(1)(c) considered in conjunction with the factors in s114(1)(d)—see *Maher* (2006), where the court considered that the trial judge should have considered this section as well as s114(1)(d). The defence may rely on *R v Thakrar (Miran)* (2010), which concerned incriminating statements made to the authorities in North Cyprus by a fugitive (D1) who with his brother (D2) was charged with a murder in England. The Court of Appeal held that the statements, in the form of confessions, were correctly admitted as prosecution evidence under s121(1)(c) CJA 2003. The defence may also seek to apply on the grounds available in *R v Musone* (2007). The case involved the admissibility of multiple hearsay, here a statement identifying M as his killer told by a dying prisoner to a fellow prisoner who passed the information to a prison officer, Patterson. The judge ruled that Patterson's evidence should be admitted in evidence, pursuant to s114(1)(d) and s121(1)(c).

M's appeal against conviction failed. The statutory test is whether the court is satisfied that, taking into account how reliable the statement appears to be, the statement is so high that the interests of justice require it to be admissible to prove that the earlier statement was made.

Section 120 does admit multiple hearsay as previous statements and applies where a witness is called to give evidence in criminal proceedings. However, Anna's statement contained in the text message does not appear to fall within s120(3) or (4), which is memory refreshing, identification evidence, or complaint by a victim. It is unlikely Anna could rely on the common law principle that an accused's reaction to an accusation may be admissible as evidence of consistency (see *R v Storey* (1968)) since there is no evidence given that her statement was such a reaction. Section 116 does not apply since it only covers first-hand hearsay.

(iii) Harry gives information to Gloria which may be relevant to the prosecution. It is arguably hearsay if it is being adduced to suggest that Anna, Fred, and John were involved in a fight. On the facts it appears to fulfil the requirements of s117 CJA in that Harry has personal information which he gives to Gloria, who is acting under a duty as allotment secretary and who hands it to a council official also acting under a duty. If Harry refuses to be summonsed as a witness he may be liable in contempt. It is possible that his evidence may be admitted under s117 since it is in a document prepared under a duty. There does not have to be a reason for Harry's absence since it does not appear to be a statement gathered as part of criminal proceedings.

Chapter 7

Problem answer

You should take each witness in turn:

• Can John testify against Janet and Janet against John?

• Is the compellability of spouses dependent on the nature of the offence?

• Does the situation change if either plead guilty?

• Is Tim eligible as a witness and will his age affect how he gives evidence?

- Is Agnes competent to give evidence?
- What are the evidential consequences if the defendants choose not to testify? (It is easy to overlook this last point since it strictly goes beyond the rules on competence and compellability but you will gain extra marks if you show you know the connection between compellability and evidential consequences.)
- What sanctions are available if a non-defendant compellable witness fails to testify?

The general rule in criminal proceedings is that all witnesses are competent and compellable (s53(1) YJCEA). We are not given any details of the age or mental state of Janet and John but it is obvious they are adults and it is assumed that they do not suffer from mental or physical incapacity. If they are jointly charged then neither are competent or compellable to give evidence for the prosecution, see s53(4) YJCEA and s80(4) PACE. Both are competent to give evidence for their own and the other's defence (s53(1) YJCEA) but neither is compellable (s80(4) PACE).

The situation will change if Janet pleads guilty since she will no longer be a co-defendant. She will be competent to give evidence for the prosecution but *only* compellable for the assault on Tim (s80(3) PACE). She will not be compellable for the prosecution for the attack on the dog since it is not a specified offence. She will be competent and compellable to give evidence on behalf of John for the attack on the dog (s80(2) PACE).

If Janet and John, as defendants, do not testify, they risk an adverse inference being drawn (s35 CJPOA). The failure of a spouse of a person charged to testify shall not be made the subject of prosecution comment (s80A PACE).

Tim is the alleged victim and the presumption is that he is competent and compellable to give evidence for the defence or prosecution (s53(1) YJCEA). As he is under 18 years of age he will be eligible for special measures (ss16–17 and 23–30 YJCEA). He will give evidence unsworn, s55(2) YJCEA. In the unlikely event that there is a challenge to his competence he may have to satisfy the test in s53(3) YJCEA. That test may also be applied to Agnes in view of her alleged mental condition, but see *R v Sed* (2004) for the willingness of the courts to apply the provision generously. If Agnes is judged to be competent

to give evidence but does not satisfy the tests for sworn evidence (s55(2)(b) YJCEA) she may give evidence unsworn (s56 YJCEA). It is for the party wishing to have the witness sworn to satisfy the court on the balance of probabilities that the test is satisfied (s55(4)).

If a witness is held to be compellable but fails to testify (s)he will be subject to a finding of contempt (*R v Yusuf* (2003)).

Chapter 8

Problem answer

The following issues are raised all requiring knowledge of s41 YJCEA 1999, the provisions in the CJA 2003, and of the common law rule on previous consistent statements.

- Can Rory's initial denial to police be admitted?
- Can Gloria's statement to her mother be admitted?
- Are Gloria's allegedly previous false allegations admissible?

Rory's denial

Although previous consistent statements are not admissible at trial this denial on arrest may be admissible as an exception to this rule under the common law (*R v Storey* (1968)). Previous out of court exculpatory statements giving the accused's reaction to an accusation are admissible as evidence of consistency and thus to support the witness's creditworthiness. The statement does not have to be made immediately on first accusation but the length of time which has elapsed is a factor in admissibility (*R v Pearce* (1979)). Whether the statement is admissible will in part depend on whether there is other adequate evidence of Rory's reaction (*R v Tooke* (1990)). It is admissible only as evidence of consistency. Alternatively, the statement may be admissible as an exception to the rule against hearsay if it satisfies the 'interests of justice' test in s114(1)(d) CJA. Then it would be evidence of the truth of its contents.

Gloria's statement to her mother

This is arguably a 'previous statement', which forms an exception to the inadmissibility of

Outline answers

✳✳✳✳✳✳✳✳✳✳

previous consistent statements in s120(7) CJA 2003. The following statutory conditions appear to apply:

- Gloria claims to be the person against whom an offence was committed;
- the alleged attempt is the subject matter of the trial;
- her complaint was not made as a result of a threat or a promise. It does appear to have been prompted by a leading question from her mother but this is not fatal to admissibility (s120(8)); and
- before the statement is adduced, Gloria must give oral evidence in connection with its subject matter. If it is admitted the statement is evidence of its truth (s120(4)).

Gloria's previous allegations

The defence will wish to bring these in. The question is whether s41 is engaged.

The defence face four hurdles in seeking to bring evidence of Gloria's alleged false allegations. First, as a question of fact there has to be a reasonable basis that the complainant made the statements and they were not true. In *R v Davarifar* (2009) the Court of Appeal held that it was for the court to pronounce on whether there was a proper evidential basis that the claim was false. A decision by the Crown Prosecution Service not to prosecute was not decisive. *R v M* (2009) is authority for the proposition that there does not, however, have to be a strong factual foundation but rather some material which would support the allegation of falsity.

Secondly, the question is raised whether adducing the allegations is precluded by s41(1) on the grounds that they are 'past sexual behaviour'? In *Davarifar* the Court of Appeal held that making a false allegation is not 'sexual behaviour' under s41(1), although the section may be engaged if the evidence details actual sexual behaviour as part of the content of the claim. In *R v S* (2003) a defence allegation that the claimant had lied about her virginity at the time of the rape which was the subject of the charge was held to be an allegation of past sexual behaviour. On the other hand, in *R v P* (2013), questions about an abortion that the complainant had undergone were not, on the facts, past sexual behaviour since they were

relevant to the accused's claim of emotional support for his alleged victim.

The third hurdle the defence will face is whether the allegation of making a false complaint is 'impugning the credibility of the complainant' under s41(4). In two conjoined appeals *R v T; R v H* (2002) the trial judge was held to have been wrong in *H* refusing to admit evidence on these grounds. They were relevant in the normal, non-statutory sense.

Finally, the defence should be reminded that the requirements of s100 CJA 2003 in such a situation must be satisfied, see *R v V* (2006); and it may be necessary for the defence to seek leave under s100(4) CJA 2003 to admit the evidence since Gloria is a non-defendant witness.

Proffered defence evidence cannot be excluded under s78 PACE.

Chapter 9

Problem answer

The issues in this problem are:

1. The admissibility of expert evidence in civil cases and the application of the relevant statutes and Civil Procedure Rules (CPR), particularly in cases where experts disagree.

2. Whether the court will allow evidence on credibility.

3. Whether experts' evidence can rely on the work of others.

Rule 35.1 CPR 1998. Expert evidence is restricted to that which is reasonably required to resolve the proceedings, see tests in *Kennedy v Cordia Services Ltd* (2016).

- The judge must establish the expertise of the experts. There is no need for formal qualifications such as doctorates.

- It is arguable that Sprog is giving evidence on the ultimate issue, namely how the injuries were caused, but this rule has been abolished in civil proceedings (s3(1) CEA 1972).

- The psychiatric evidence from Friend is more problematic since it relates to the credibility of the witness. There is much controversy over whether credibility is a matter for the court. In *Re M and R (Minors)* (1996) the court allowed expert evidence on the credibility of a child witness. Arguably the evidence was relevant on whether alleged sexual abuse had occurred. Special circumstances appear to apply to vulnerable witnesses such as children. The key issue here is whether the credibility of Pat is disputed, in which case, arguably, evidence may be taken on it.

• Experts are allowed to rely on the work of others and such hearsay statements are admitted in civil proceedings (CEA 1995). Thus, the work of the US professors is admissible.

• Here, since the experts disagree, the court may consider whether to give permission for them to appear in court. If permission is not granted they must give evidence in writing.

• The parties must follow the notice rules.

• The judge must give reasons if his judgment prefers one expert over another.

Chapter 10

Problem answer

The question requires you to apply (i) the law on public interest immunity (PII), (ii) the possibility that witness anonymity may be appropriate, and (iii) to consider if a stay of prosecution may be ordered.

English law protects the identity of informants in matters concerned with public prosecutions. Public interest immunity certificates are issued in order to protect the public interest in keeping such flows of information secret. See *Marks v Beyfus* (1890).

There is a presumption of non-disclosure here and it will be for James to convince the court of the need for disclosure.

On the other hand, *R v Ward* (1993) established that the prosecution is obliged to disclose to the defence all material on which the prosecution is based.

Section 21(2) CPIA 1996 states that the common law rule on non-disclosure in the public interest is preserved.

Under s3 CPIA (as amended by the CJA 2003) the procedure for the judge to hear argument in cases about contested disclosure is set out. On the facts this would not appear to be a situation in which an *ex parte* hearing was appropriate.

James may rely on *R v Agar* (1989), where it was held on appeal that disclosure of the name of an informer in a drugs case was necessary where the defendant claimed to have been set up by the informer and police acting together.

In reaching a decision on whether to allow disclosure, the court can take into account the alleged informer's willingness to be named but this is not conclusive (*Savage v Chief Constable of Hampshire* (1997)).

Here, James is claiming that he was framed, not just informed upon and he must put up some evidence to convince the court that it is necessary to name Joan.

James may find some support in the robust approach to PII claims taken in *Rowe and Davis v UK* (2000) and *Edwards v UK; Lewis v UK* (2005).

The House of Lords considered how to apply these rulings in *R v H; R v C* (2004), where the test was set out for considering PII claims. It is possible to make use of a special advocate in the preliminary hearing. If the defendant cannot be adequately protected by limited measures and a fair trial would be impossible without full disclosure then disclosure must be ordered even if the prosecution stays the proceedings.

The Corners and Justice Act 2009 sets out the grounds on which witness anonymity may be ordered. In *R v Mayers* (2008) the Court of Appeal held that knowledge of the true identities of undercover police officers was rarely of importance to the defendant.

If the prosecution wish to protect their sources in the face of a disclosure order they may apply to stay the proceedings. In *R v Barkshire* (2011) the non-disclosure of the activities of a police informer led to a miscarriage of justice.

Chapter 11

Problem answer

The question involves the application of legal professional privilege in civil proceedings. You will need to explain its scope and whether it can be waived.

The general principle is that communications between client and solicitor are privileged. If the 'dominant purpose' of the communication is litigation the privilege is wider in that it embraces communications between the potential litigant and third parties, ie non-lawyers. The question here is whether the email is covered by this privilege and therefore should not be disclosed by Freda. The leading case is *Waugh v British Railways Board* (1980). The widow of a man killed in a railway accident sued BRB and sought disclosure of an internal accident report which engineers had sent to BRB lawyers. She failed since the House of Lords ruled that this was not a case where the dominant purpose of the correspondence was litigation. This does not mean that the sole purpose of the email sent by the insurers has to be preparing the litigation but the courts, eg, will examine whether the litigation was a likelihood if it had not already been set in motion at the time the email was sent. If the 'dominant purpose' is to make changes to staffing policy in PHC then the email will not be privileged.

Thus, Freda may be advised that she may be able to use the email in her claim if litigation privilege is held not to apply here and correspondence with the insurers is not privileged. More information is needed about the background to their letter to Fixit and if it pre-dated the litigation. If on the other hand litigation privilege is held to apply then several other courses of action are possible. First, Freda should take note of r31.20 Civil Procedure Rules 1998. These provide that privileged documents which are revealed by mistake cannot be used without the consent of the court. It appears, however, that Martin sent the correspondence deliberately and so the section does not apply. Freda should be advised that she could argue that she has obtained only a copy of the correspondence and that privilege does not extend to secondary evidence. It was held in *Calcraft v Guest* (1898) that copies of a privileged document could be put in evidence. Freda may finally fail, however, in that if PHC act promptly they could apply for an injunction to prevent the production of admissible evidence on grounds of breach of confidentiality. The case of *Ashburton v Pape* (1913) is authority for the granting of a discretionary injunction in such circumstances. The facts of that case were, however, somewhat different in that the defendant had obtained the information by trickery and so the injunction as an equitable remedy redressed an unconscionable act. It does not appear from the facts that Freda has acted in an improper way. A final consideration is that the injunction would only be granted if the evidence had not already been used.

Glossary

actus reus the criminal act, contrasted with '*mens rea*' the guilty mind

adduce evidence putting evidence before the court either at trial or in preliminary proceedings

adverse inference is an inference of guilt which the judge may, in certain circumstances, direct the jury that they are permitted to draw

advice privilege a sub-species of legal professional privilege which protects from disclosure communications made with the **dominant purpose** of seeking or obtaining legal advice

agent provocateur a person acting for the authorities who sets out to provoke others into committing a crime. The use of an agent provocateur may make it unfair to prosecute the crime they have provoked

caution must be given by police before questioning to persons whom there are grounds to suspect of an offence. The current words of the caution, to be found in PACE Code C para 10.5(b), 'You do not have to say anything. But it may harm your defence if you do not mention when questioned something which you later rely on in court. Anything you do say may be given in evidence.'

civil partner partner in a relationship analogous to marriage sanctioned by the state for homosexual partnerships

Civil Procedure Rules body of rules governing procedure in civil courts

come up to proof used of a witness whose evidence in court matches what was said before the trial

corroboration is additional evidence or evidence of a different kind that supports a proof already offered in a proceeding

Court of Star Chamber this court sat in Westminster until its abolition in 1641 and became a byword for unfairness and a symbol of royal tyranny. The court sat in secret to try state cases with no indictment or right of appeal

credibility the extent to which an assertion or a witness can be believed

Criminal Cases Review Commission (CCRC) the independent public body set up in 1995 to investigate possible miscarriages of justice in England, Wales, and Northern Ireland and consider whether to refer them for appeal

Criminal Procedure Rules body of rules governing procedure in criminal courts

Crown privilege (now called Public Interest Immunity (PII)) a claim for exemption from disclosure for government documents

disclosure procedure by which a party to litigation gives lists to the opposing party of relevant documents (including privileged documents) which are or were in his possession

discovery procedure by which non-exempt documents previously disclosed by a party to litigation are handed over to the other side

DNA (deoxyribonucleic acid) unique genetic material found in a person's body cells and secretions

dominant purpose documents qualify for legal professional privilege if made for the main reason of giving legal advice or conducting litigation

double jeopardy the principle that once a verdict has been delivered at a defendant's trial, he cannot be tried again for the same offence. In English law it took the form of a procedural defence of *autrefois acquit* (or *autrefois convict*). The principle has the status of a constitutional right in the United States, but was abolished in England in 2003

ear-printing finding a match for the impression left by a criminal's ear at the scene of a crime

entrapment a procedure whereby a person may be tricked into committing an offence by undercover actions of a state official or non-state actors such as journalists. It is not recognised as a specific defence in English

Glossary

✳✳✳✳✳✳✳✳✳✳

law, unlike the position in the United States, but abuse of the procedure may require stay of prosecution or exclusion of evidence under s78 PACE

equality of arms part of the concept of fair trial under Art 6 European Convention on Human Rights (ECHR). Each party must have a reasonable opportunity to put his case under conditions which do not place him at a substantial disadvantage compared with his opponent. Includes the requirement that a party should be able to see all the evidence before the court

ex parte used for hearings in which one side appears without notice to the other

exculpatory statement a statement tending to exonerate its maker

facial mapping a technique for matching a suspect or the image of a suspect with a photograph or video image

fact-finder/trier of fact a jury is often referred to loosely as the trier of fact on the basis that the judge decides issues of law and leaves determination of the facts to the jury. A judge or tribunal without a jury acts as fact-finder as well as deciding issues of law

free proof is a mode of legal reasoning advocated by Jeremy Bentham which is based on common sense rather than strict rules of evidence

gravamen of an offence the weighty or serious part of an offence

hostile witness a witness is presumed hostile if he testifies for the opposing party. A party can have one of his own witnesses declared hostile if the witness's evidence turns out to be openly antagonistic or clearly prejudicial. The witness can then be asked leading questions

identification parades (including video) procedure by which a witness chooses from among a number of similar-looking persons, one of whom is the suspect, regulated by PACE Code D

inculpatory statement a statement tending to incriminate its maker

interlocutory appeal an appeal on some point arising before the final determination of the

issues at trial An appeal against the judgment is called a final appeal

litigation privilege a sub-species of legal professional privilege which protects from disclosure communications made with the dominant purpose of use in litigation

mens rea (Latin for 'guilty mind') the state of mind required to commit an offence. Contrasts with the criminal act ('*actus reus*' in Latin). The general principle is that the act does not make a person guilty unless the mind is also guilty

mischief rule a rule of statutory construction requiring the court to interpret a statutory provision by reference to the wrong which the statute was intended to put right

nolle prosequi decision by the prosecution to dismiss the charges. Possible grounds for this might include new evidence coming to light or the non-appearance of a witness

peculiar knowledge by its nature is only available to the individual concerned. A party relying on peculiar knowledge may be put to proof of the fact concerned

principle of orality refers to the oral examination of witnesses as a fundamental feature of the trial in English law. Oral evidence contrasts with evidence given by affidavit

propensity evidence is that which shows a pattern of prior criminal behaviour by the defendant or suspect

proscribed organisations under the Terrorism Act 2000, are officially designated by the authorities as terrorist organisations, making membership or financial support of the proscribed organisation a criminal offence

psychological profiling a method of predicting the psychological make-up of the perpetrator on the basis of the nature of a crime

res gestae a common law exception to the rule against hearsay, making a statement admissible as evidence of any matter stated, if its maker was so emotionally overpowered by an event that the possibility of concoction or distortion can be disregarded

res ipsa loquitur (Latin 'the matter speaks for itself') a plea in the law of negligence signifying that further details are unnecessary: the negligence is self-evident on the facts. The classic case is the scalpel left inside the patient after surgery

reverse burdens (of proof) the normal rule for allocating the burden of proof is that 'he who asserts must prove'. Where there is a reverse burden the party against whom a fact is asserted must disprove it, which in criminal cases detracts from the presumption of innocence since it places the burden of proof on the defendant

right to confrontation the right of a defendant to see, hear, and question his accuser in person

similar fact a rather misleadingly named principle that evidence of the accused's past misconduct may be admissible as evidence of guilt; since the similarity between the earlier behaviour and that in the current case is so similar, it is unlikely to be a coincidence. Previously a common law rule now covered by CJA 2003 in criminal trials and by the common law in civil cases

special advocates appointed by the government and given security clearance to represent the interests of suspects and defendants who cannot be allowed to see the evidence themselves. Primarily but not exclusively used in terrorism cases. The advocate may not reveal to the suspect sensitive materials he has seen

stay of proceedings an order of the court which has the effect of preventing any further moves in the case either indefinitely or for a fixed period

sunset clause a term in a statute which has the effect of repealing a provision after a certain time unless additional specific legislation extends it

sworn evidence evidence given on oath

term of art a word or phrase that has a specialised meaning within a particular occupation or field

third party to a trial used loosely to describe parties who are not directly involved in the primary dispute between defence and prosecution in criminal cases or claimant and defendant in civil suits

voir dire a 'trial within the trial' to determine, eg, the admissibility of evidence or the defendant's fitness to plead. Also describes the process of selecting a jury, especially in the United States

Wednesbury unreasonableness conduct so unreasonable that no reasonable person (or body) could do it, after the public law case *Associated Provincial Picture Houses Ltd v Wednesbury Corpn* (1948)

weight of a piece evidence is the extent, if any, to which the jury find it convincing of guilt

Index

Index
✳✳✳✳✳✳✳✳✳✳

Index

✳✳✳✳✳✳✳✳✳✳✳✳

Index

✱✱✱✱✱✱✱✱✱✱

Index

****

Concentrate QUESTIONS & ANSWERS

Revision & study guides
from the **No. 1** legal education publisher

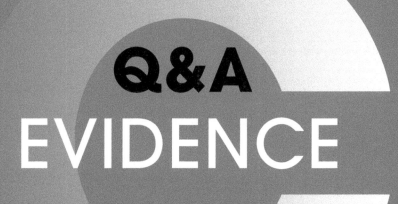

Q&A
EVIDENCE

Maureen Spencer & John Spencer

Practise technique › Boost your confidence › Achieve success

OXFORD

9 Examination and Cross-Examination

KEY DEBATES

Debate: in rape trials is the prior sexual experience of the complainant with the defendant relevant to the instant charge?

Under s. 41 of the Youth Justice and Criminal Evidence Act 1941 (YJCEA) leave of the court is required before questioning the complainant on prior sexual experience with other partners including the defendant. Some commentators condemned the decision in *R v A (No. 2)* [2001] UKHL 25, allowing judicial discretion in determining the relevance of questioning a complainant about previous sexual behaviour with the defendant. They argue that this entrenches a male perspective that a woman who has engaged in consensual sexual activity with a particular man is more likely to be consenting to sex with the same man, the subject of the instant charge.

⊙

Debate: is it good practice to prepare witnesses for the experience of cross-examination before the trial?

Witness prior familiarisation with the demands of the adversarial system has been given judicial approval in *R v Morodou* [2005] **1 WLR 3442** but in practice it rarely happens. Arguably this means that many witnesses are not assisted to testify effectively. A distinction must be drawn between such familiarisation by means of mock questioning and the coaching of witnesses on the evidence in the forthcoming trial. The former is acceptable but the latter is objectionable.

QUESTION | 1

Daniel, a police constable, in response to a call on his radio, went to investigate an alleged burglary at Henfield Road. As he drove up to the scene of the crime, he saw Henry dressed in a T-shirt and running shorts and carrying a holdall on his back, running in the opposite direction. Daniel chased after him but soon lost him. Daniel made a note of what he had seen in his notebook, but did not do so until nearly six months later, just before the trial. Just after the incident, following an appeal for witnesses, Henry went voluntarily to the police station and was interviewed. He said that the reason that he was in the area at the material time was because he had been out jogging, as he was training for the London Marathon and that the holdall contained bricks to weigh him down. Henry is subsequently arrested and charged with the burglary.

Advise on the following evidential matters:

(Each part of the question is worth equal marks.)

(a) Can Daniel refresh his memory from his notebook outside court before giving evidence? If Daniel then gives evidence for the prosecution without referring to the notebook can the defence cross-examine him as to the contents of the notebook?

(b) Can Daniel refresh his memory from his notebook in court? And if so, can it be put in evidence?

(c) What use can the defence make of Henry's voluntary statement at the police station?

! CAUTION!

▦ Make sure that you have revised both the common law and statutory provisions under **s. 120 of the Criminal Justice Act (CJA) 2003** on refreshing memory.

▦ In assessing evidential worth you need to be aware of how evidence of consistency differs from evidence of the truth stated.

DIAGRAM ANSWER PLAN

Identify the issues	▦ The legal issues are: (a) law relating to refreshing memory out of court and whether witness can be cross-examined on source; (b) law relating to refreshing memory in court; (c) admissibility and evidential worth of previous consistent statements.
Relevant law	▦ (a) The relevant statutory section is **CJA 2003, s. 120(3)** and related case law; (b) **s. 139** covers this area and **s. 120(3)** also applies; (c) see common law cases since **CJA** has not affected the law on the admissibility of previous consistent statements but note that **s. 114** inclusionary discretion for hearsay statements may apply.
Apply the law	▦ (a) This concerns the use by Daniel of a memory-refreshing document out of court and needs consideration whether it is necessary for the document to be contemporaneous; (b) the judge will have to agree that Daniel can consult the document in court, apply **CJA 2003, s. 139**; (c) **Henry's statement is admissible.**
Conclude	▦ Assess the outcome for each witness.

SUGGESTED ANSWER

(a) Refreshing Memory Outside Court

It is common for witnesses, such as Daniel as a prosecution witness, to look at written statements which they have made, in order to refresh their memory, before testifying on the witness stand. This practice was recognised by the Court of Appeal in *R v Richardson* **[1971] 2 QB 484.**[1]

In *Richardson*, four prosecution witnesses were given their statements prior to their testimony. The statements were not sufficiently contemporaneous for them to be used to refresh their memory in court. The accused argued on appeal that as the statements were not contemporaneous for the purpose of the rule on refreshing memory in court, their evidence should not have been admitted. The Court of Appeal rejected this argument and approved the dicta in *Lau Pak Ngam v R* **[1966] Crim LR 443.** In that case, the Supreme Court of Hong Kong stated that if witnesses were deprived of the

[1] You could point out that such a rule would probably be unenforceable.

opportunity of checking their recollection beforehand by reference to statements or notes made near to the time of the events in question, testimony in the witness box would be no more than a test of memory, rather than of truthfulness.[2] Further, refusal of access to the statements would create difficulties for honest witnesses, but would not hamper dishonest ones. Subsequently, the court held in *R v Da Silva* **[1990] 1 All ER 29**, that the judge has a discretion to allow a witness to withdraw from the witness stand in order to refresh his memory from a statement made near or at the time of the events in question. The judge has this discretion even where the statement is not contemporaneous with the events.[3] Before he exercises his discretion, the judge must be satisfied that Daniel recalls the events in question because of lapse of time, that he had made a statement near the time of the event representing his recollection of them, that he had not read the statement before testifying and that he wishes to read the statement before he continues to give evidence. In *R v South Ribble Magistrates' Court, ex p Cochrane* **[1996] 2 Cr App R 544**, the Divisional Court made it clear that *R v Da Silva* did not lay down a rule of law that all four conditions must be satisfied. So he is likely to be able to consult even if it is unclear whether Daniel made the note contemporaneously with the events in question.

Cross-examination on contents

The next issue is whether the defence can cross-examine Daniel as to the contents of the notebook if he consults it before trial.[4] The Court of Appeal in *R v Westwell* **[1976] 2 All ER 812** decided that if the prosecution counsel is aware that his witness has refreshed his or her memory outside the court, it was 'desirable but not essential' that the defence should be informed of this fact. Once the defence is aware that Daniel has refreshed his memory from his notebook outside the court, they are entitled to inspect the notebook, and cross-examine Daniel on the relevant matters contained in it: see *Owen v Edwards* **(1983) 77 Cr App R 191**. However, the court made it clear that if the defence counsel cross-examines a witness on material in the notebook or statement, which has not been used by the witness to refresh his memory, they run the risk of the notebook or statement being put in evidence. **Section 120(3) of the Criminal Justice Act (CJA) 2003** provides that if a witness's memory-refreshing statement becomes admissible as a result of cross-examination then it is admissible evidence of any matter stated of which oral evidence by the witness would be admissible.[5] See also *R v Chinn* **[2012] EWCA 501** where the Court of Appeal addressed the construction of this section.

[2] Note that this area is not closely regulated by law. Arguably there is a case for reform.

[3] In relation to the witness refreshing his/her memory in the witness box under the **CJA 2003**, there is no need for the document to have been made contemporaneously with the event.

[4] It is important you organise your answer to cover the two issues separately.

[5] There are a number of reasons why it might be relevant evidence which are set out in **s. 120(2)(e)**.